Warblers Then & Now

A Pictorial History

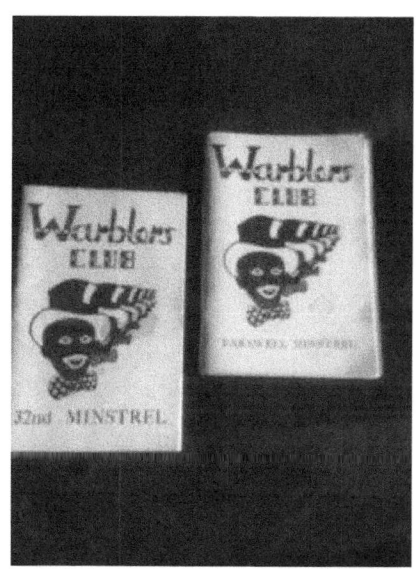

Dr. James E. Martin

ISBN-13: 978-1530630844

ISBN-10: 1530630843

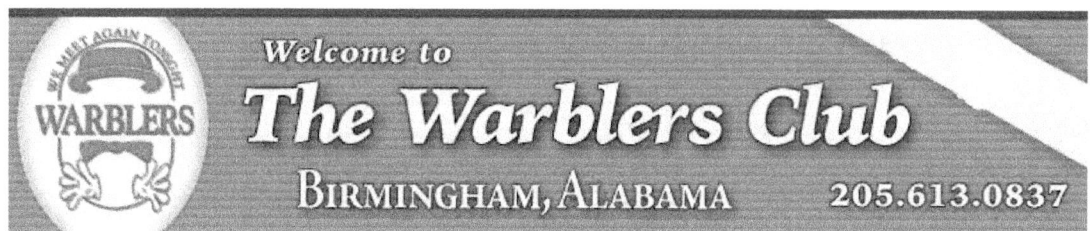

Introduction

The Warblers Club had its beginning at Woodlawn High School, in Birmingham, Alabama, in 1929. It is a male chorus that specializes in a very unique blend that has been described by many as a similar but not exactly barbershop style blend of four part male voices. Over the years the club, while in existence at Woodlawn averaged around fifty voices. They have been privileged to participate in many differing venues and performances such as minstrel shows, hobo shows, city competitions, etc. Today the club, after reorganization in 1988, sings at various churches, patriotic events, etc. Special performances, which are generally done every couple of years features the club performing in a similar fashion to the former days of minstrel and hobo shows. There are usually near or complete sell-out crowds that gather to hear this rich sound.

In this book I have gathered photos from various contributors that focus on group pictures as well as individual pictures. They are arranged in miscellaneous order to provide much variety. These photos are representative of all that is associated with the Warblers Club over its many years of existence. Many of the pictures are not identified since I was unable to find anyone who could provide applicable information. Many of those who read will, undoubtedly, recognize some of the participants. You may even see yourself in one. I apologize for the poor quality of some of the pictures but it was the best I could get.

I wish to offer my sincere appreciation to all who have contributed pictures, encouragement, suggestions, etc. to make this possible to come to fruition. It is hoped that you, the viewer, will be reminded of much as you view these photos that will stir your memories to a greater appreciation of all who have served in any capacity in this wonderful organization.

Jim

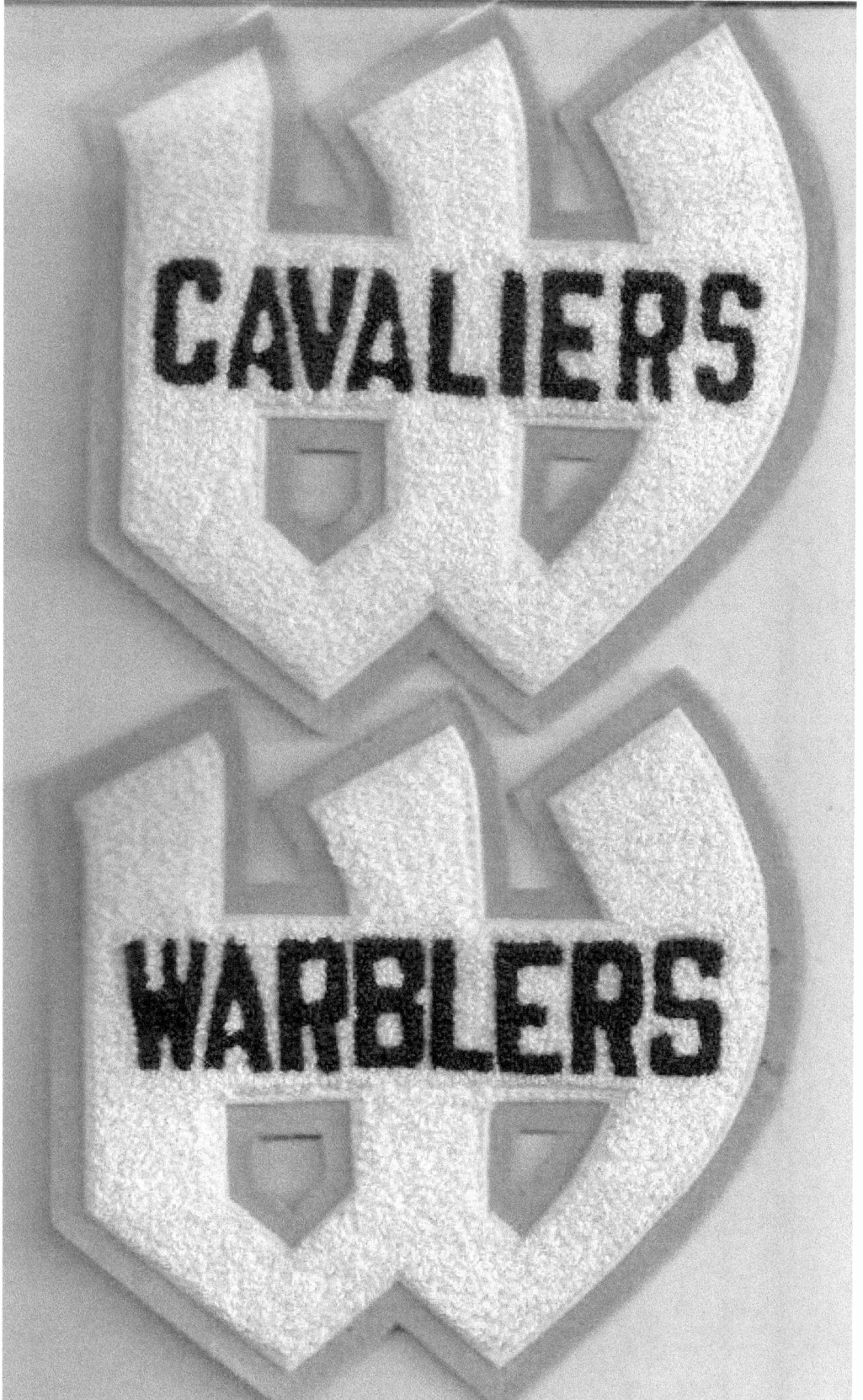

Warbler's Creed

I believe in the high ideals which form the basis of the Warbler's Club and will do my best to uphold them.

I will think only the best, work only for the best, and expect only the best from others.

I will forget the mistakes of the past and so strive to improve myself physically, mentally and morally that I have no time to criticise others.

I will try to keep a ready smile and never lose my sense of humor.

I will support the club wholeheartedly in any club activity.

I will take pride in the fact that I am a member of Woodlawn High School, give my unqualified support to all its activities, and at all times strive to be a good sport.

FAREWELL MINSTREL

WARBLERS
..CLUB..

recorded live in
IRMINGHAM, ALA.
1961

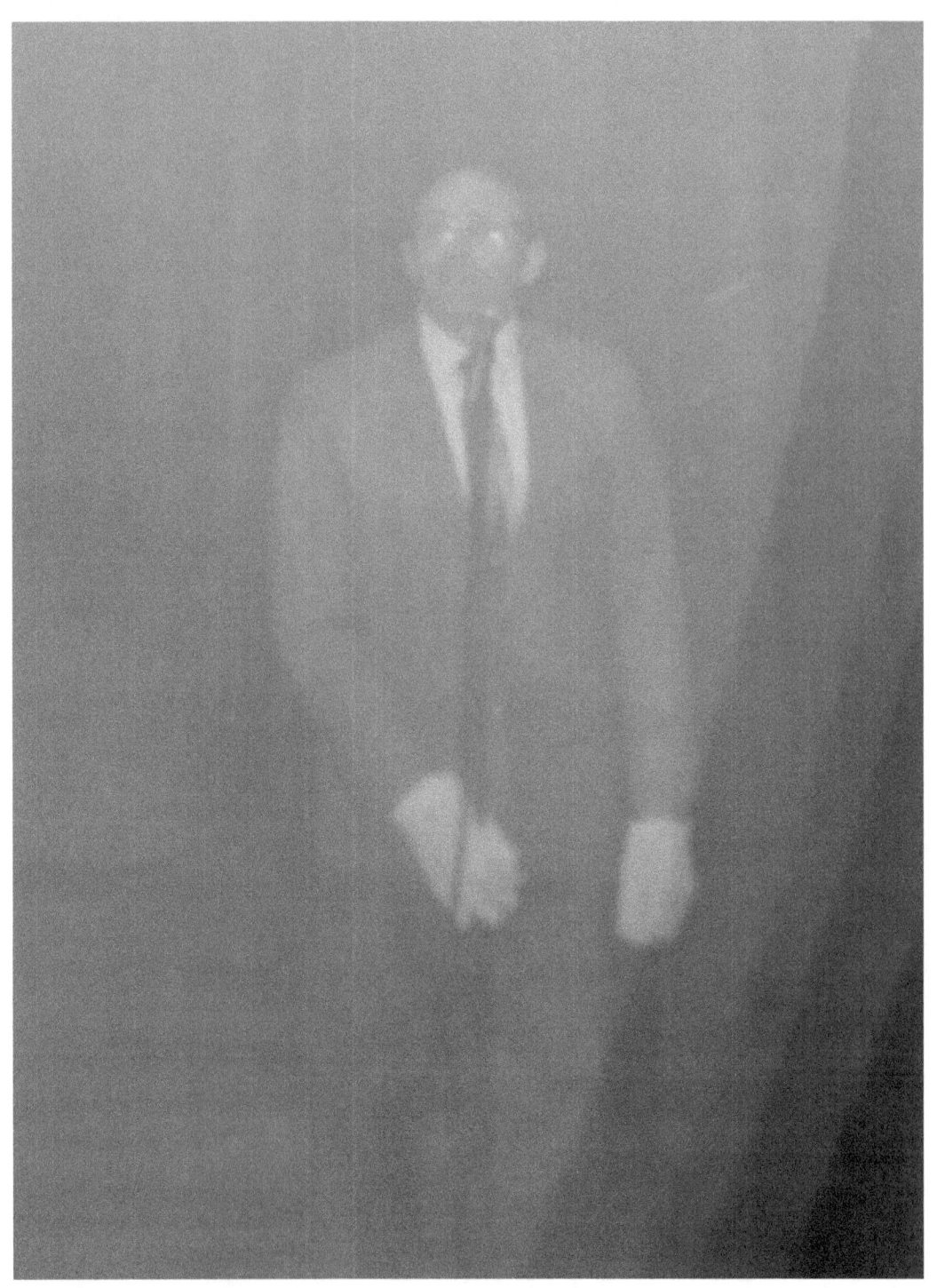

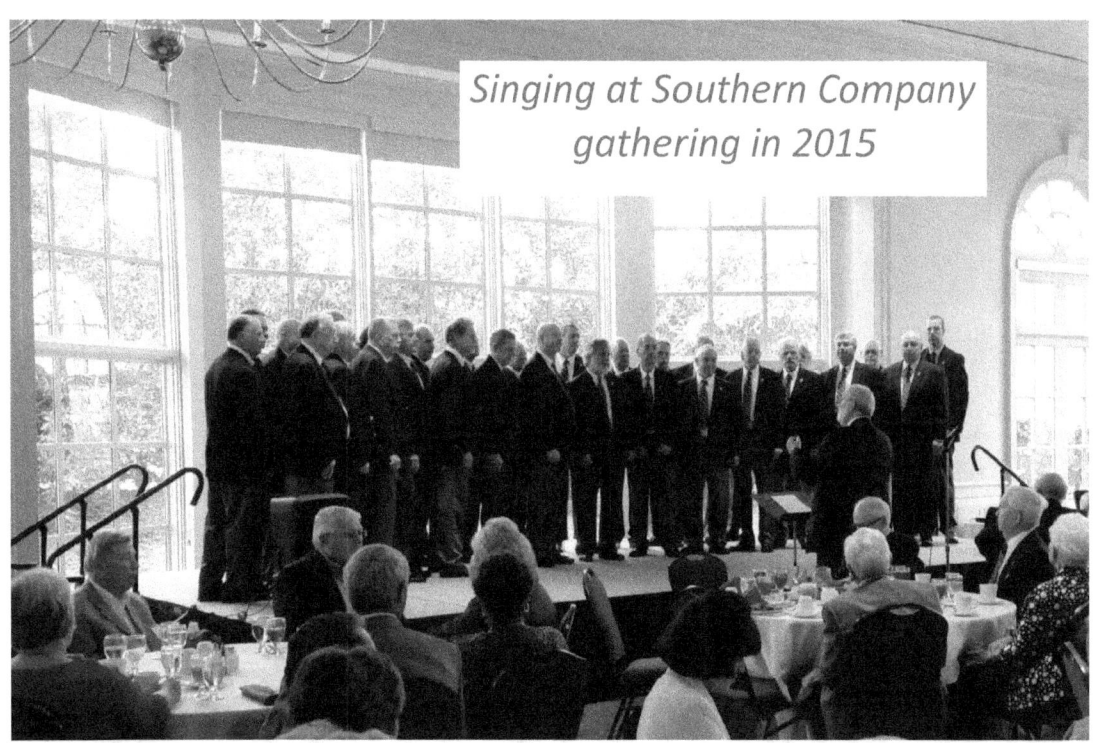

Singing at Southern Company gathering in 2015

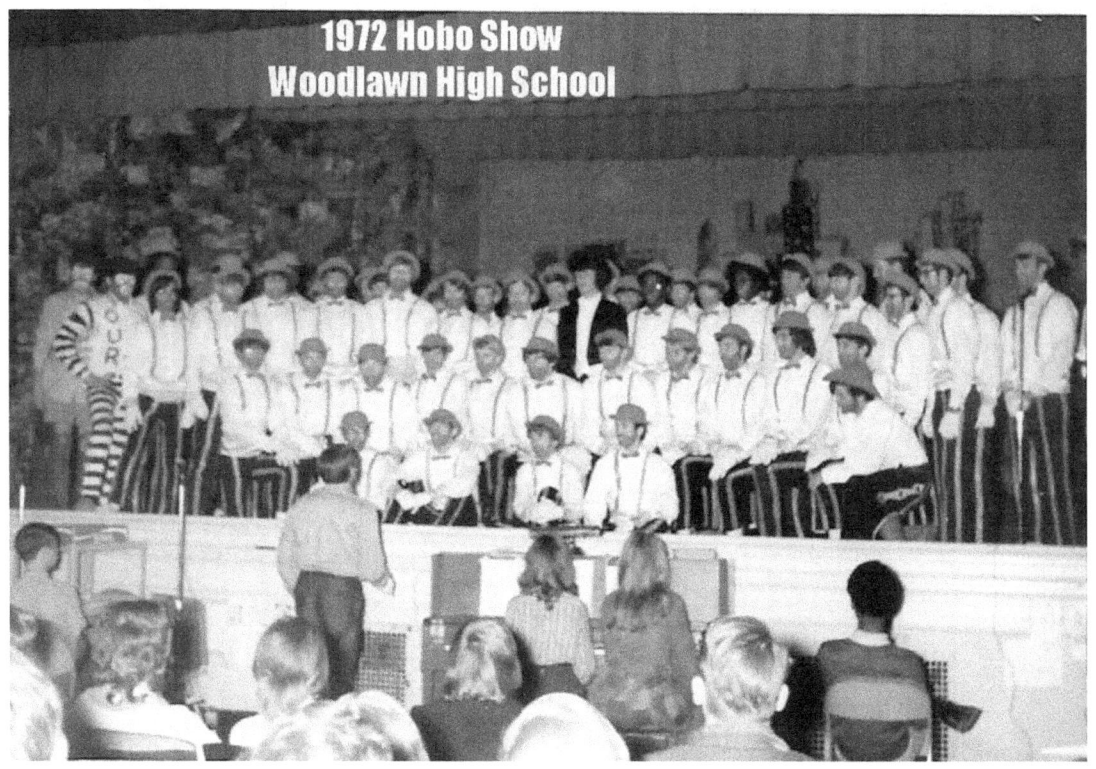

1972 Hobo Show
Woodlawn High School

Warblers 1977

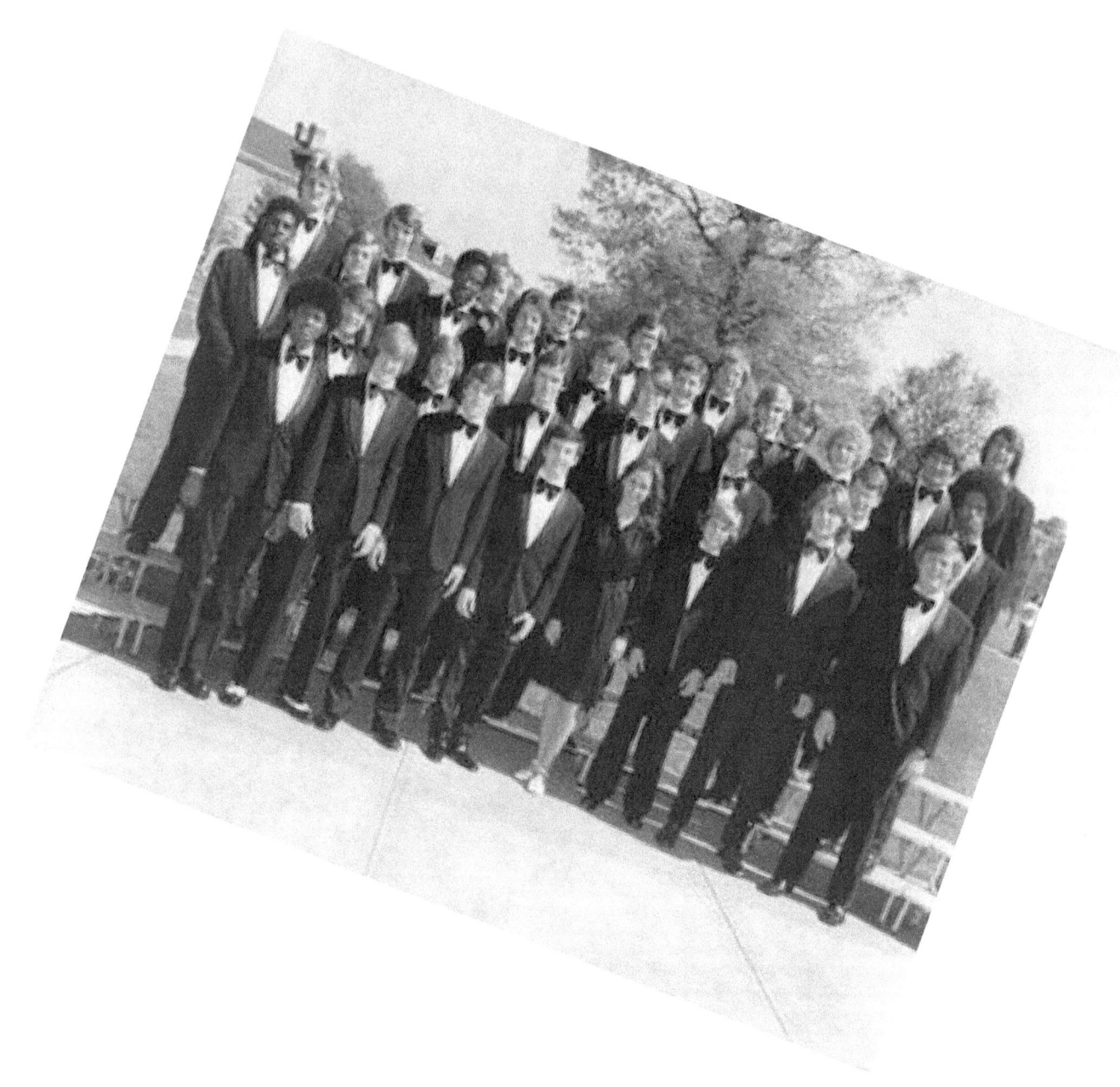

2014 Show

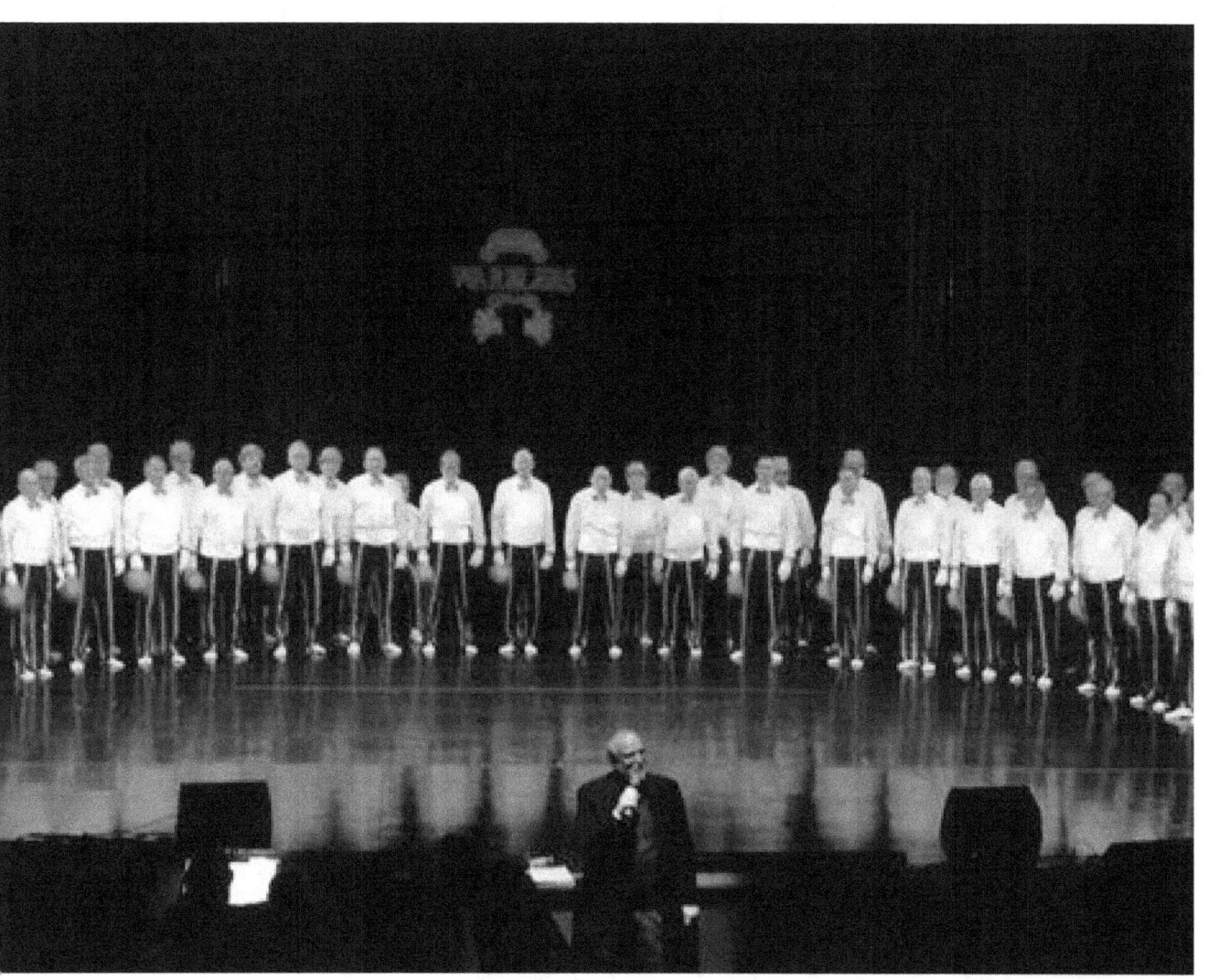

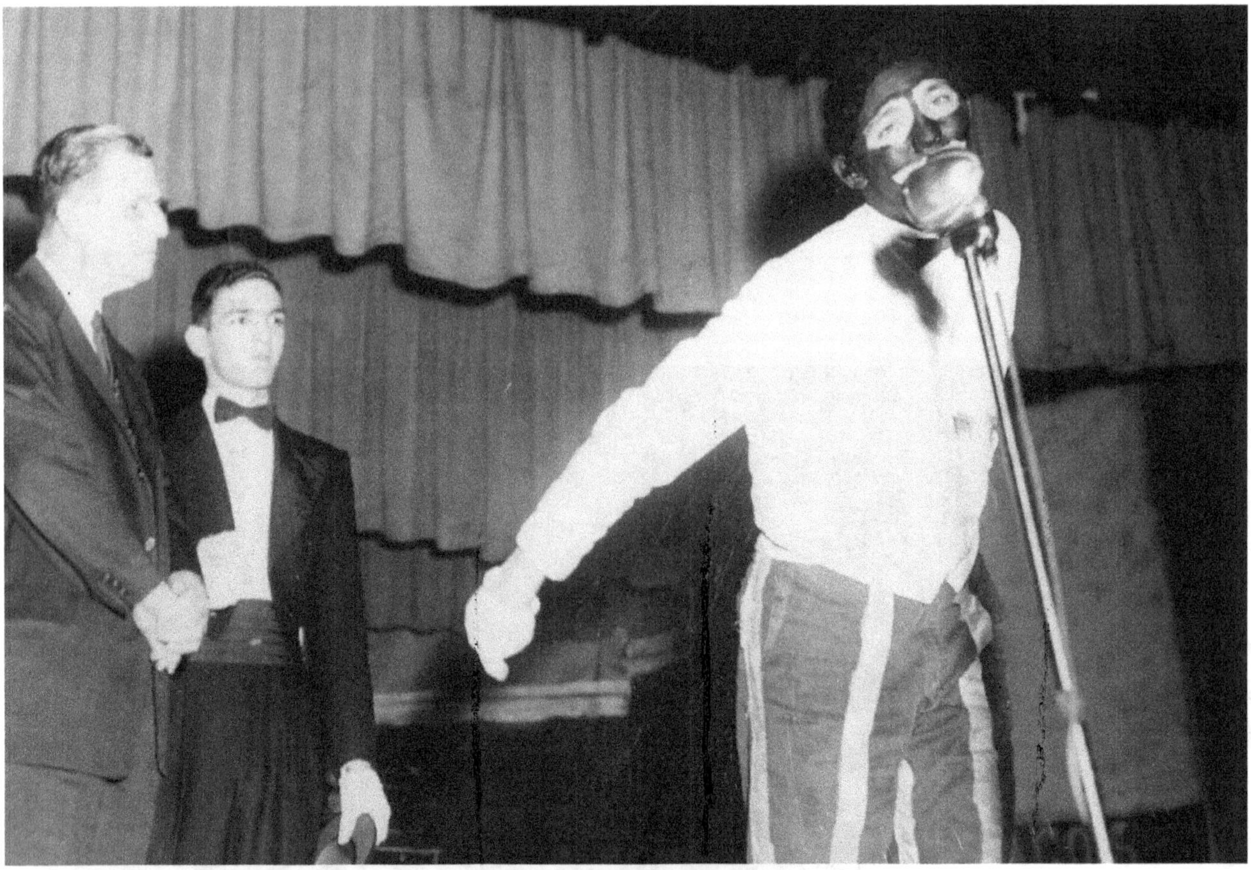

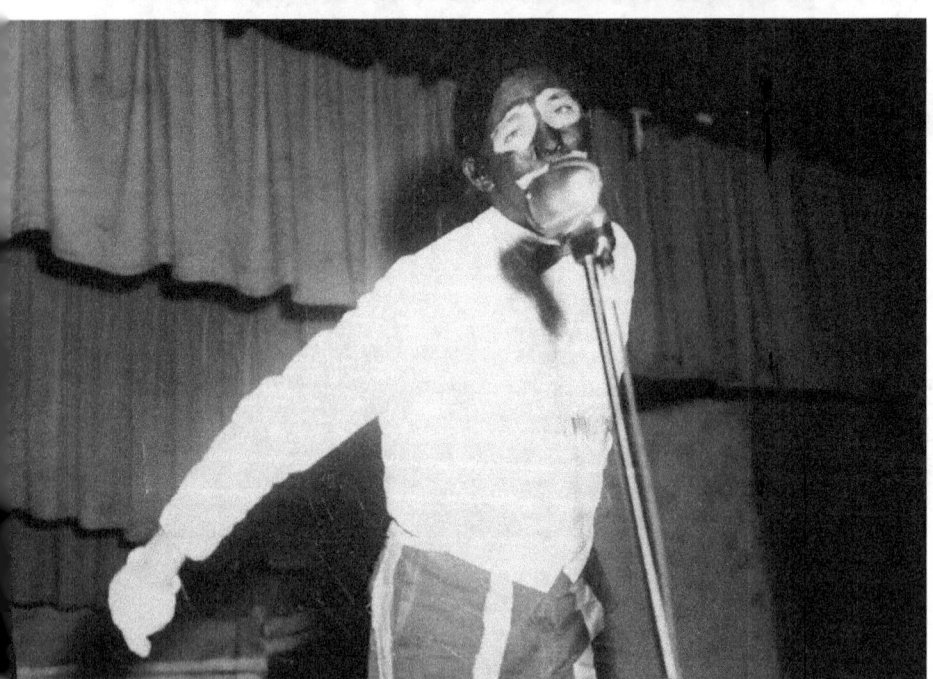

1948 Uncle Joe

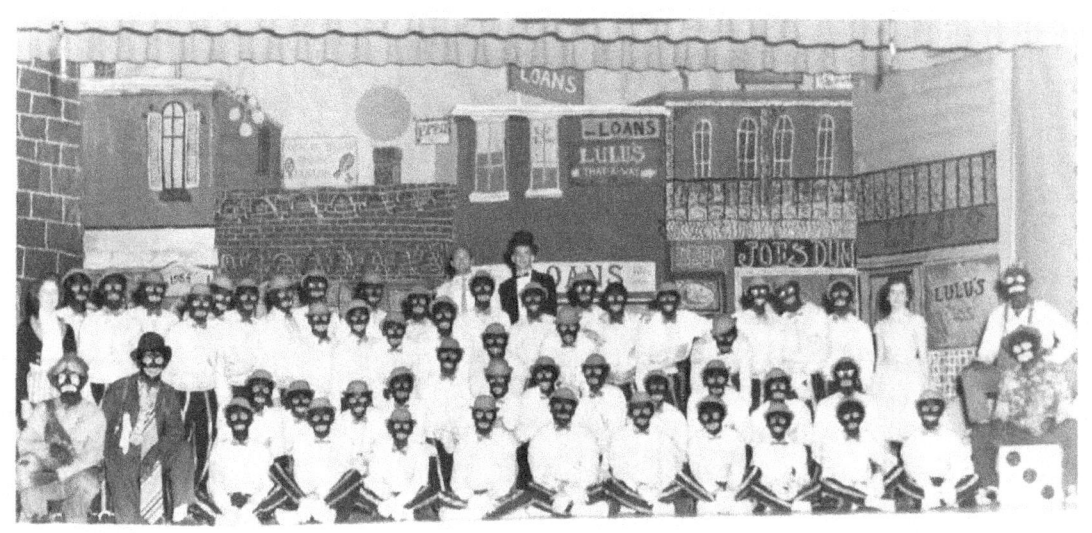

WARBLERS CLUB 32nd MINSTREL

Center back: Director, Joe Turner: Interlocutor, Jimmy Headley

Row One: End Men, J. T. Calfee and Charles Yessick; Lawrence Corley, Dan Davis, George Broom, Mike Huston, Robert Wilson, Wayne Turner, Claude Holter, Donald Garrett, Jimmy Rye, Larry Contri; End Men, John Sanders, and Harold Morgan.

Row Two: Jimmy Gibson, Wayne Carlisle, Eddie Muglach, Wayne Brand, John Reedy, Dewey Markates, Mike Mitchell, Roy Dunn, Herb Dayton, Kenneth Harris.

Standing: Sharon Walsh, Joe Morgan, Melvin Coberly, Tommy Johnson, Butch Waldrop, Paul Price, Buddy Kelly, Winston Long, Earnest Burdette, Gary Hyche, Donnie McBrayer, Charles Roberts, John Compton, Malcolm Youngblood, Jack Fincher, Johnny Aycock, Tommy Loveless, David Nichols, Wayne Miller, Jack Marchant, Jim Lamb, David Bishop, Bill Dean, Tommy Walker, Mike Russell, Tommy Nelson, Linda Carter.

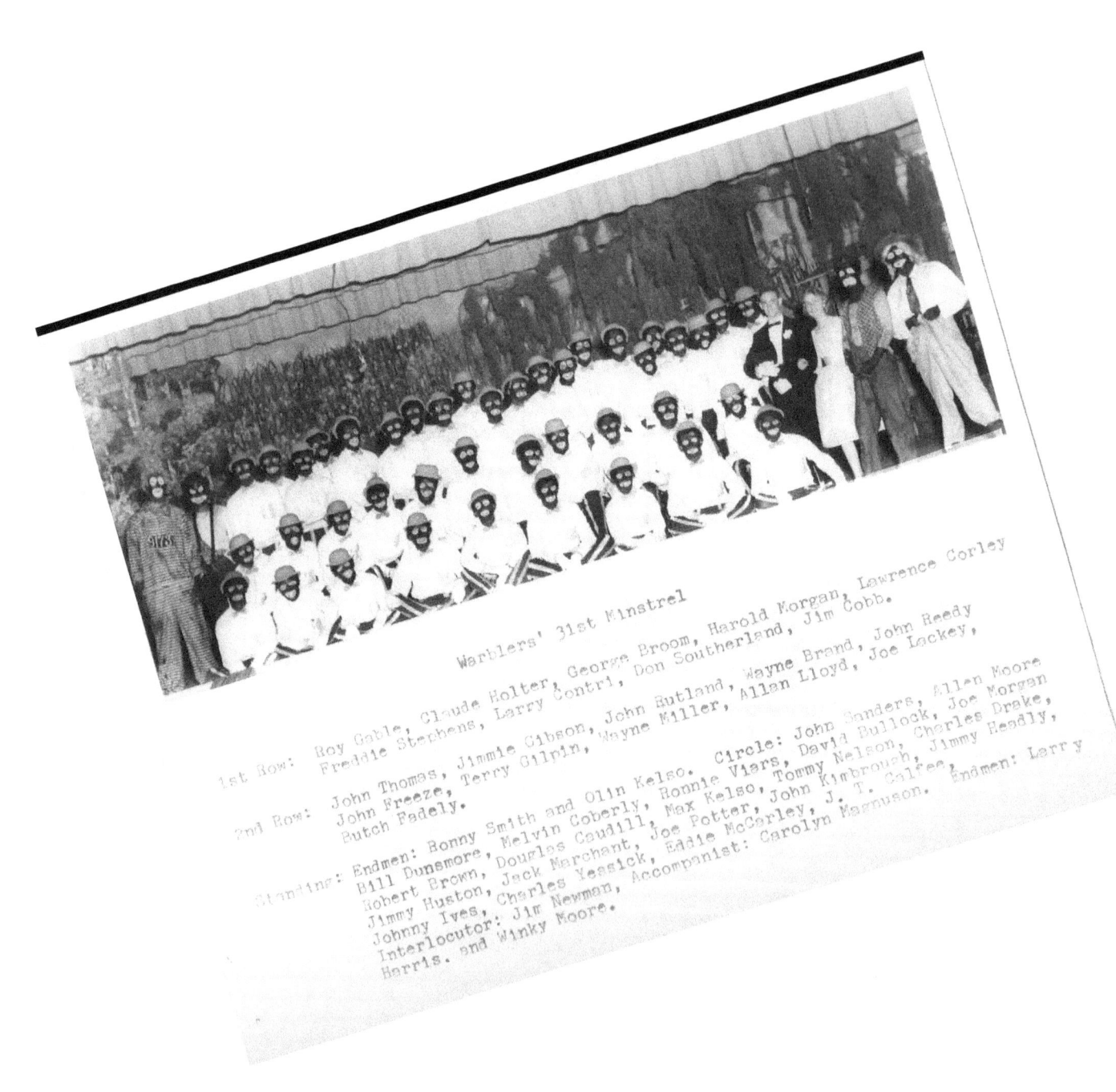

Warblers' 31st Minstrel

1st Row: Roy Gable, Claude Holter, George Broom, Harold Morgan, Lawrence Corley
Freddie Stephens, Larry Contri, Don Southerland, Jim Cobb.

2nd Row: John Thomas, Jimmie Gibson, John Rutland, Wayne Brand, John Reedy
John Freeze, Terry Gilpin, Wayne Miller, Allan Lloyd, Joe Lockey,
Butch Fadely.

Standing: Endmen: Ronny Smith and Olin Kelso. Circle: John Sanders, Allen Moore
Bill Dunsmore, Melvin Coberly, Ronnie Viars, David Bullock, Joe Morgan
Robert Brown, Douglas Caudill, Max Kelso, Tommy Nelson, Charles Drake,
Jimmy Huston, Jack Marchant, Joe Potter, John Kimbrough, Jimmy Headly,
Johnny Ives, Charles Yeasick, Eddie McCarley, J. T. Calfee. Endmen: Larry
Interlocutor: Jim Newman, Accompanist: Carolyn Magnuson.
Harris. and Winky Moore.

14

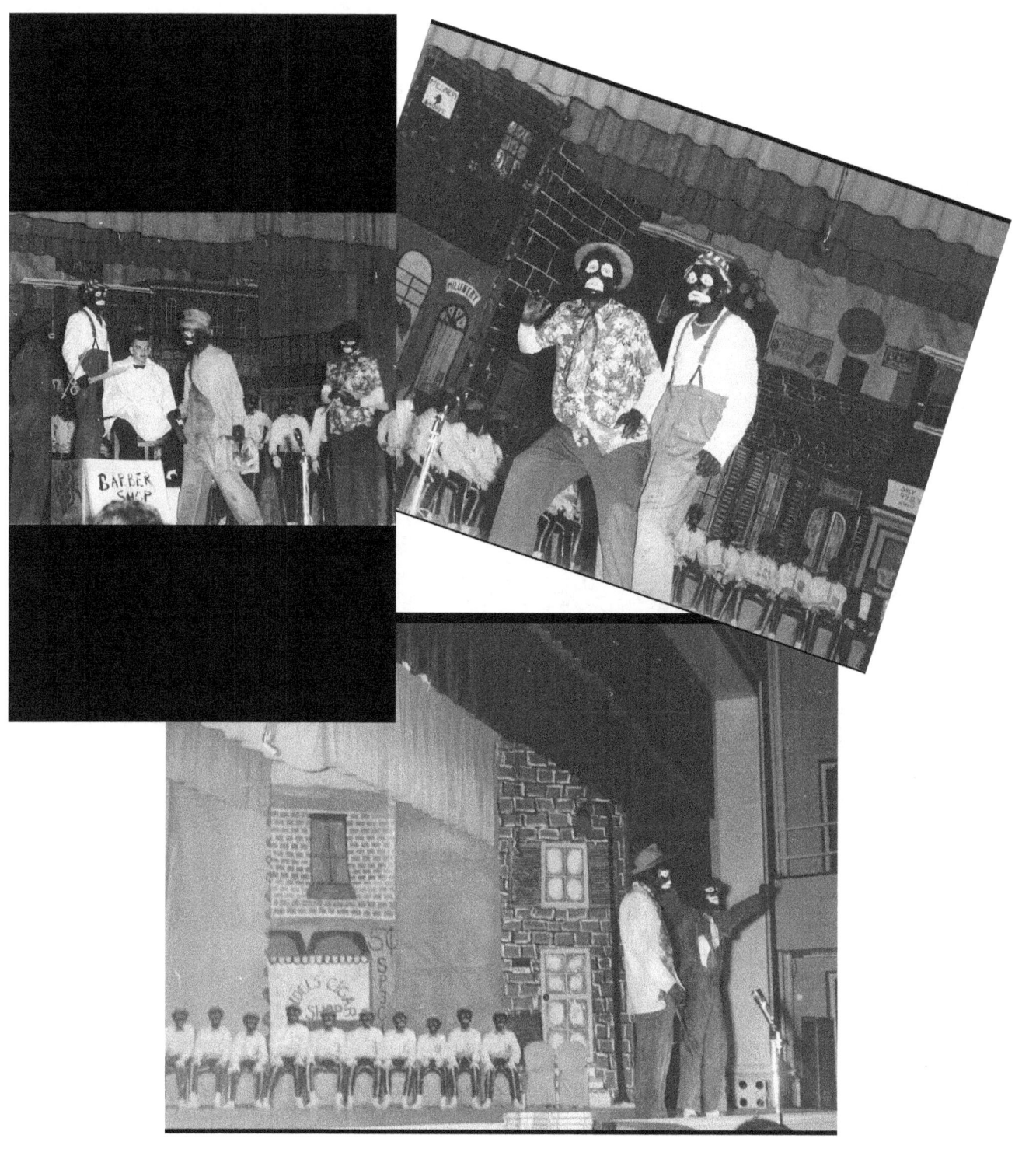

1962 Minstrel

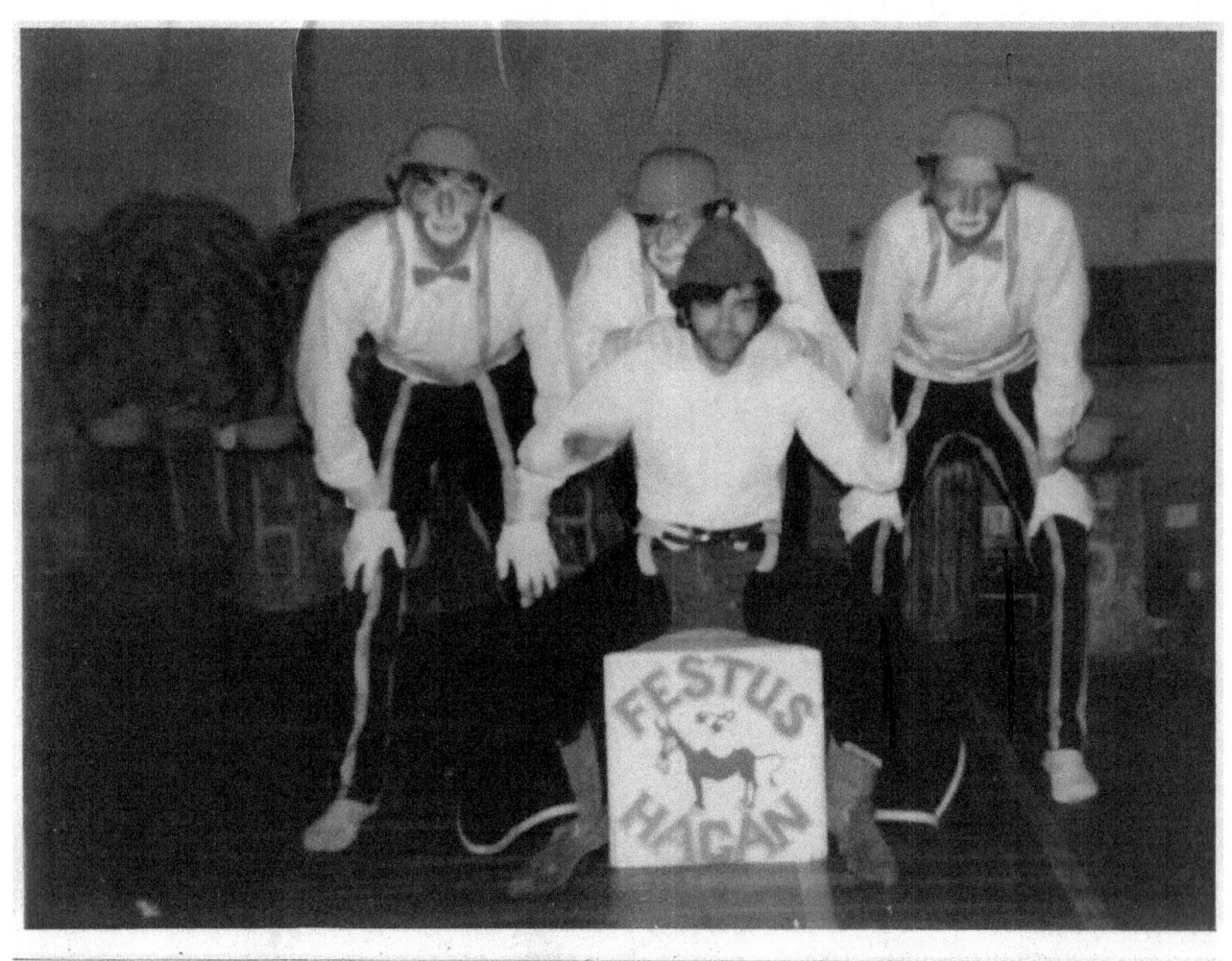

Left to Right: Steve Loggins, Mike Crawford,Robert Frew, Randy McBrayer(Festus)

From 1972 Hobo Show

WOODLAWN COUNCIL'S HIGHLIGHTS IN SOUND OF 1960

Sponsor: Mrs. Moon Gray

I would like to extend my sincere appreciation to the following people who have helped make the Record Yearbook a success:

Mr. Joseph Turner and Miss Claude Dowling.
Fred Milloit, Official Narrator
Andrew Davenport, Cover designer
Tri Hi-Y for their help in advertising
Maryvann Pilgreen for service beyond the call of duty
Bill Wheat my on the spot recorder
WBRC, Mr. Fox Lightfoot and Stan Siegel for recording all football games
Warbler's Club
Girl's Glee Club
Bomar Printing Company
Andy Robinson
Mrs. Franklin for keeping our records straight.

RECORD YEARBOOK STAFF

Narrator: Fred Milloit   Sponsor: Rose B. Johnson

Designer of Cover: Andy Davenport   Sponsor: Mrs. Black

Publicity Chairman: Maryvann Pilgreen   Sponsor: Mrs. Kinzey and Tri-Hi-Y Club

Recording Editors: Bill Wheat, Andy Robinson, Reugene Gunn
Sponsors: Mr. Turner, Mr. Youngblood

Advice Chairman: Mrs. Roger W. Long

SIDE ONE	SIDE TWO
Introduction by Fred Milliot	Cavaliers singing "Halls of Ivy"
Revue of Football Season by Artie Hanes	Girl's Glee Club "All the Things You Are"
Phillip's-Woodlawn Game	Band Revue "Trumpet Holiday"
Caroliers Cherbium Song	Highlights from minstrel
Stunt Night — Warbler's Singing	Choir singing "The Lord Bless You and
"Tumbling Tumbleweed"	Keep You"
Fall Play	
Christmas Music	
Orchestra	

My Sincere Thanks Goes To
Artist Recording Studio
Mr. Homer Milam
Who Made This Record Possible.

© R. W. Long 1960

Sincerely Yours,
Eleanor Long
Advisor Chairman

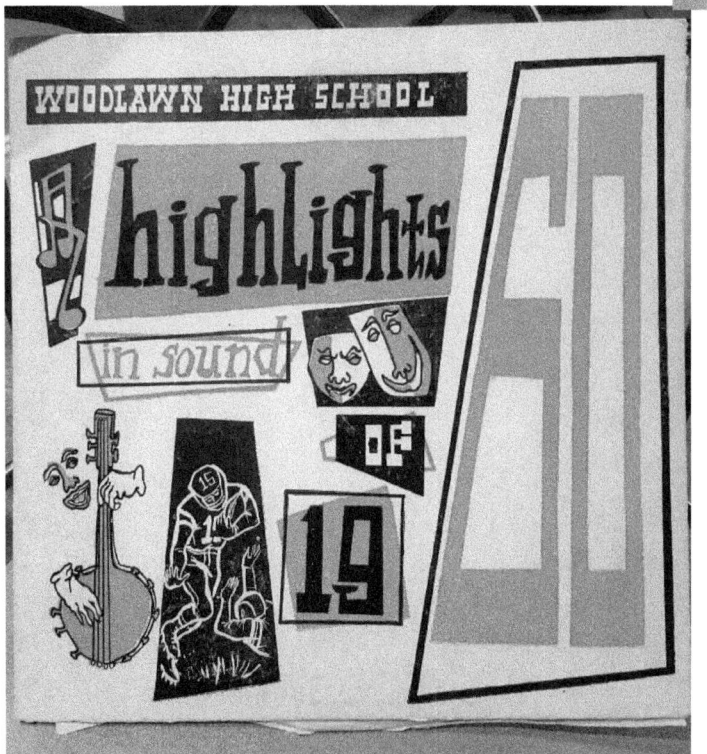

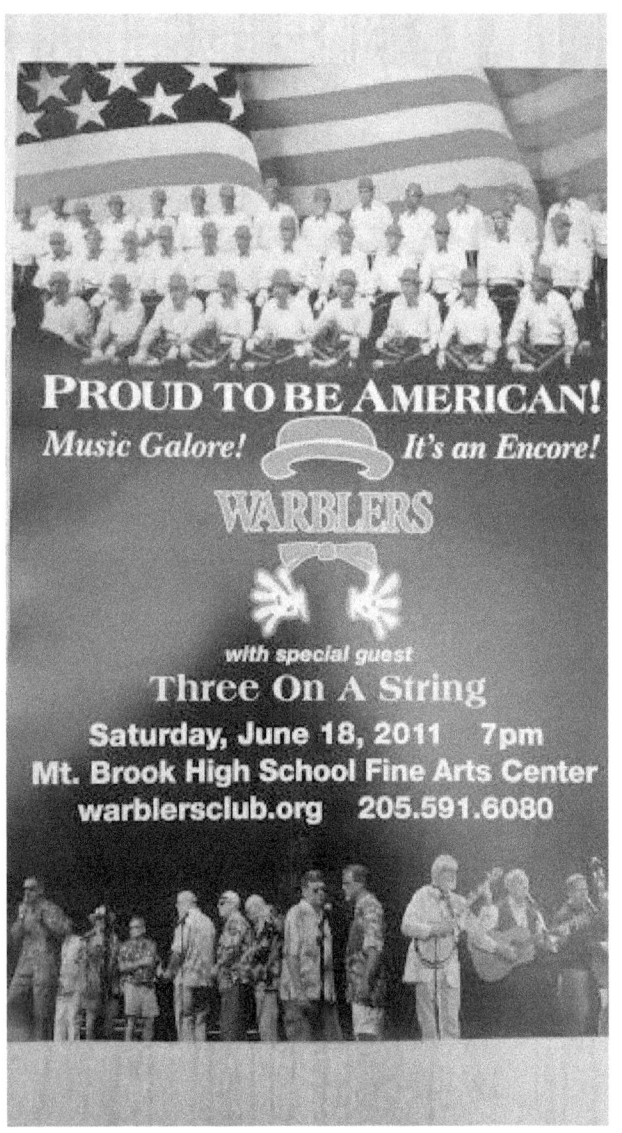

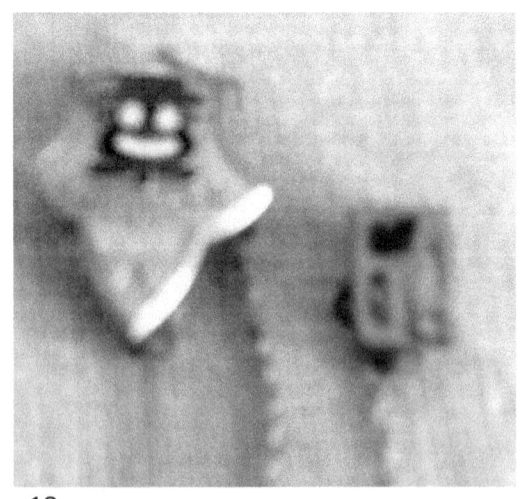

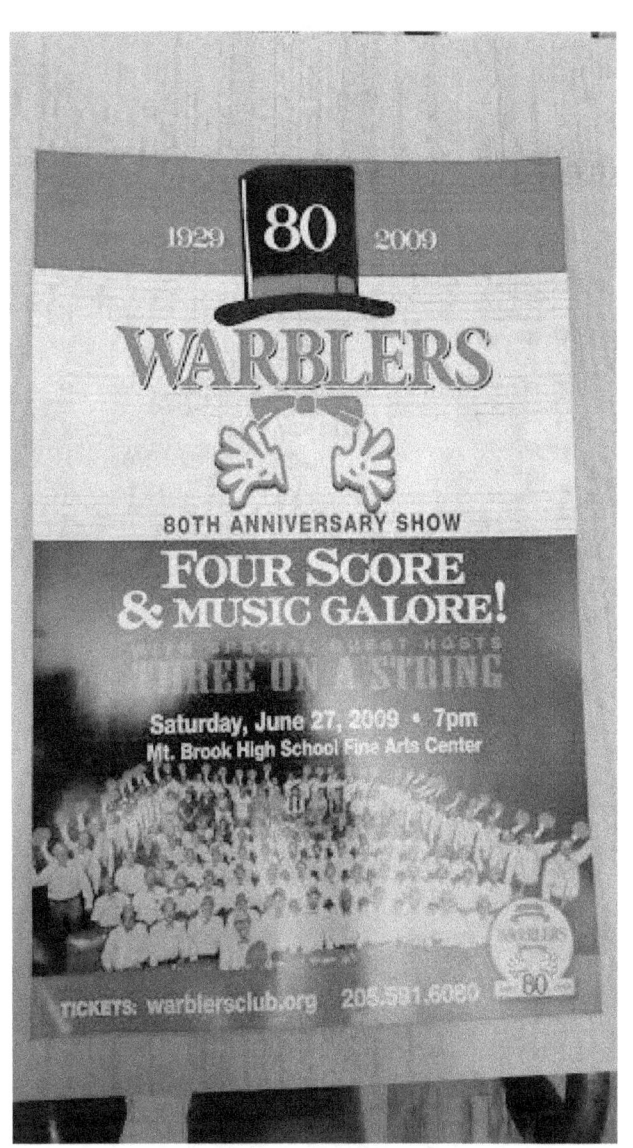

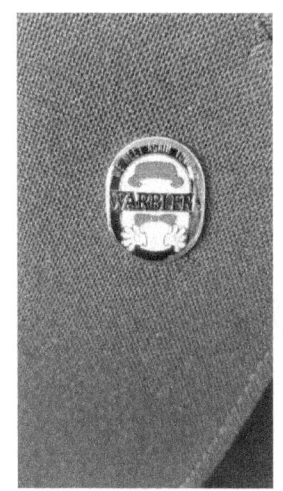

2005 Warblers at the Alabama Theater with Three on a String

(TOAS — Honorary Warblers)

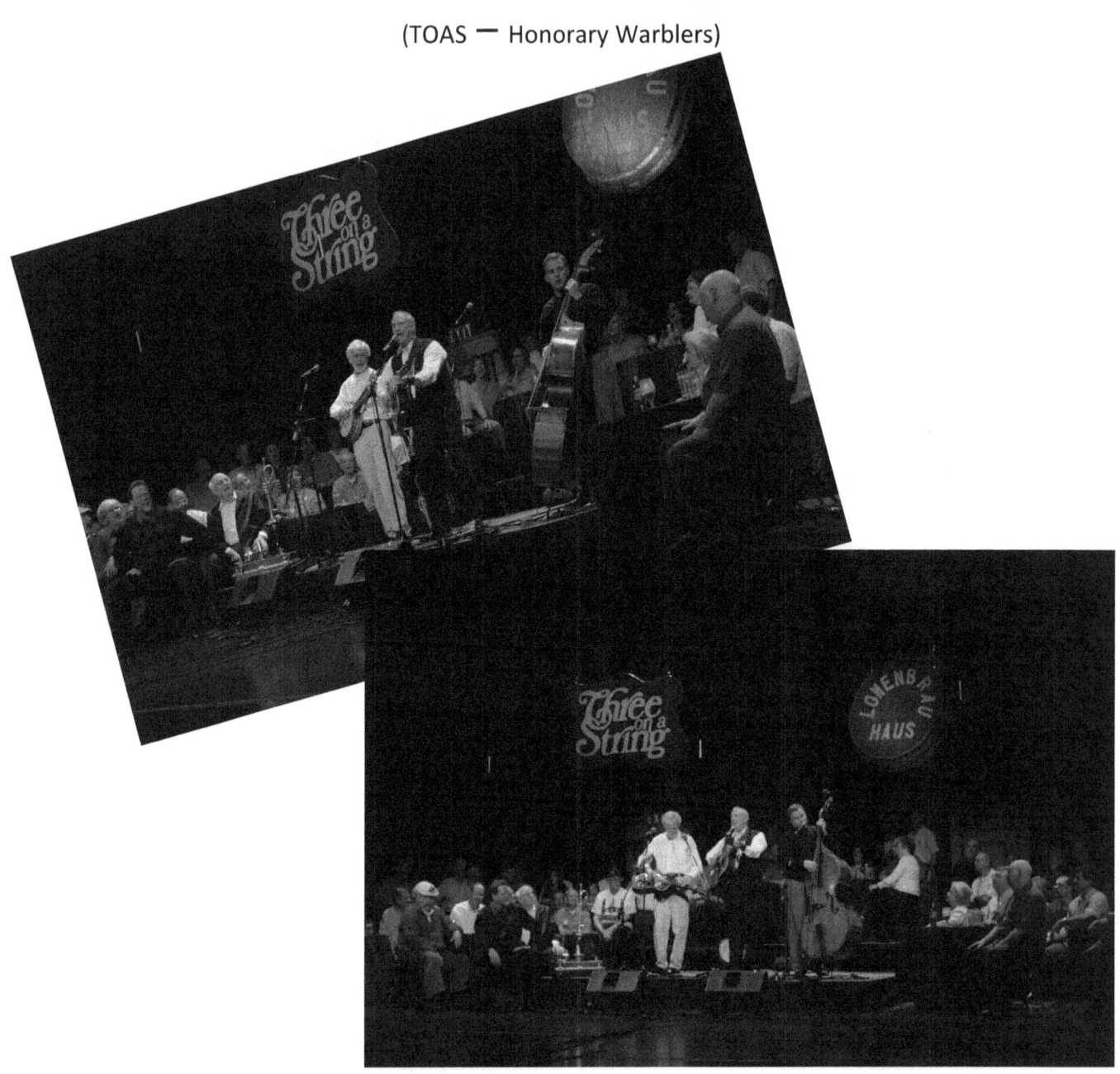

2005 at the Alabama

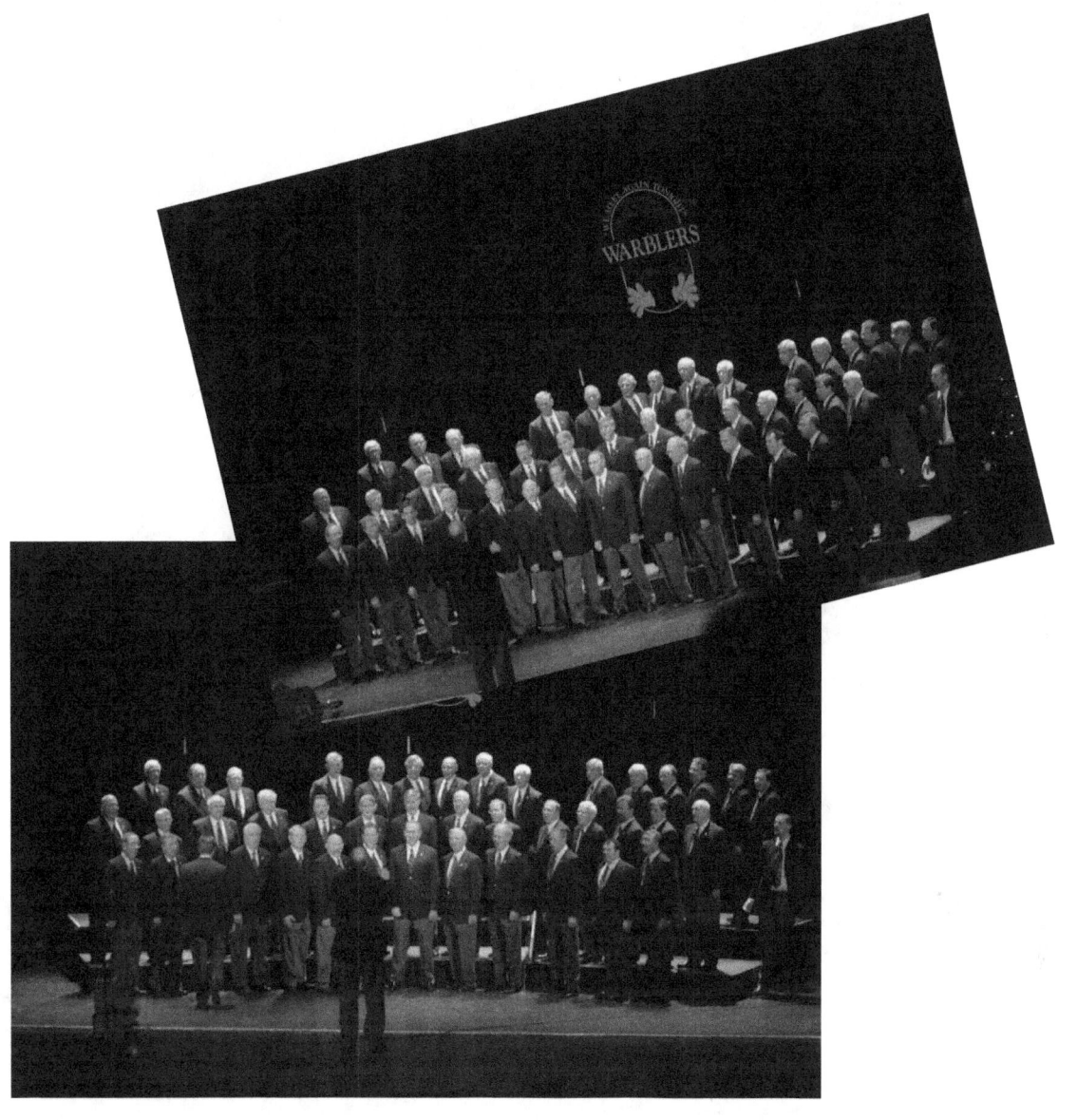

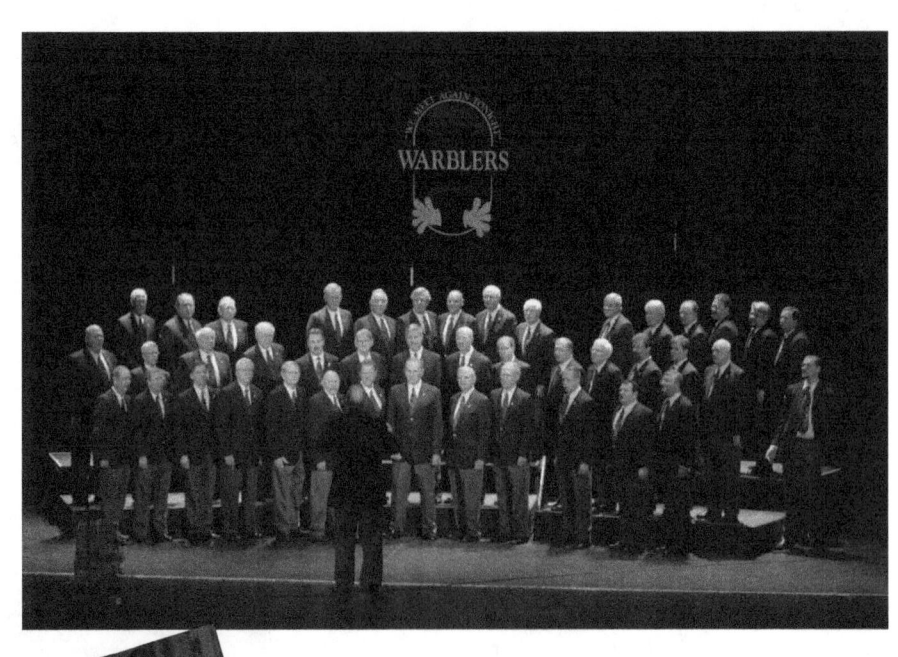

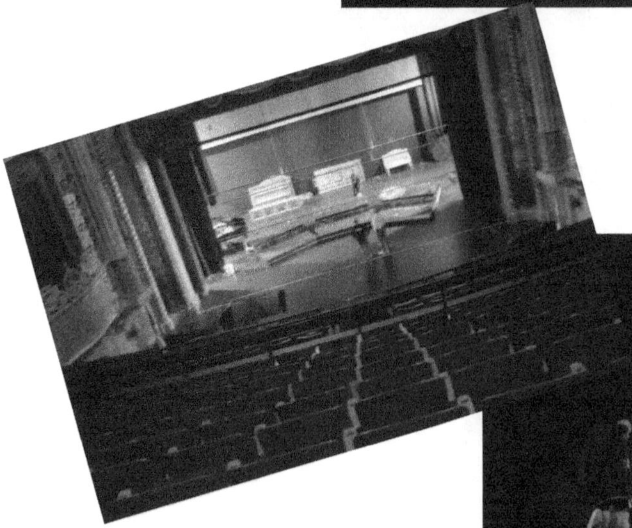

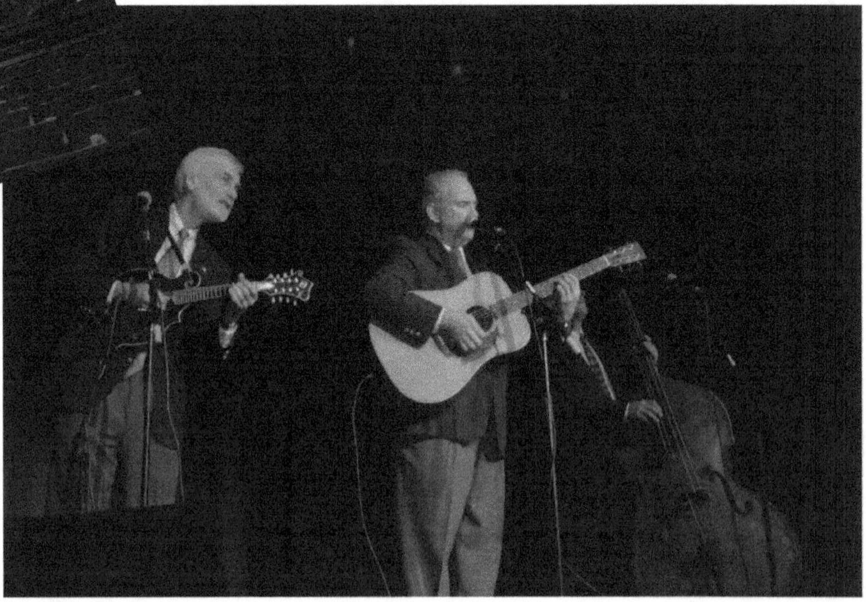

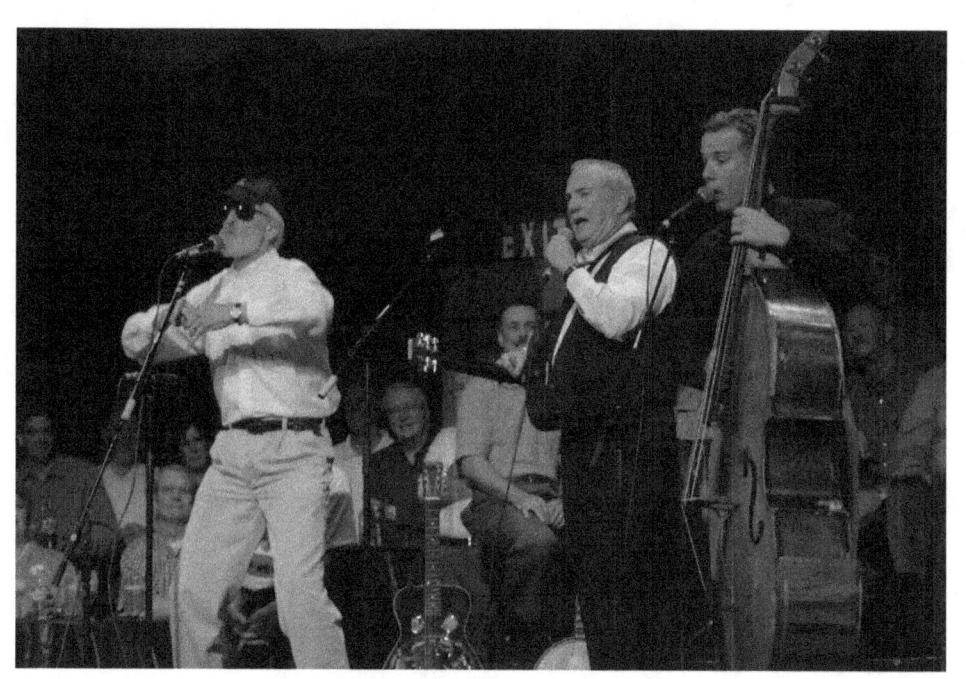

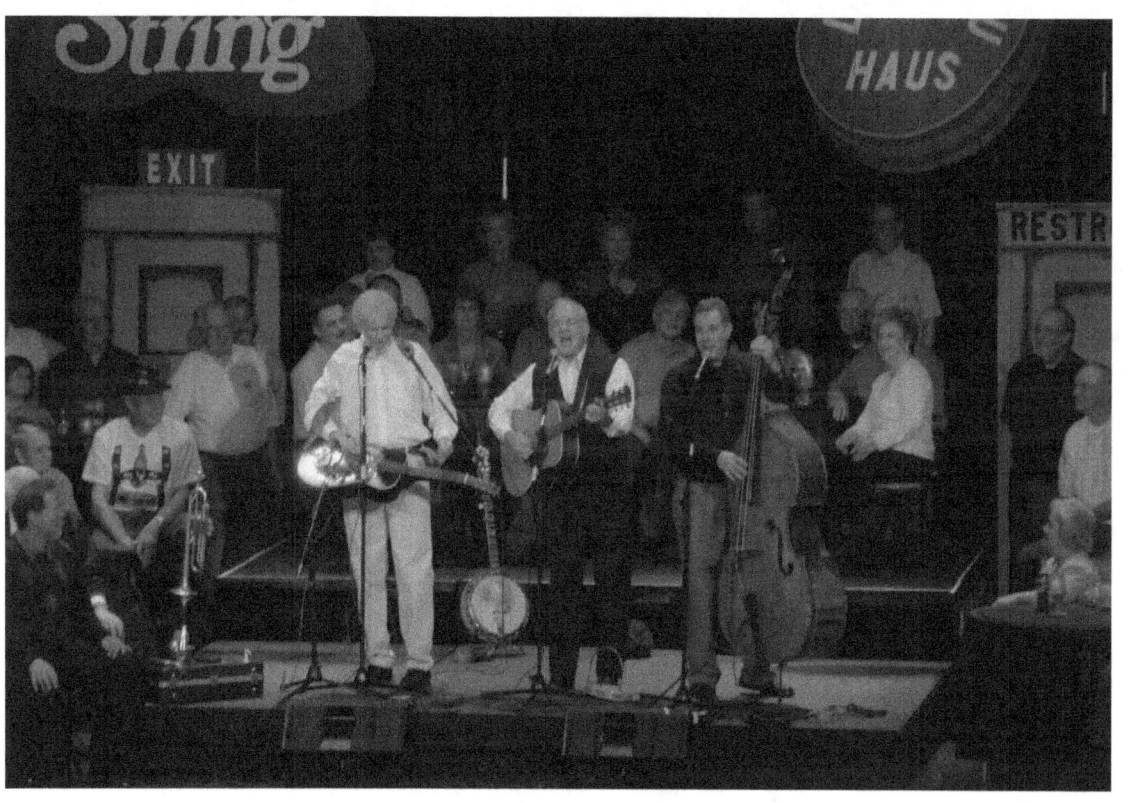

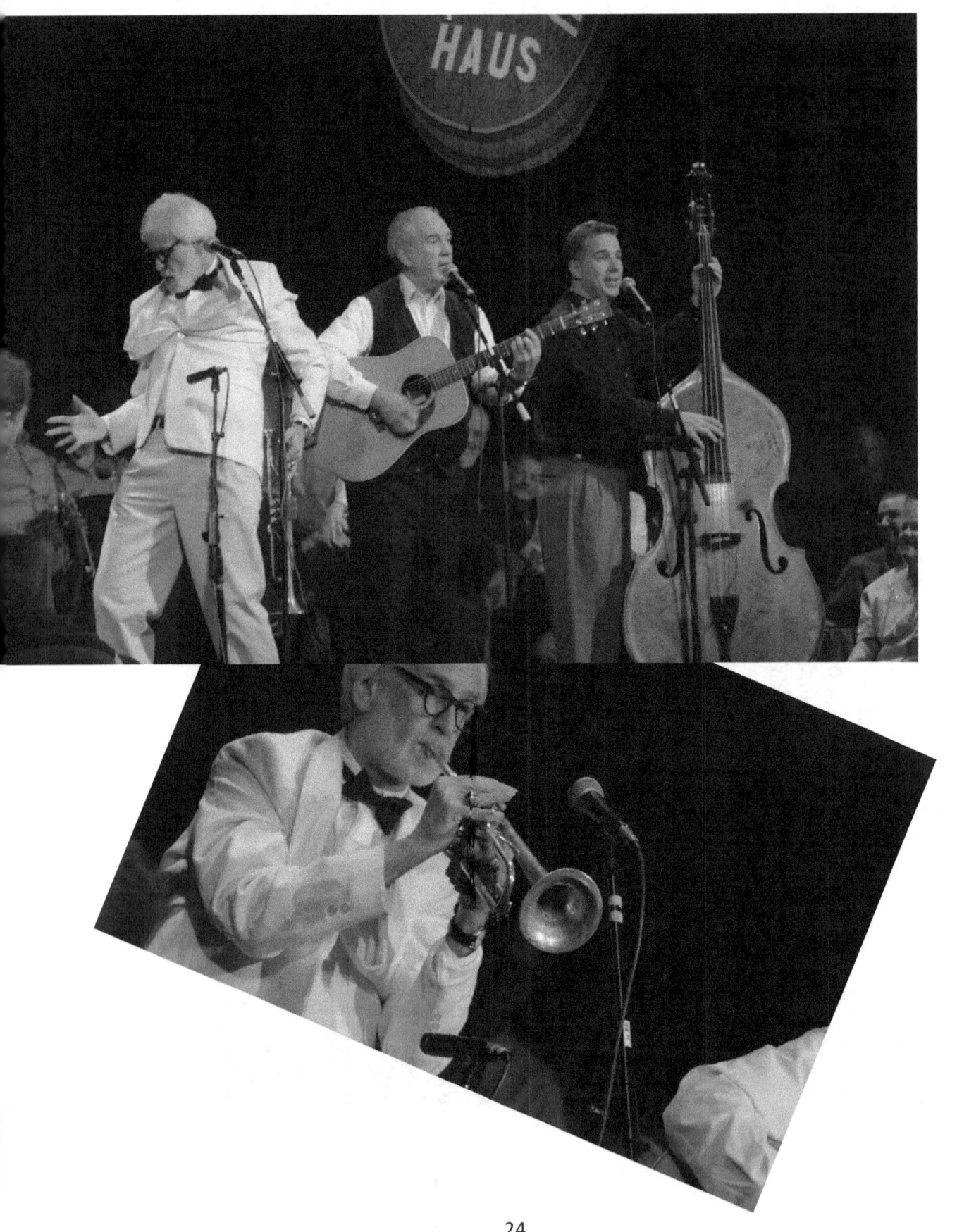

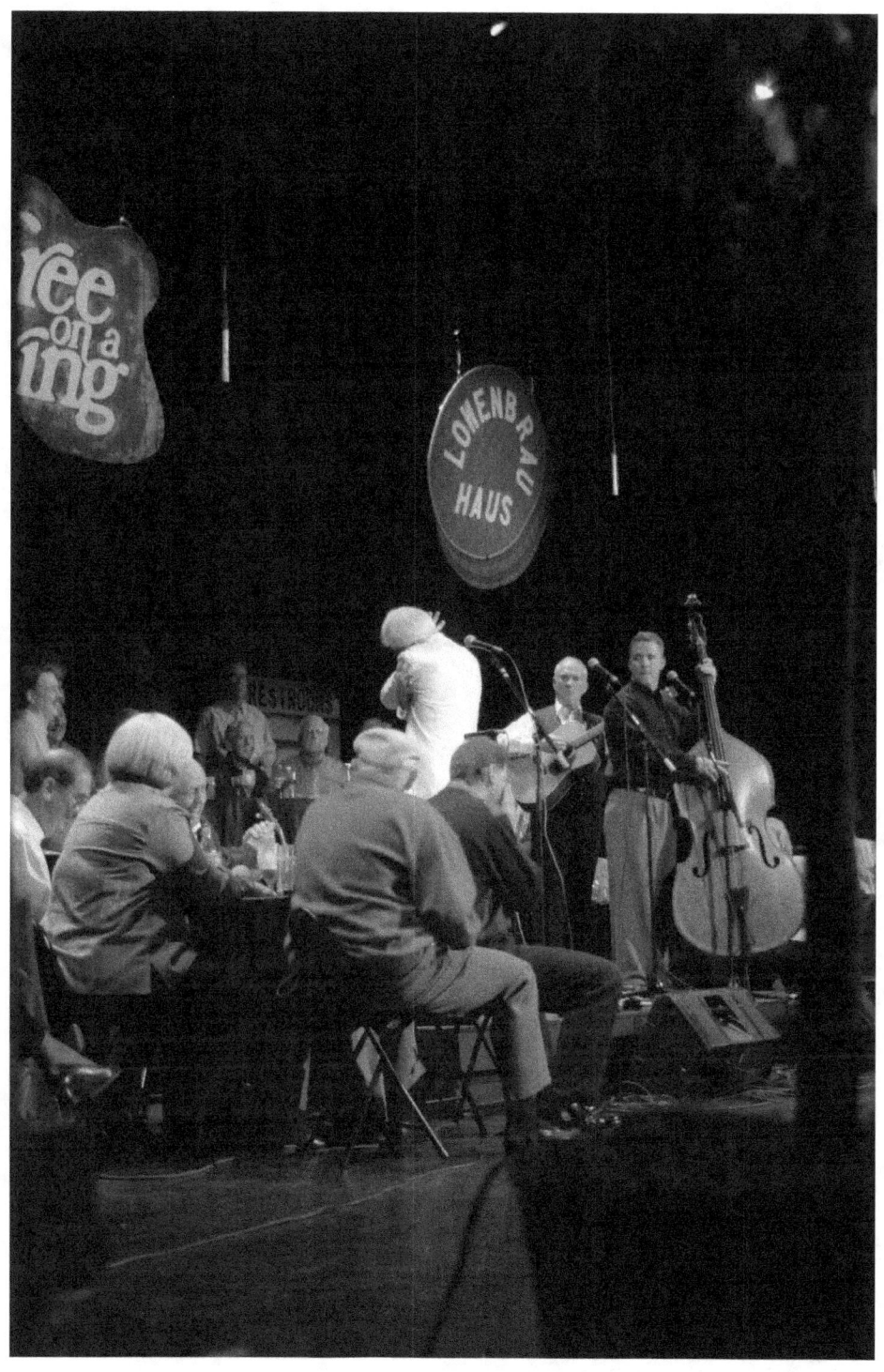

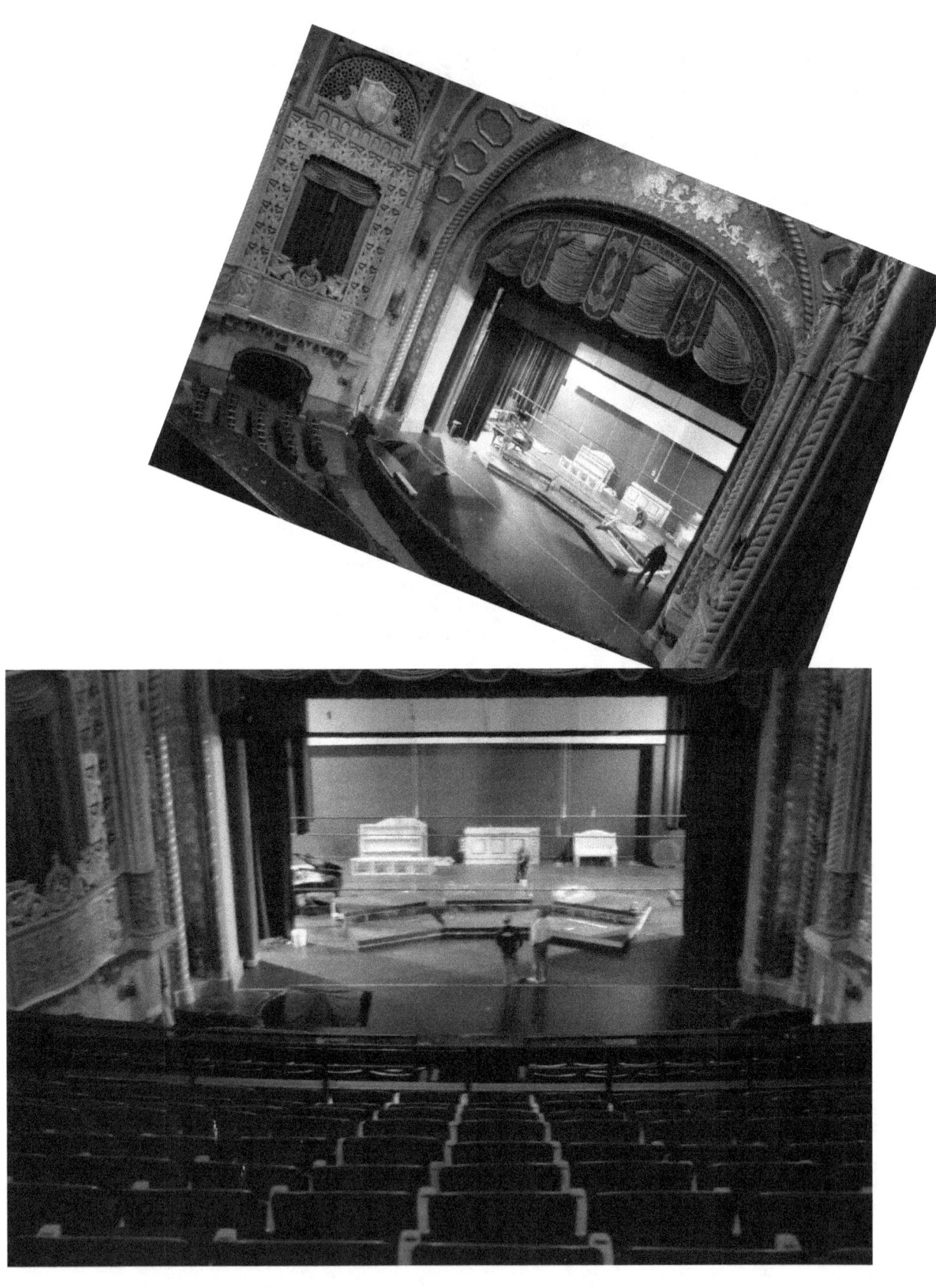

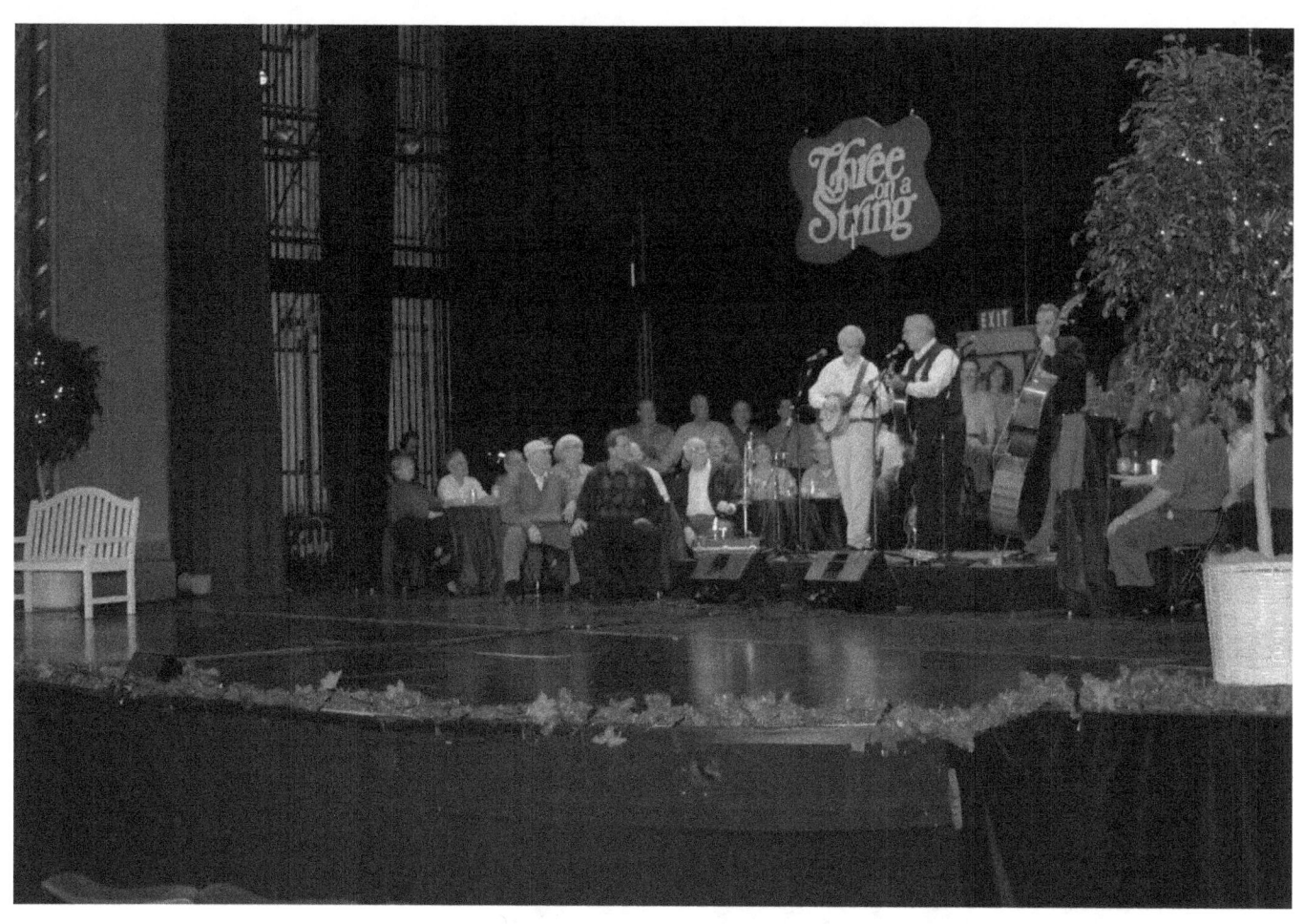

From 2011 Show

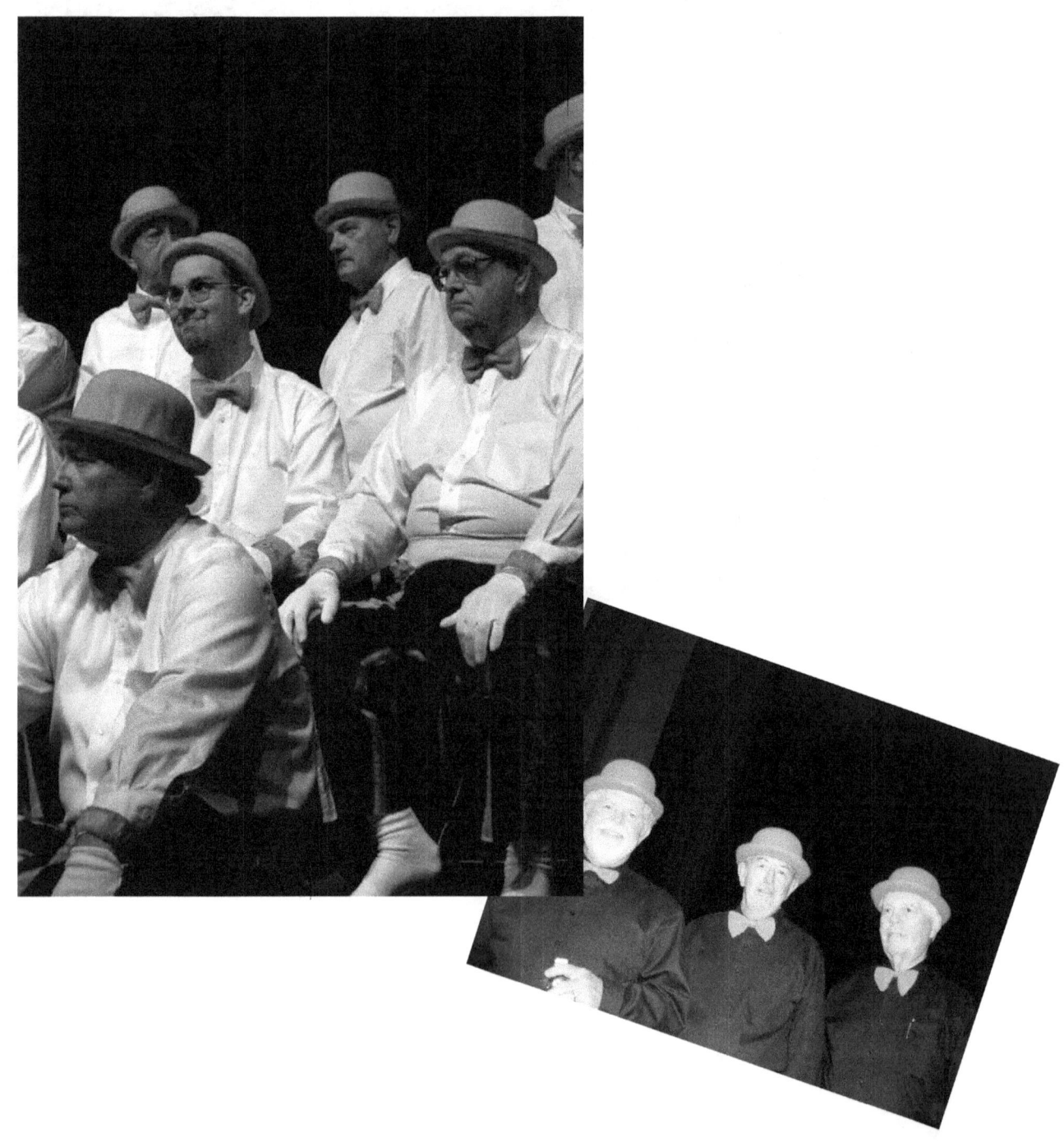

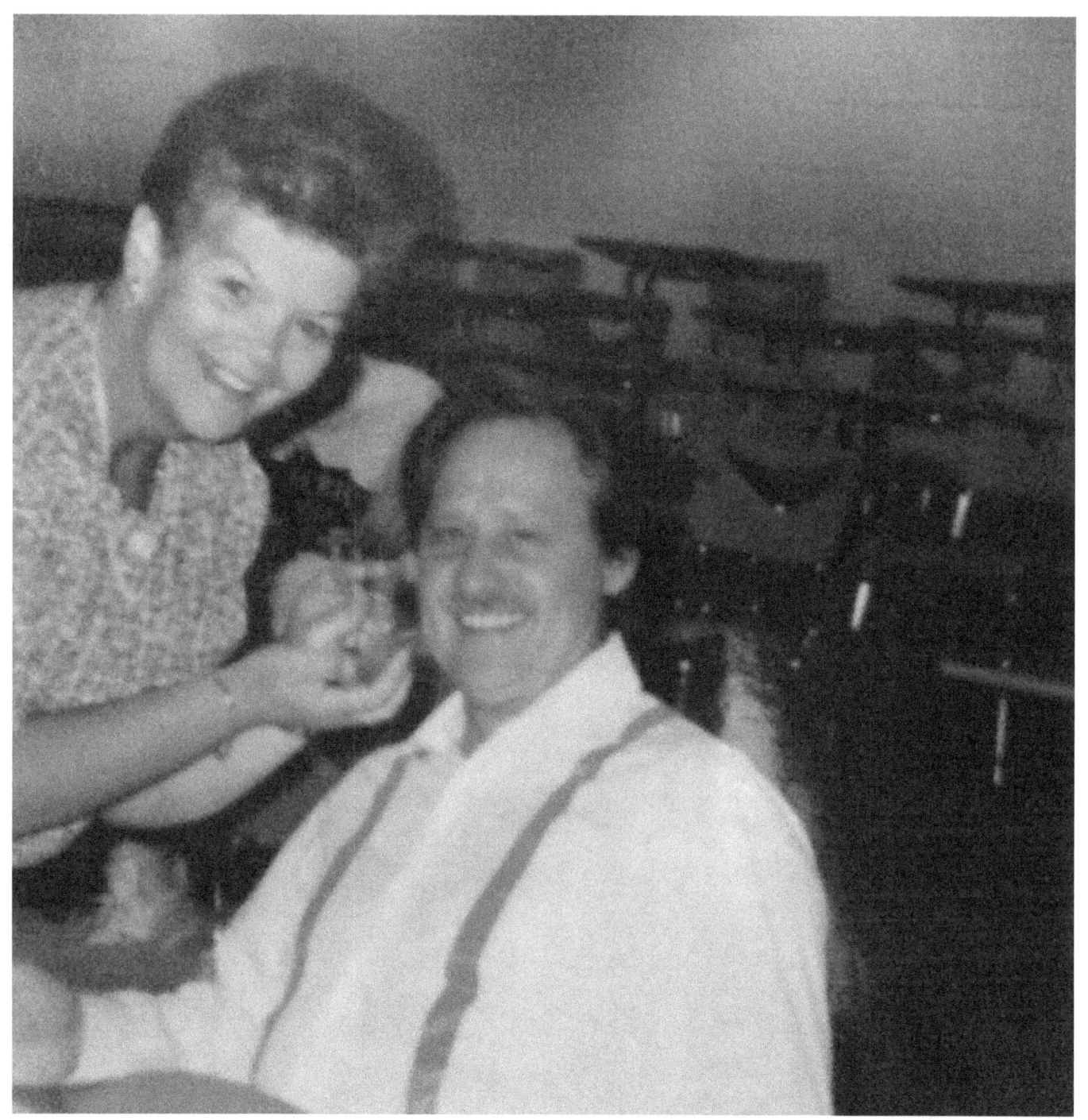

Harriet Clark and Joe Thrasher

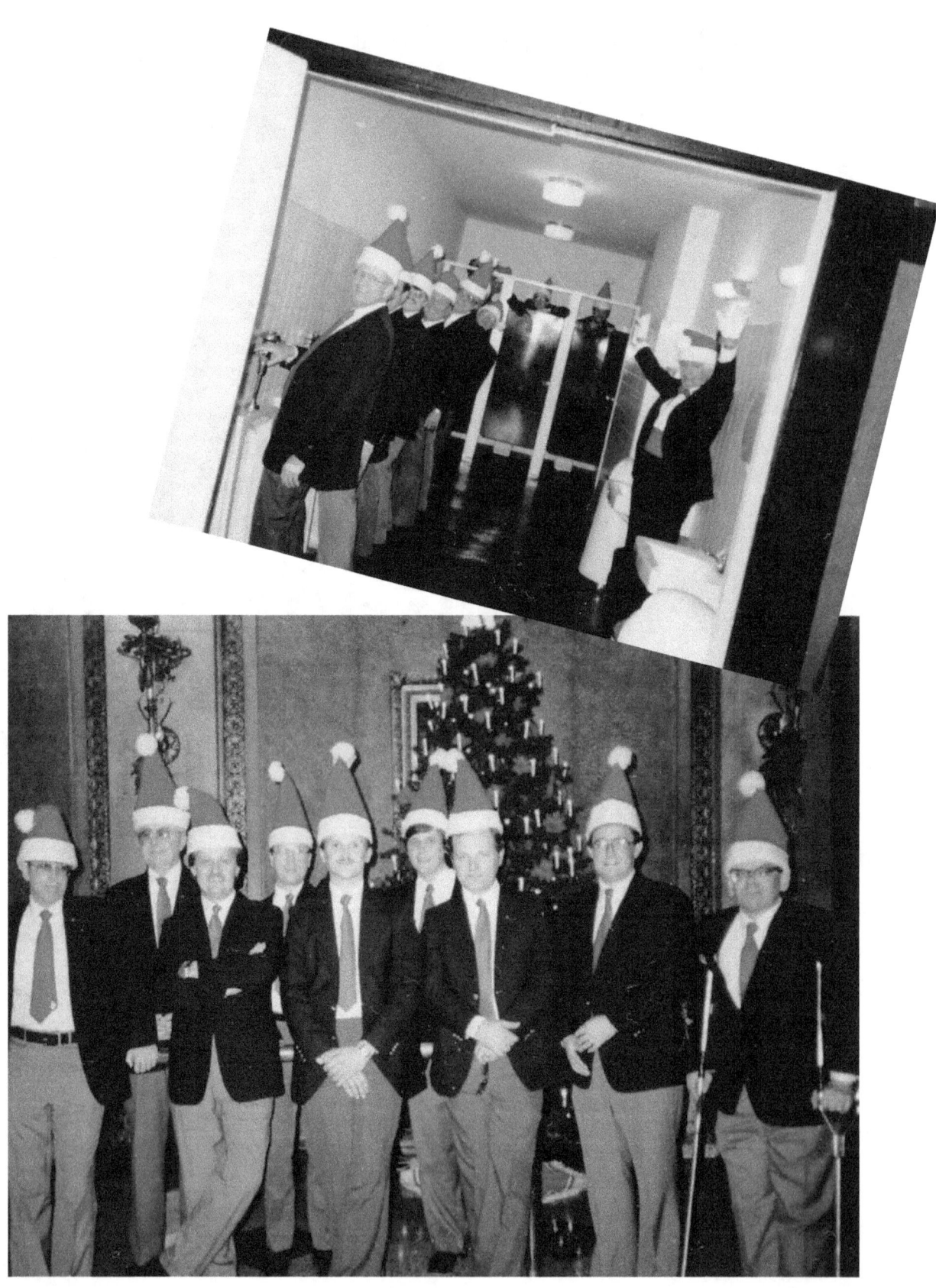

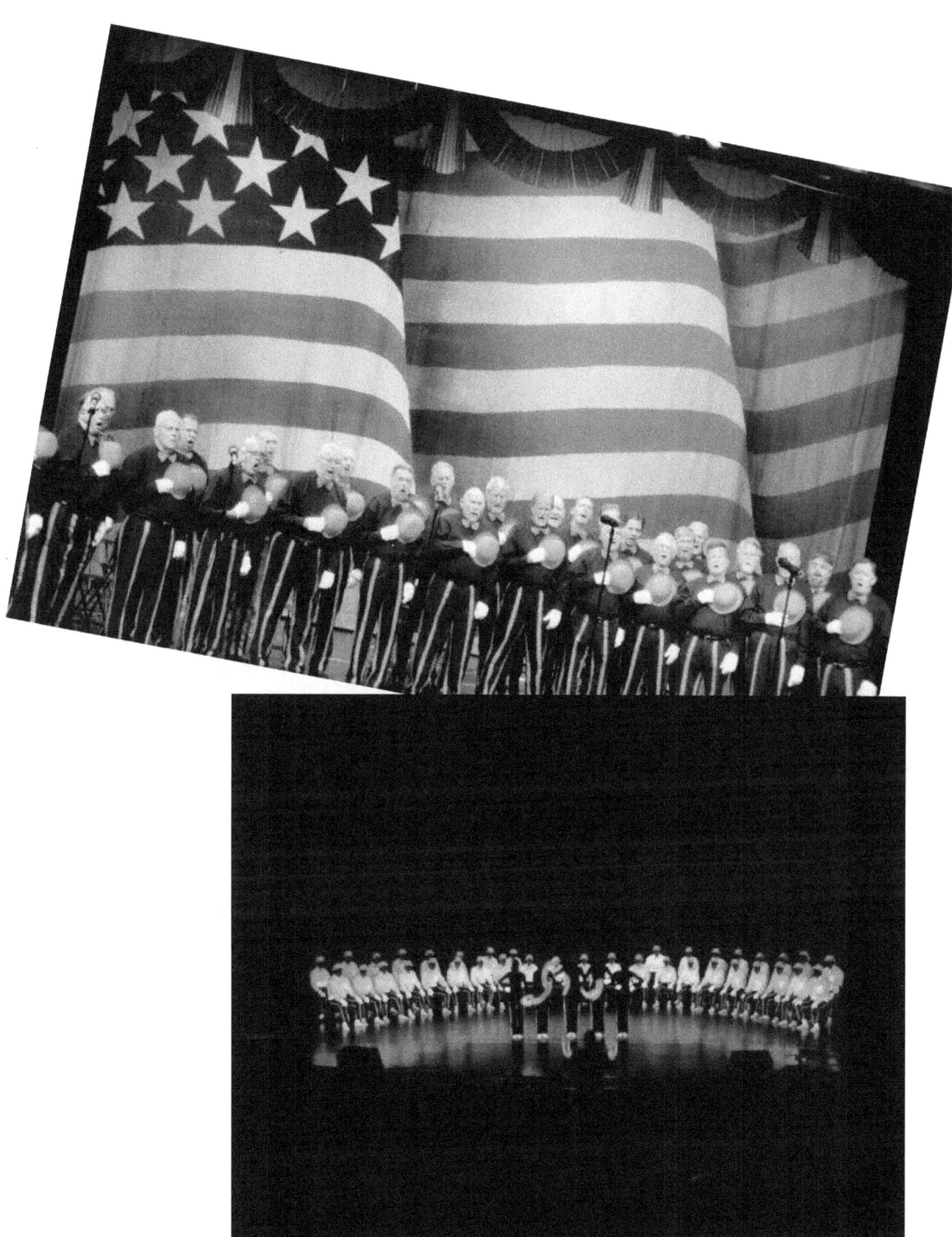

Woodlawn High School Stunt Night 1975...Warblers Club performing "What Shall We Do With A Drunken Sailor."

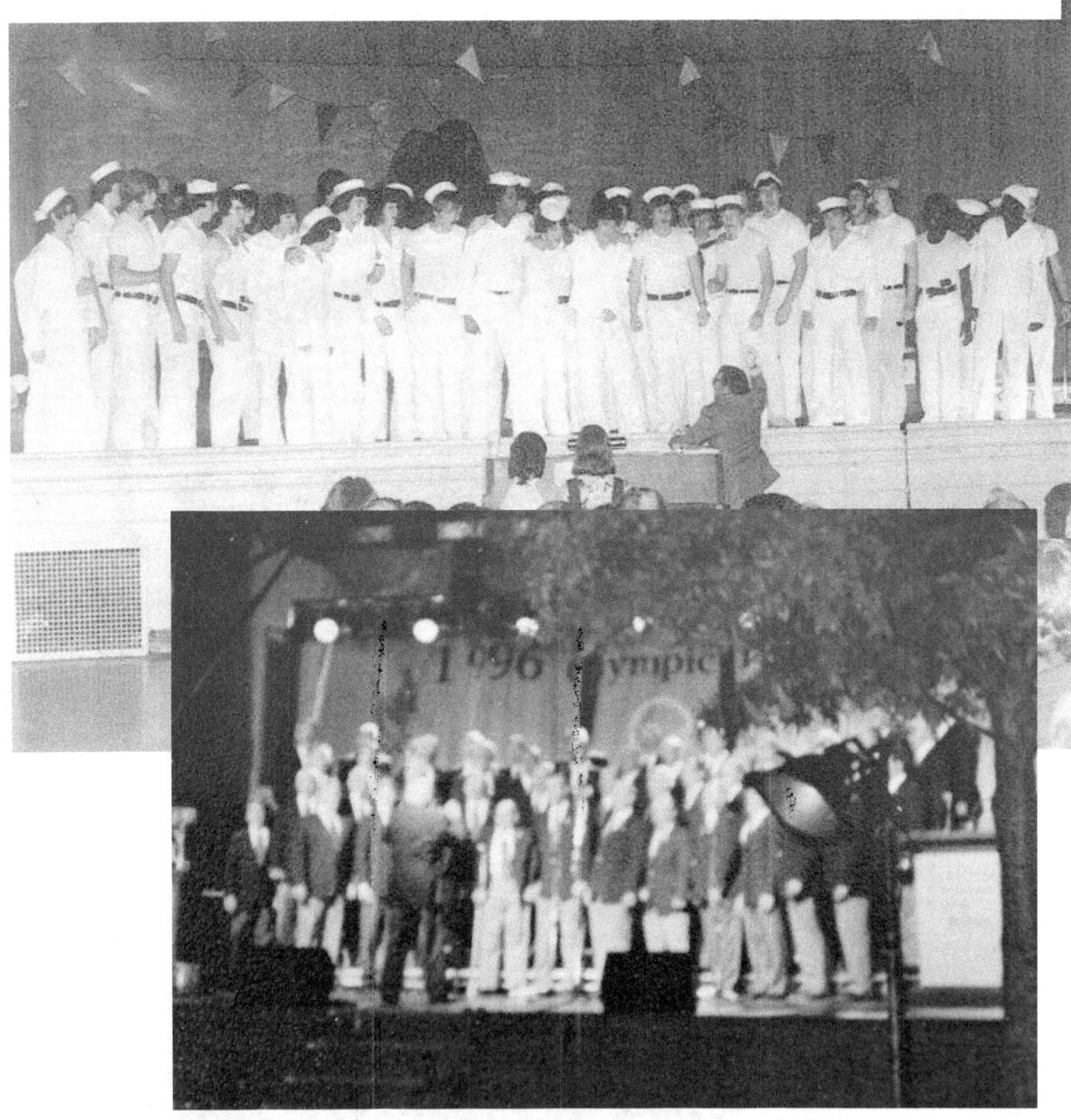

Singing at Rickwood Field

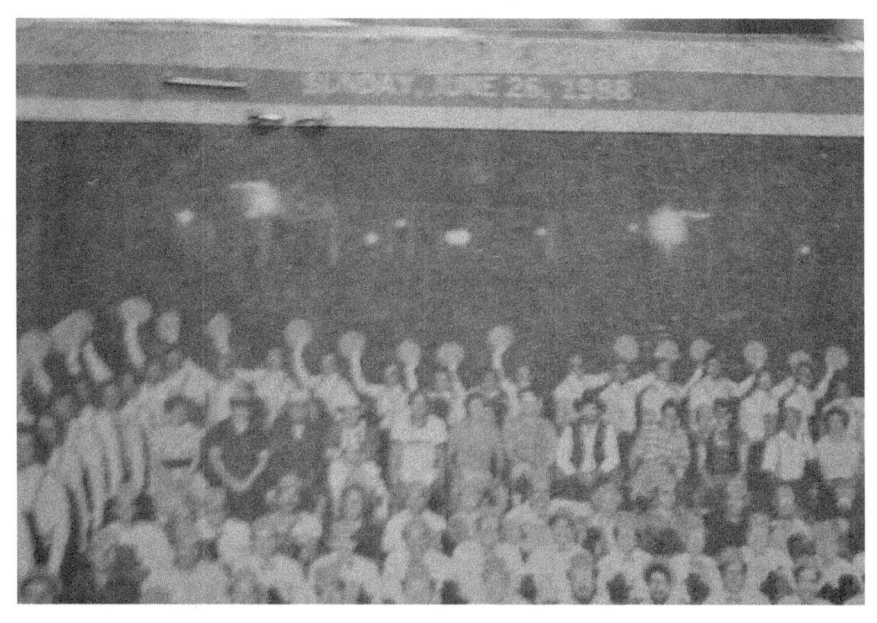

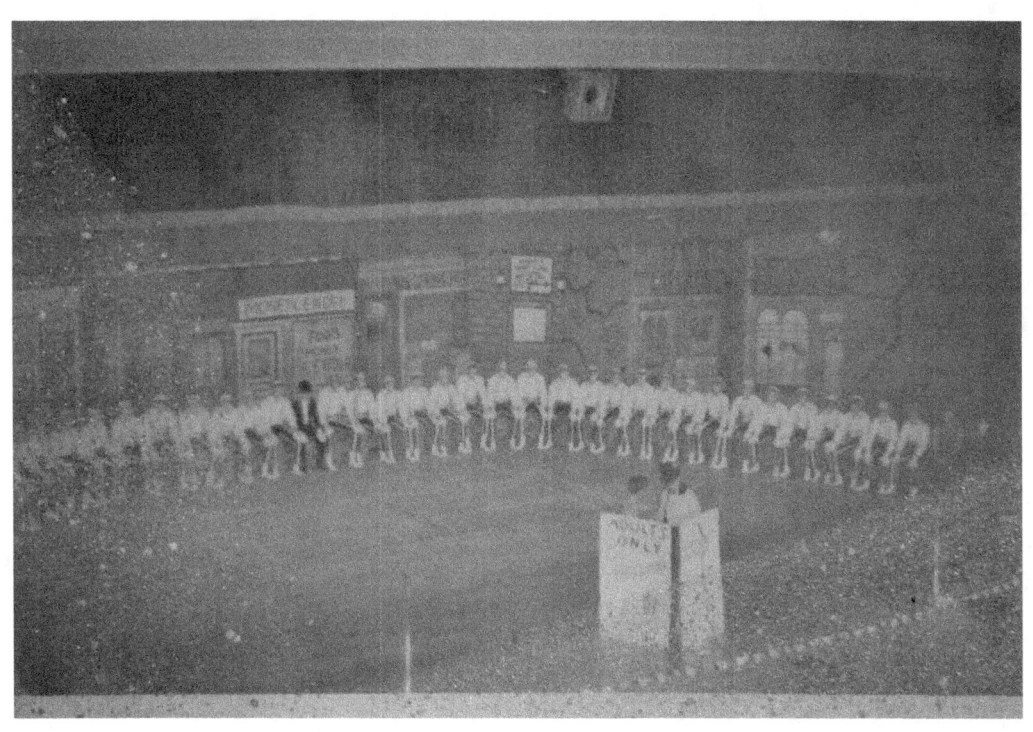

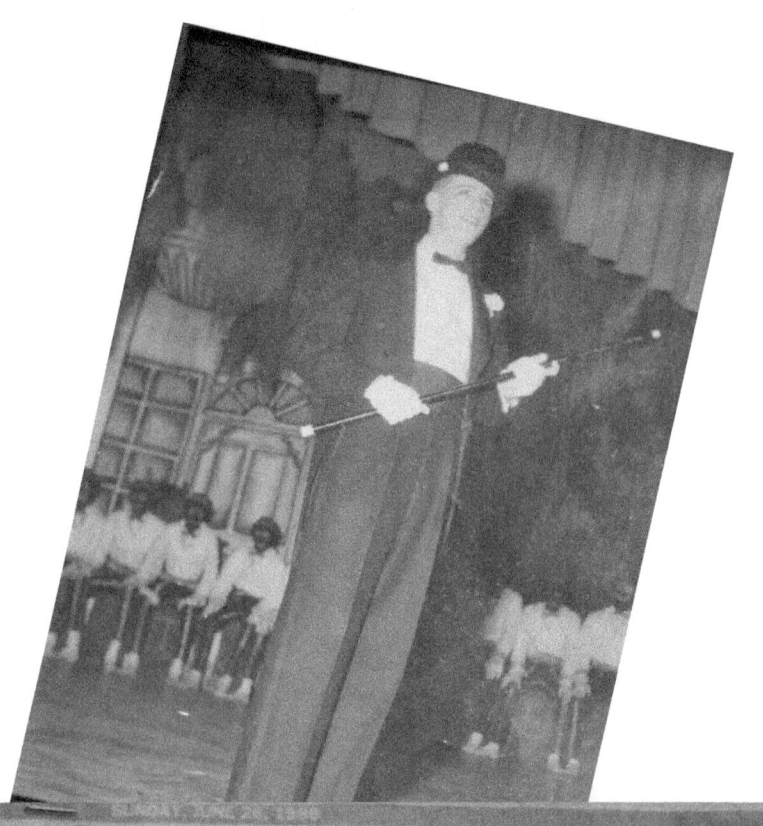

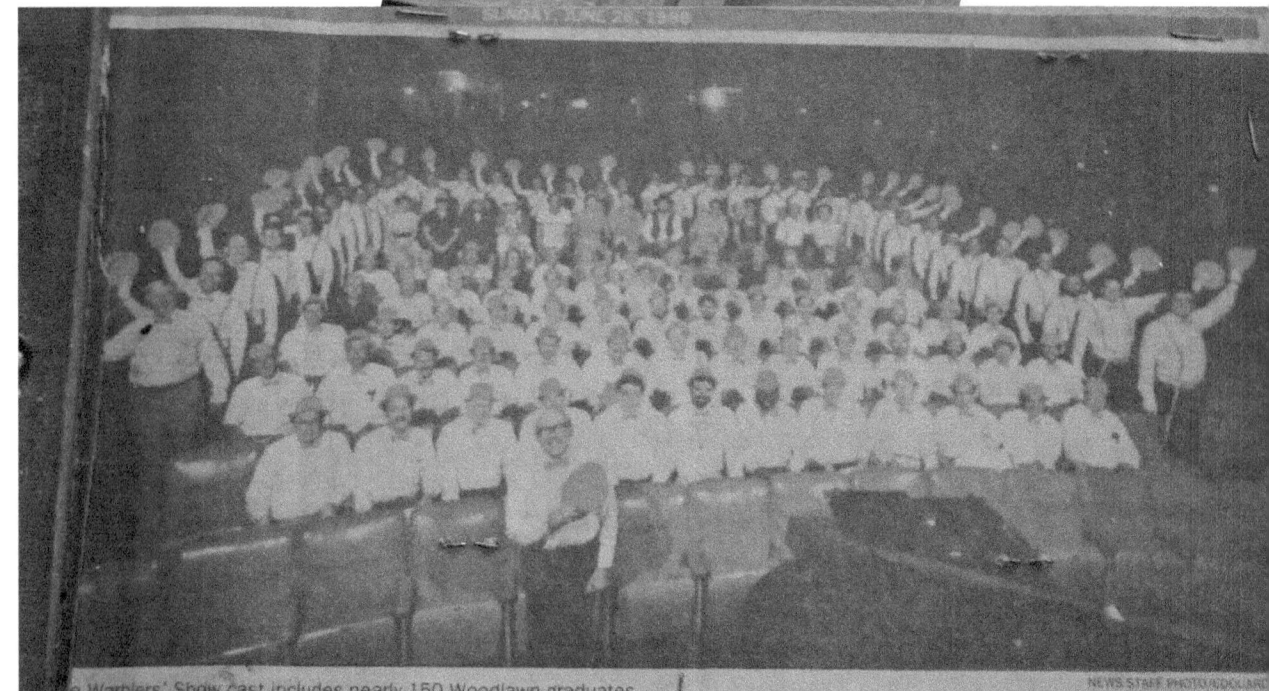

e Warblers' Show cast includes nearly 150 Woodlawn graduates.

NEWS STAFF PHOTO/GOOLARD

Warblers will journey for a sentimental sing

eunion to bring Woodlawn graduates back to Alabama Theatre

Elma Bell
's staff writer

reunion concert. The cast includes nearly 150 Warblers from across the state, and several hundred more are expected to attend.

being in the Warblers. Mr. Turner was the kind of man boys looked up to. He worked out with weights, he was a lifeguard at Cascade Plunge.

'One of the soloists in this Warb concert, Jake Antonio, was one of Hudson says.

34

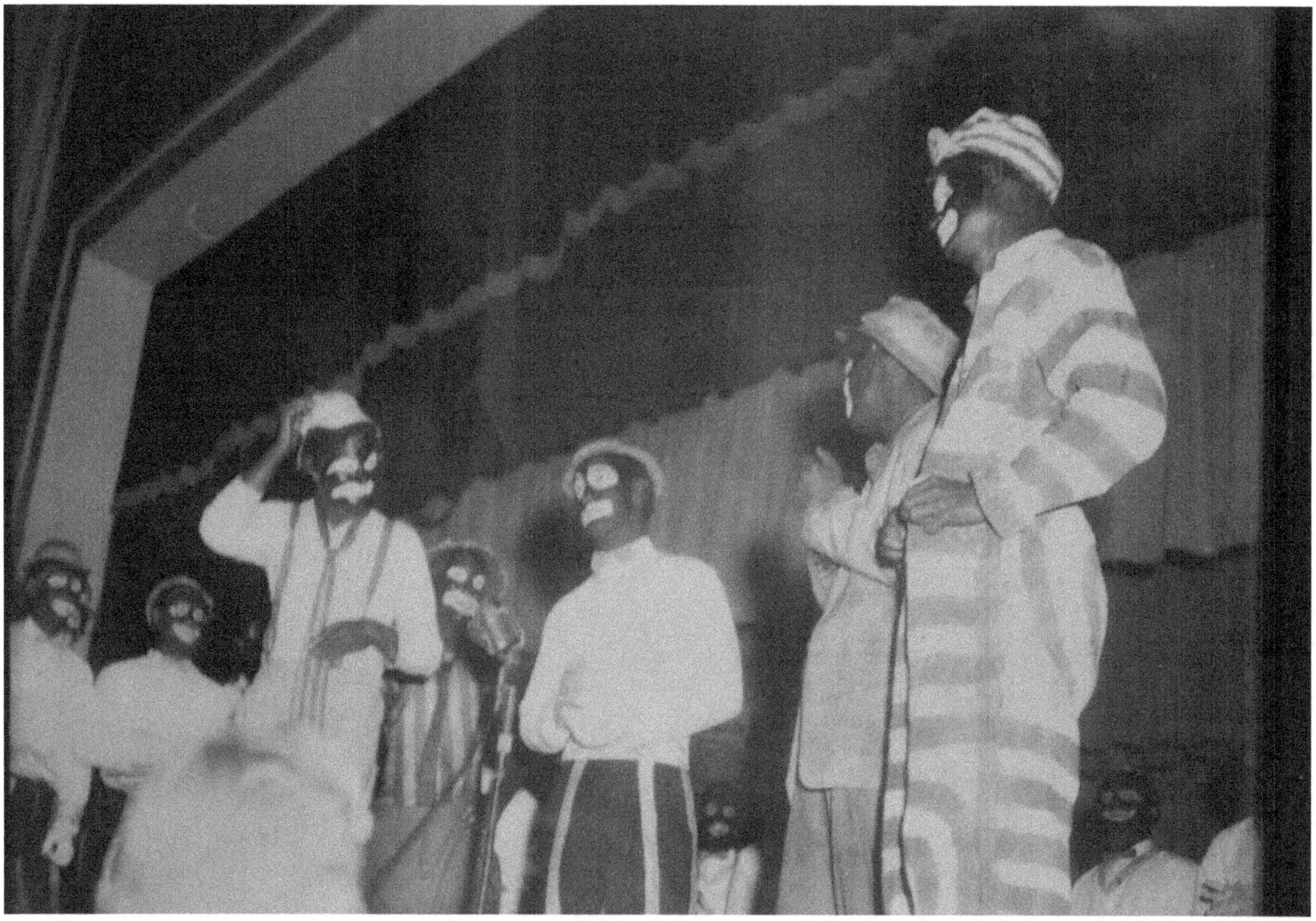

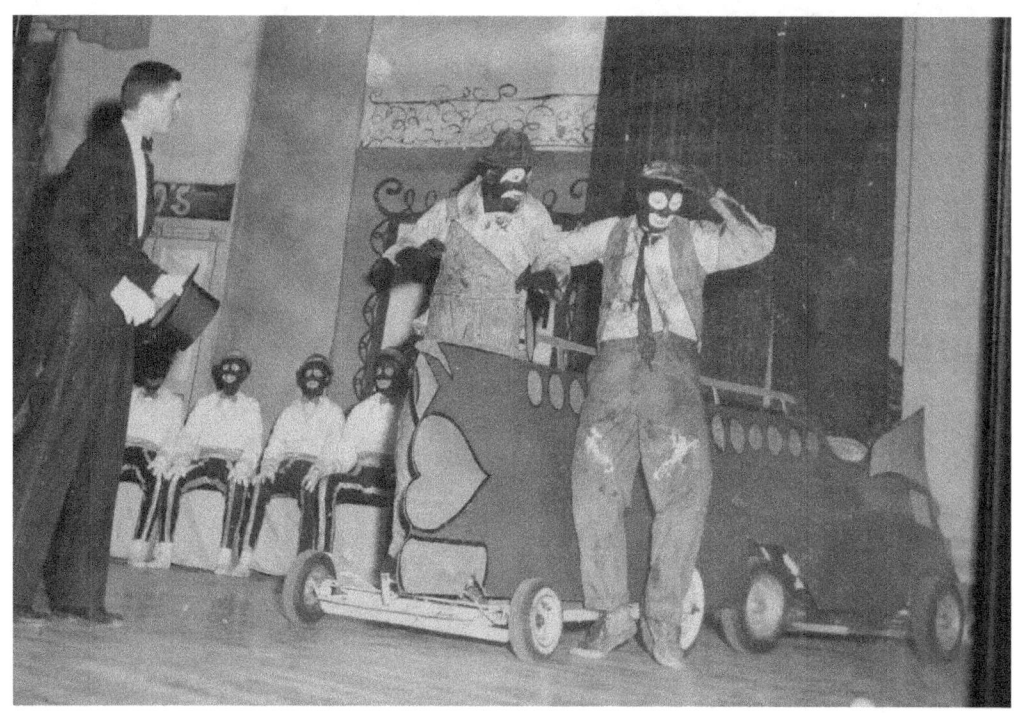

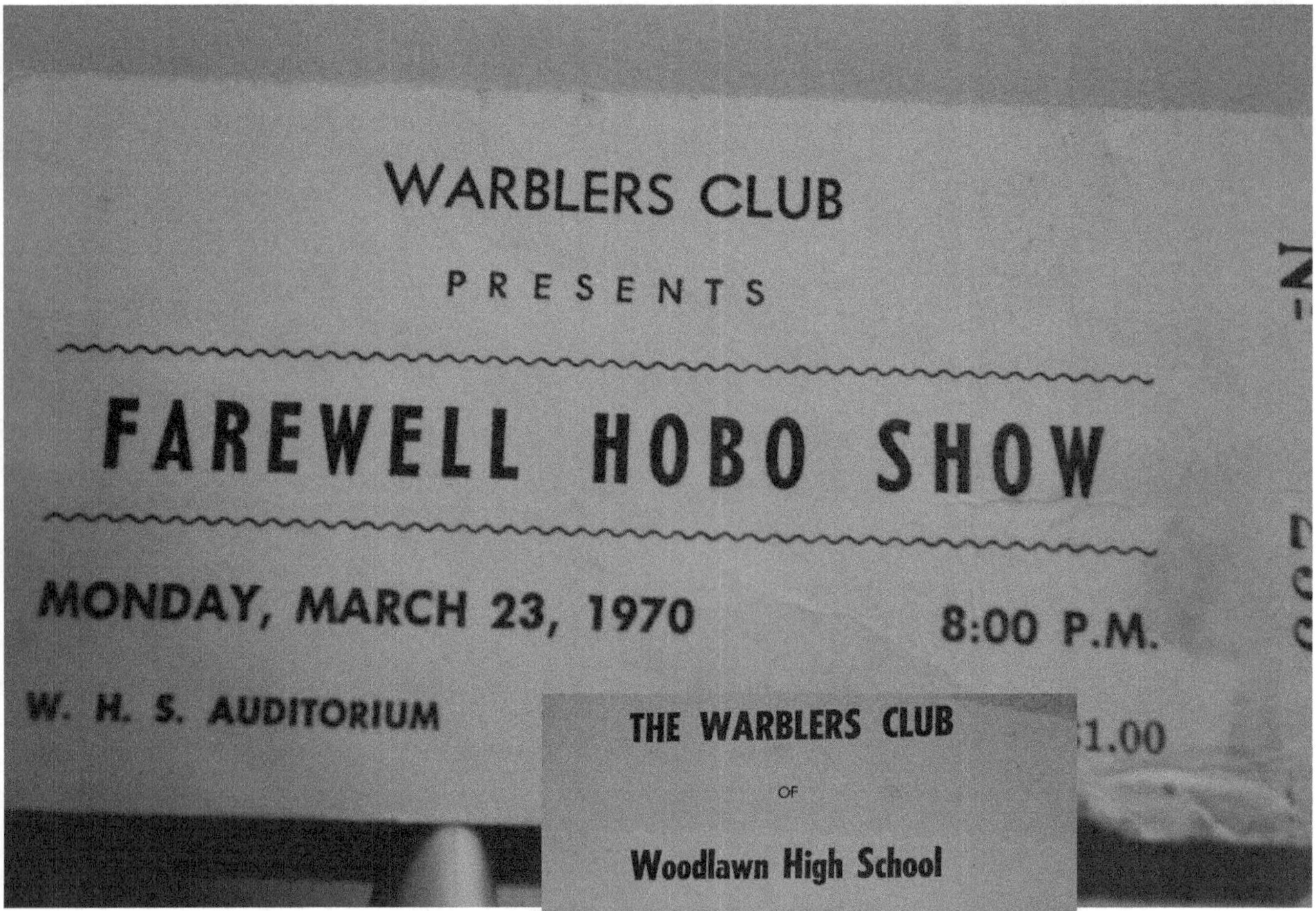

WARBLERS CLUB

PRESENTS

FAREWELL HOBO SHOW

MONDAY, MARCH 23, 1970   8:00 P.M.

W. H. S. AUDITORIUM   1.00

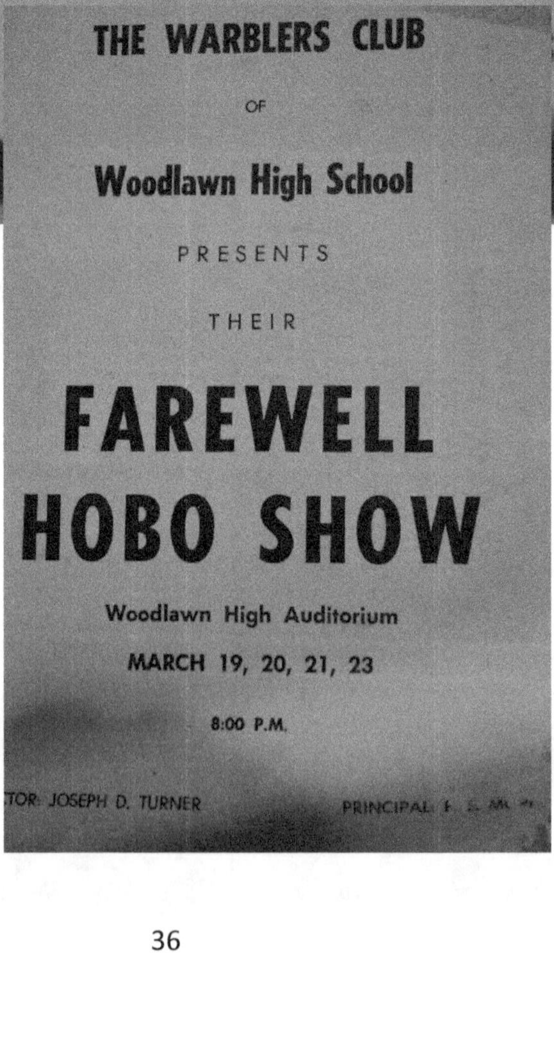

THE WARBLERS CLUB

OF

Woodlawn High School

PRESENTS

THEIR

FAREWELL
HOBO SHOW

Woodlawn High Auditorium

MARCH 19, 20, 21, 23

8:00 P.M.

TOR: JOSEPH D. TURNER   PRINCIPAL H. E. MA..

36

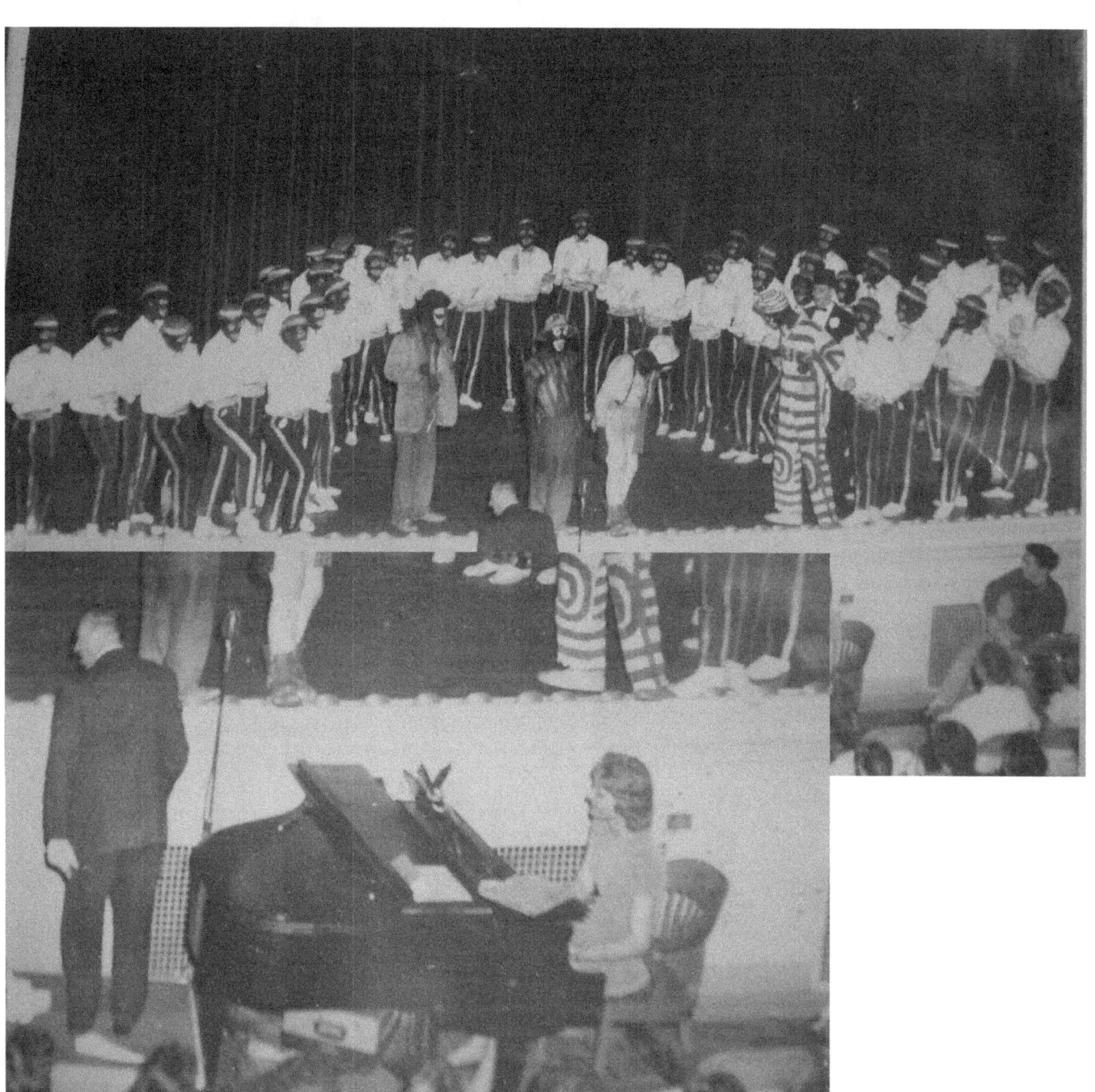

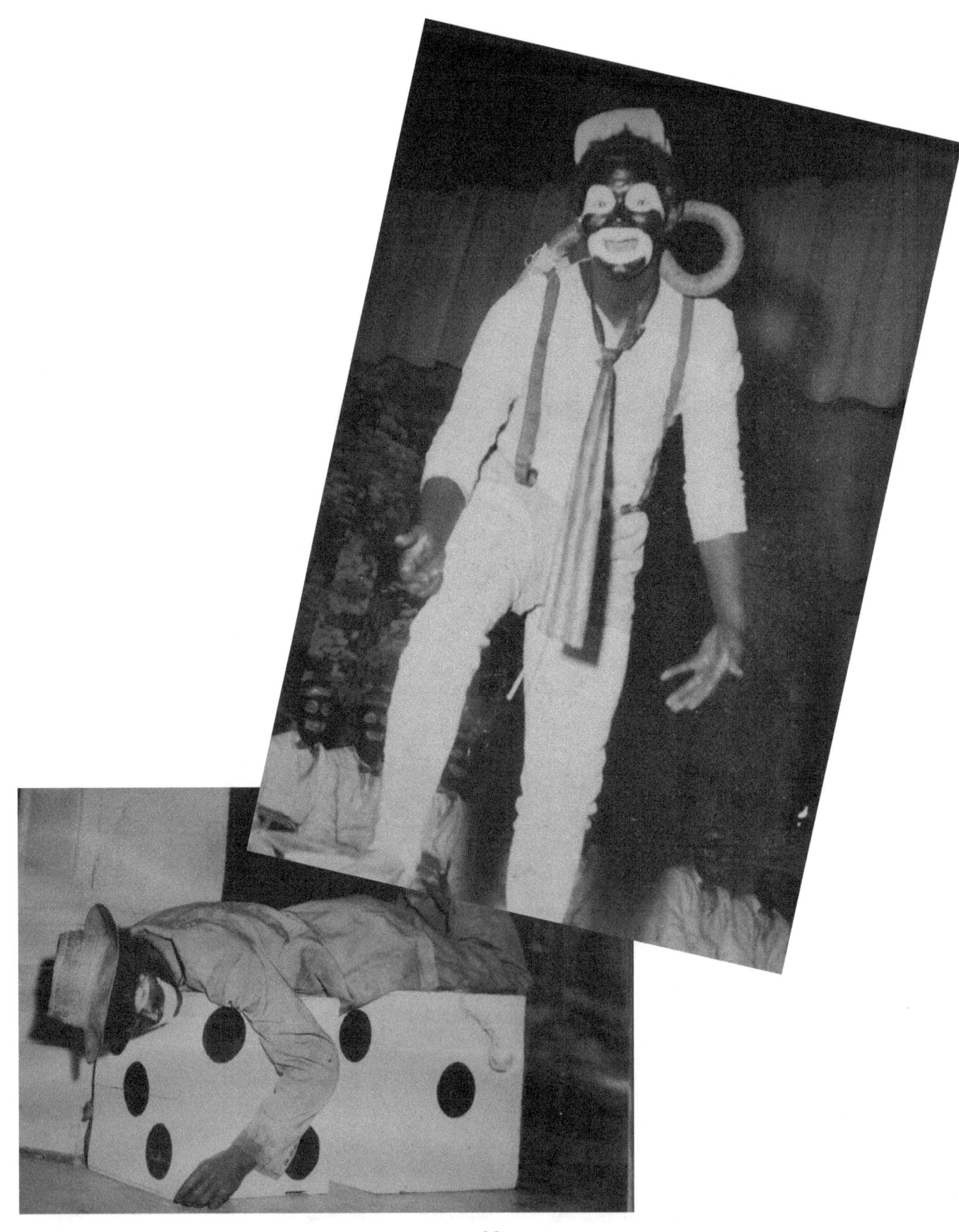

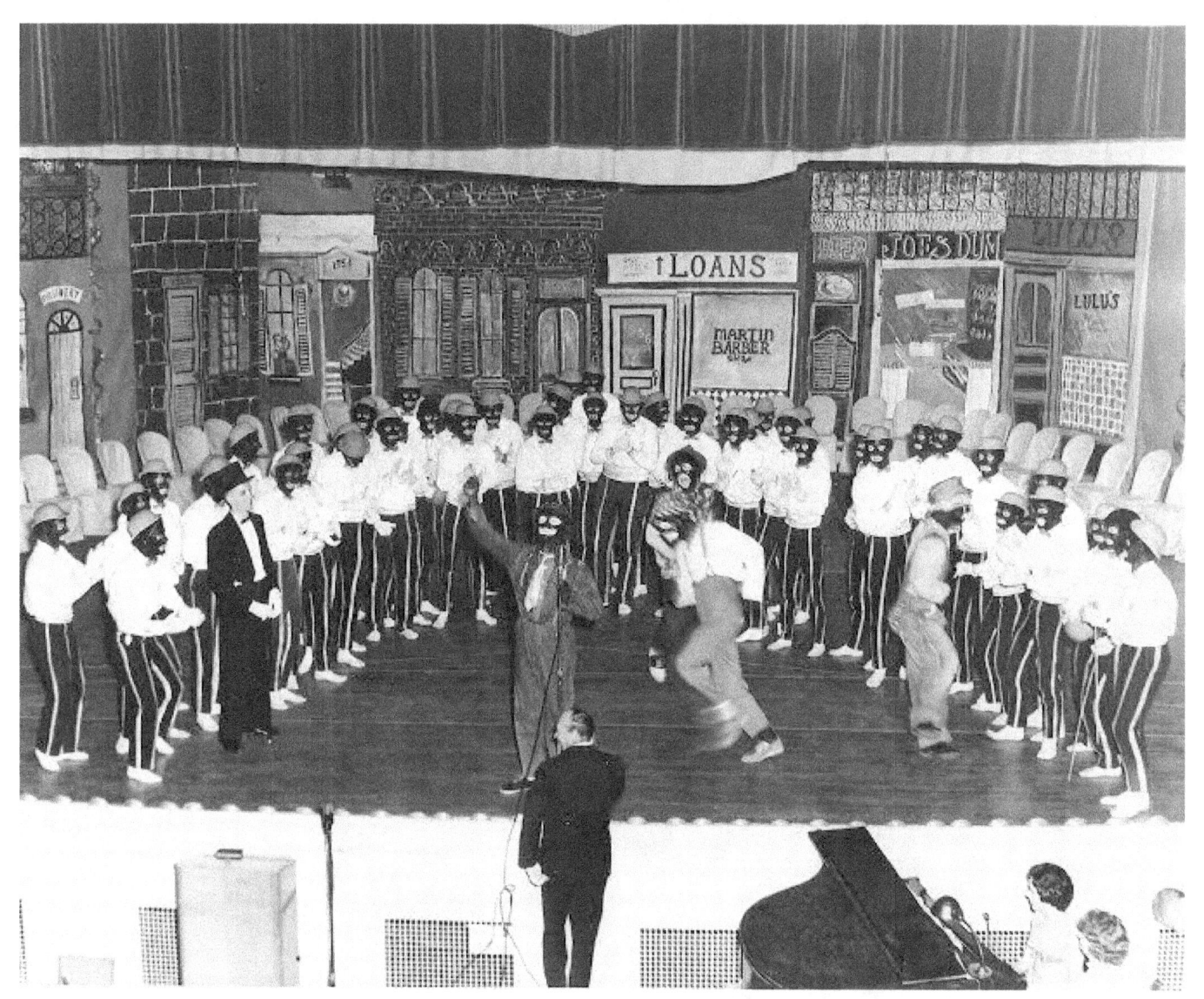

1962 Minstrel

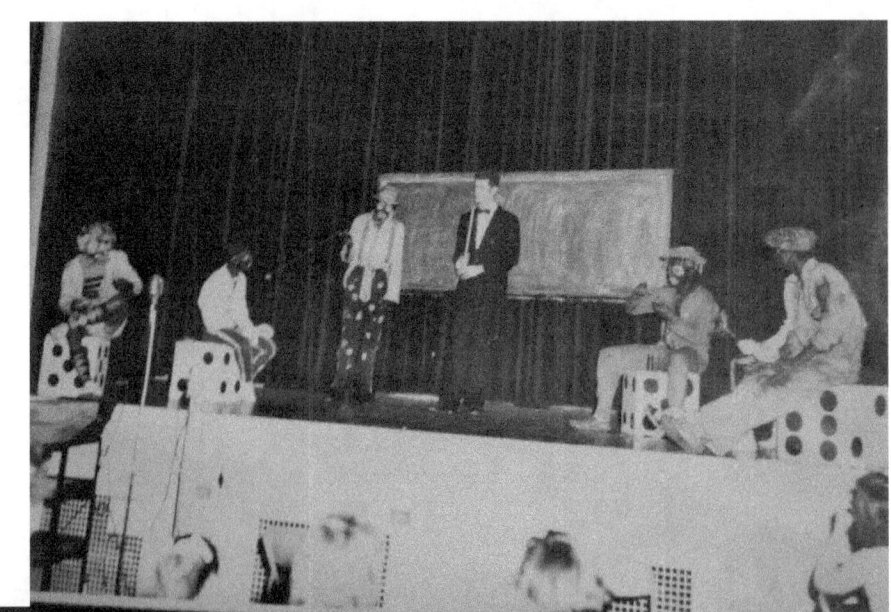

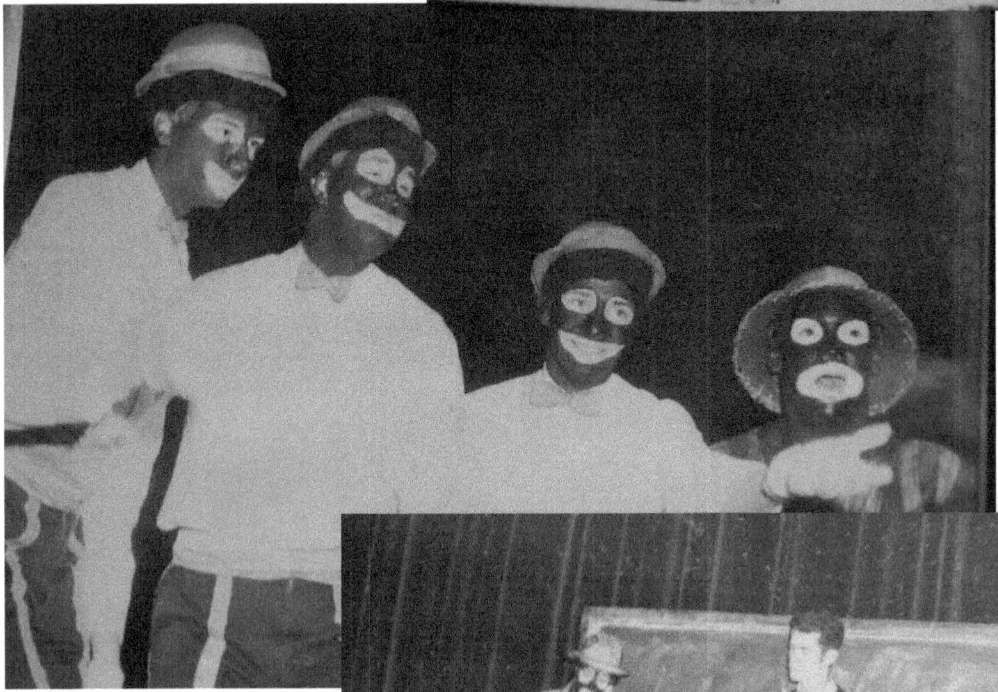

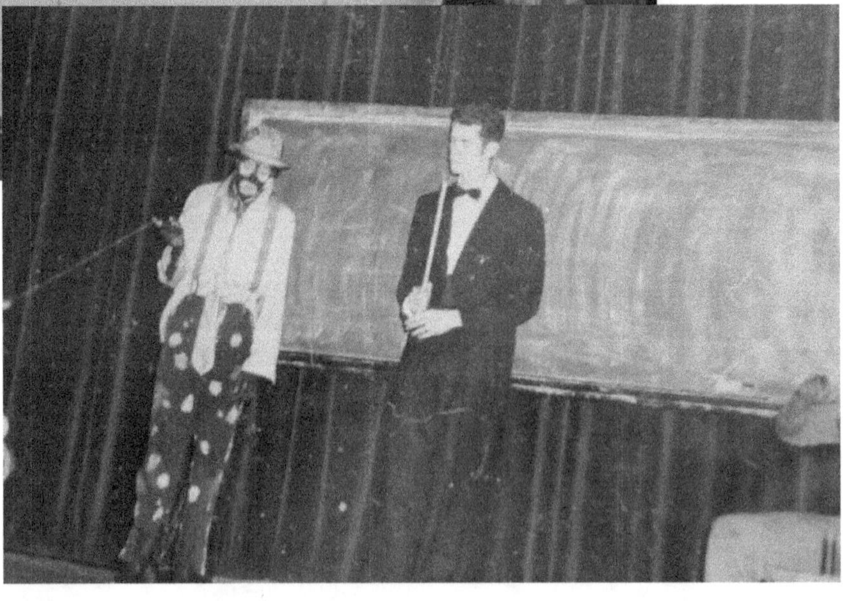

Panama City, Florida

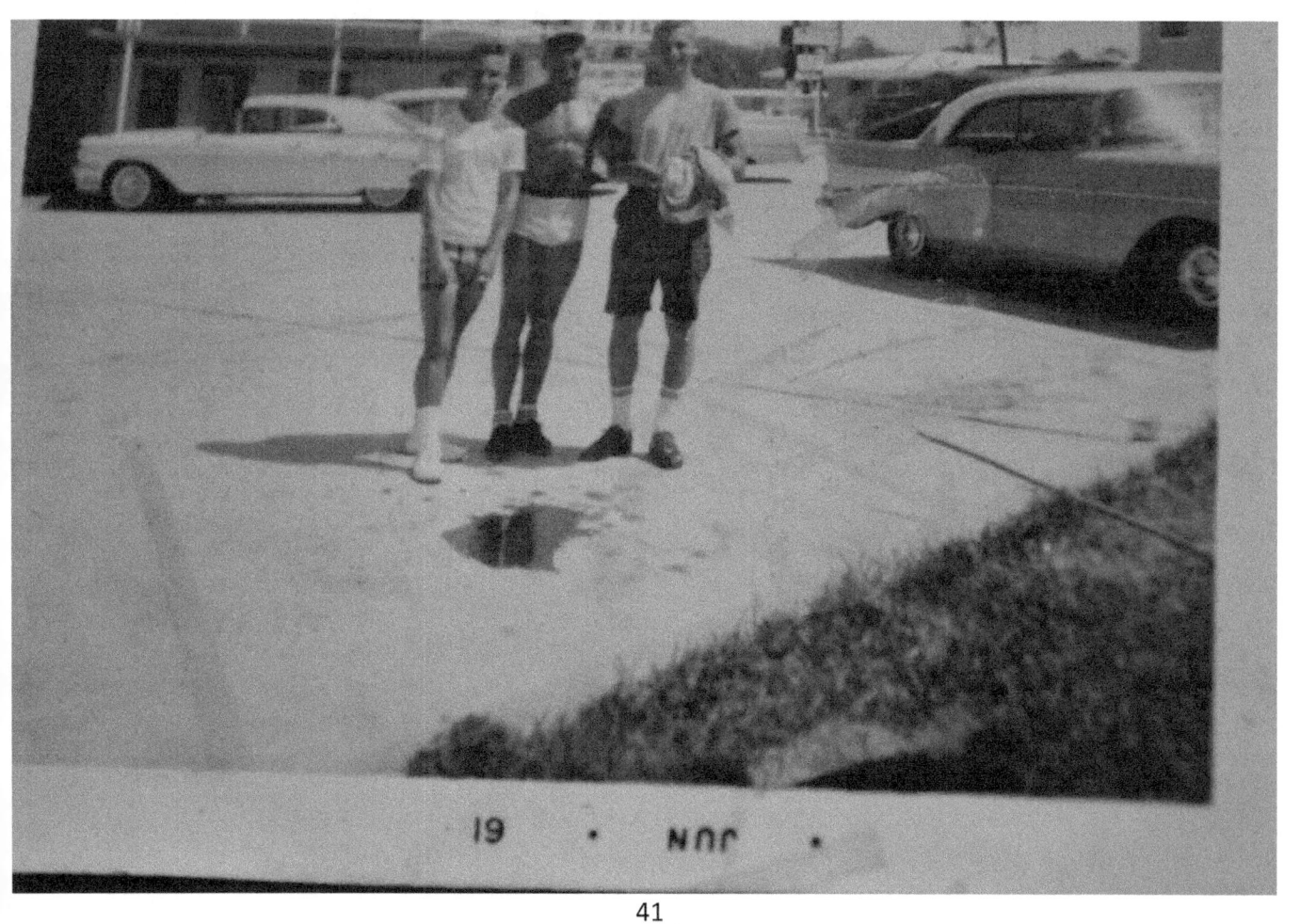

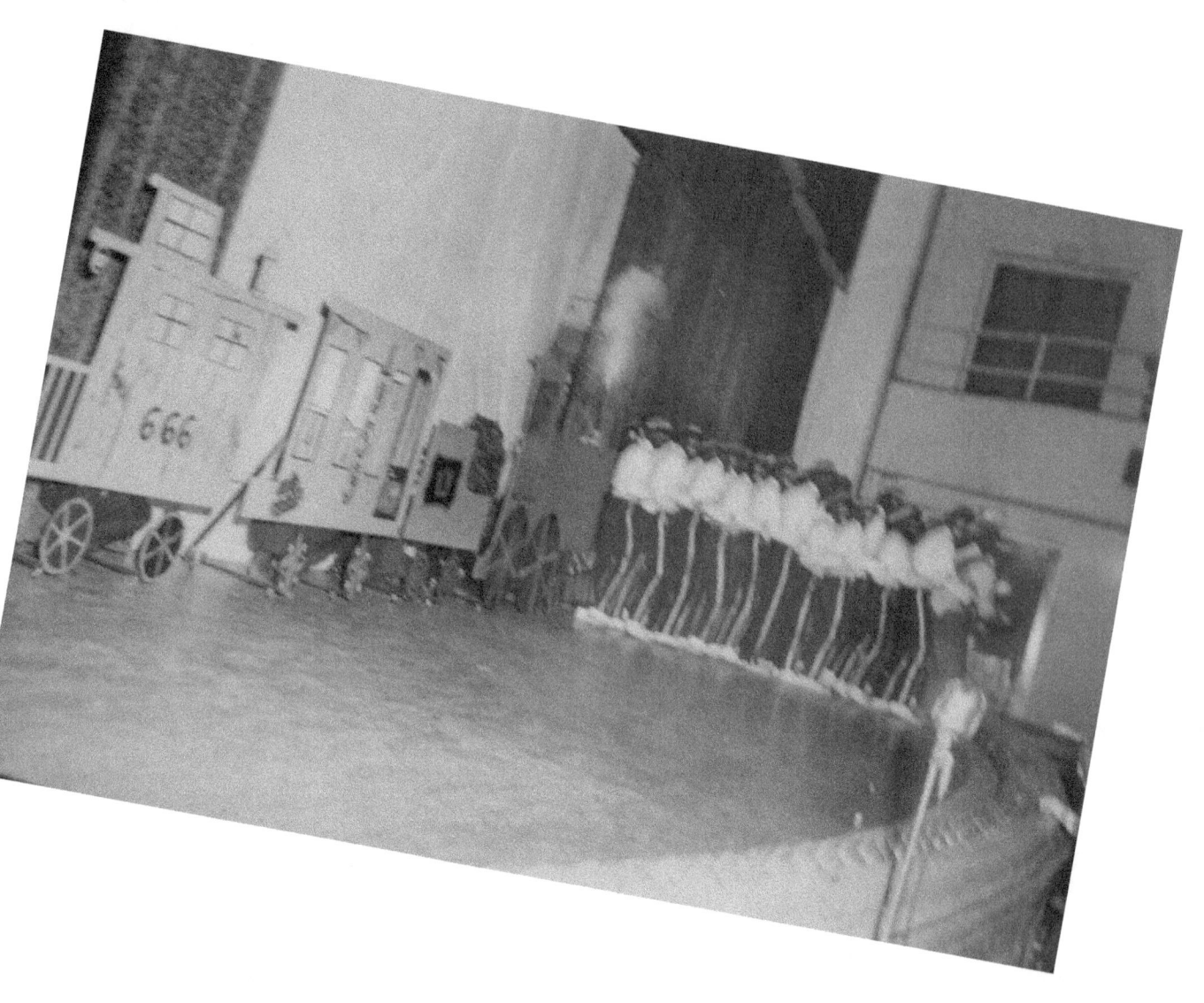

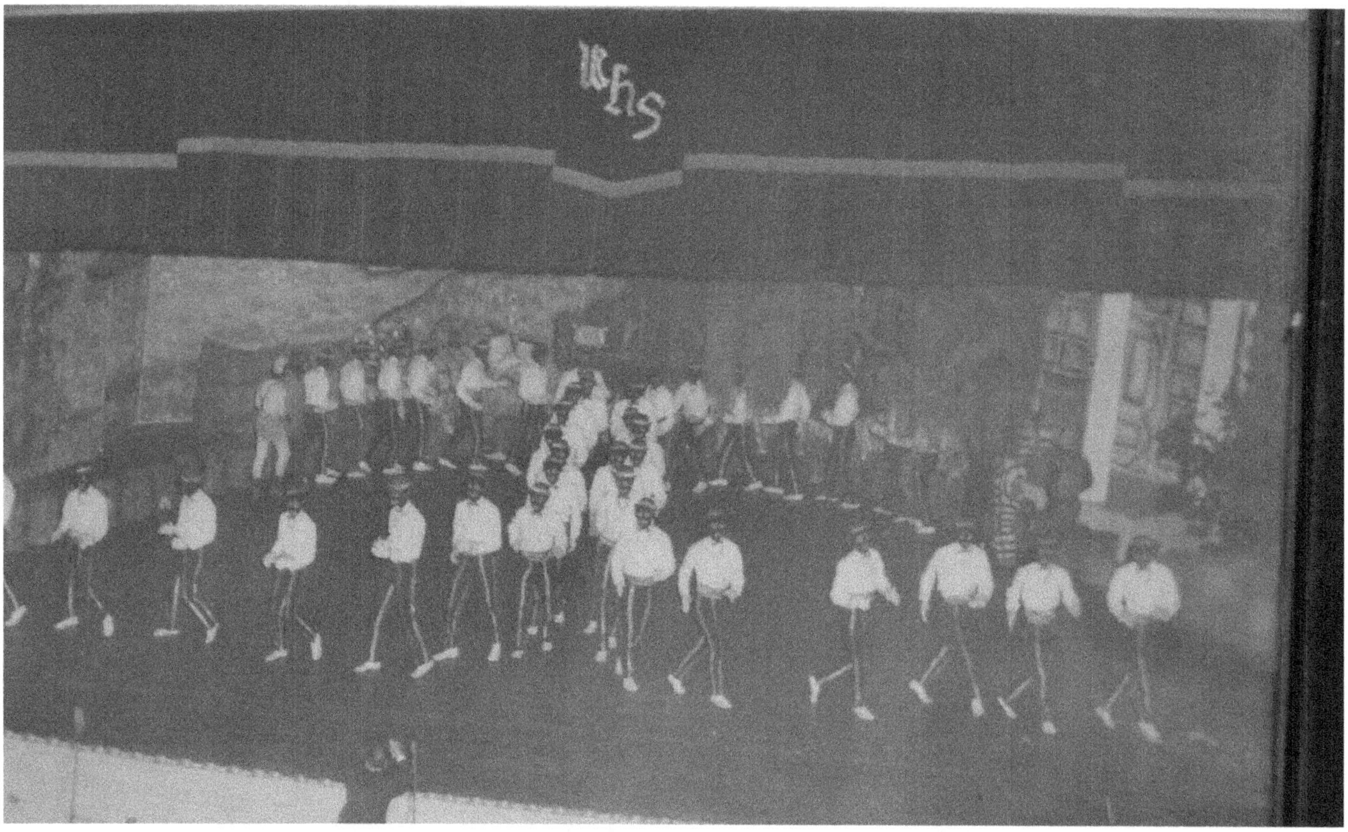

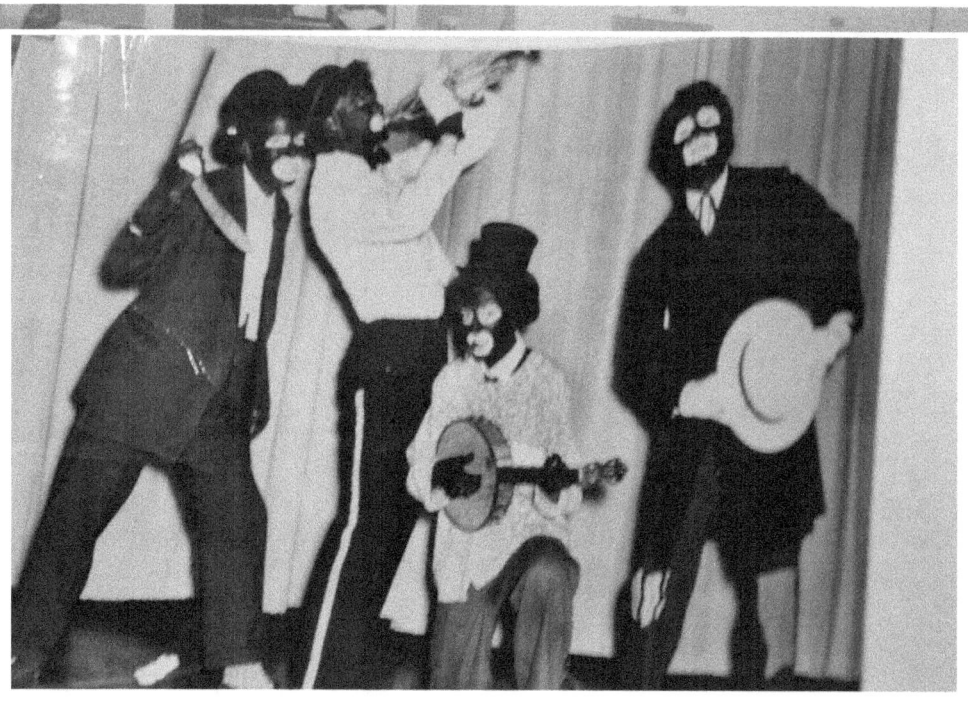

On Stage at Woodlawn High School

A Little Trivia!!!

What is the significance of this number picture???

All original Warblers from WHS should remember (with a little "brain rattlin")

All others can ask a Warbler who remembers!!!

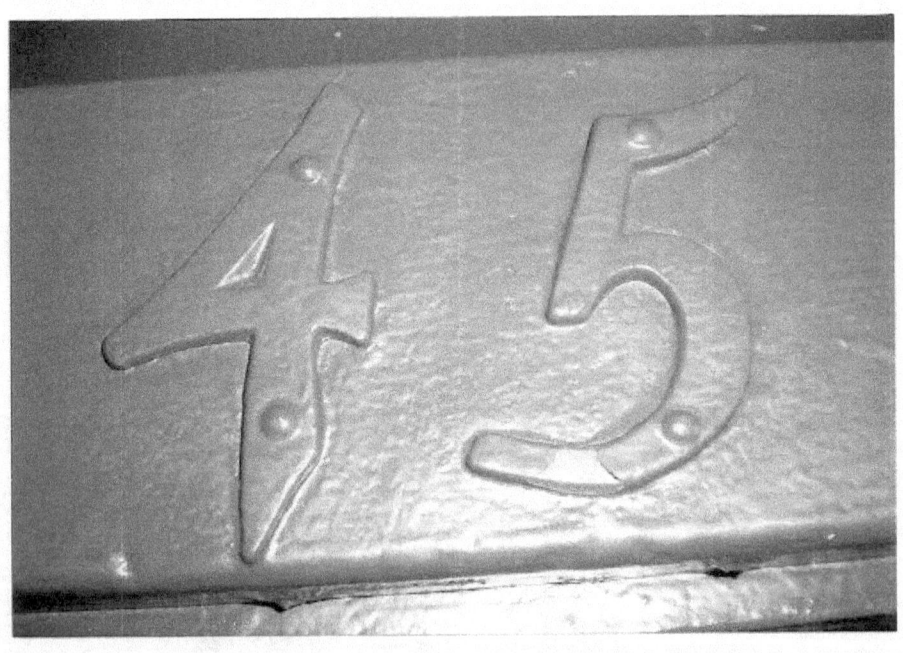

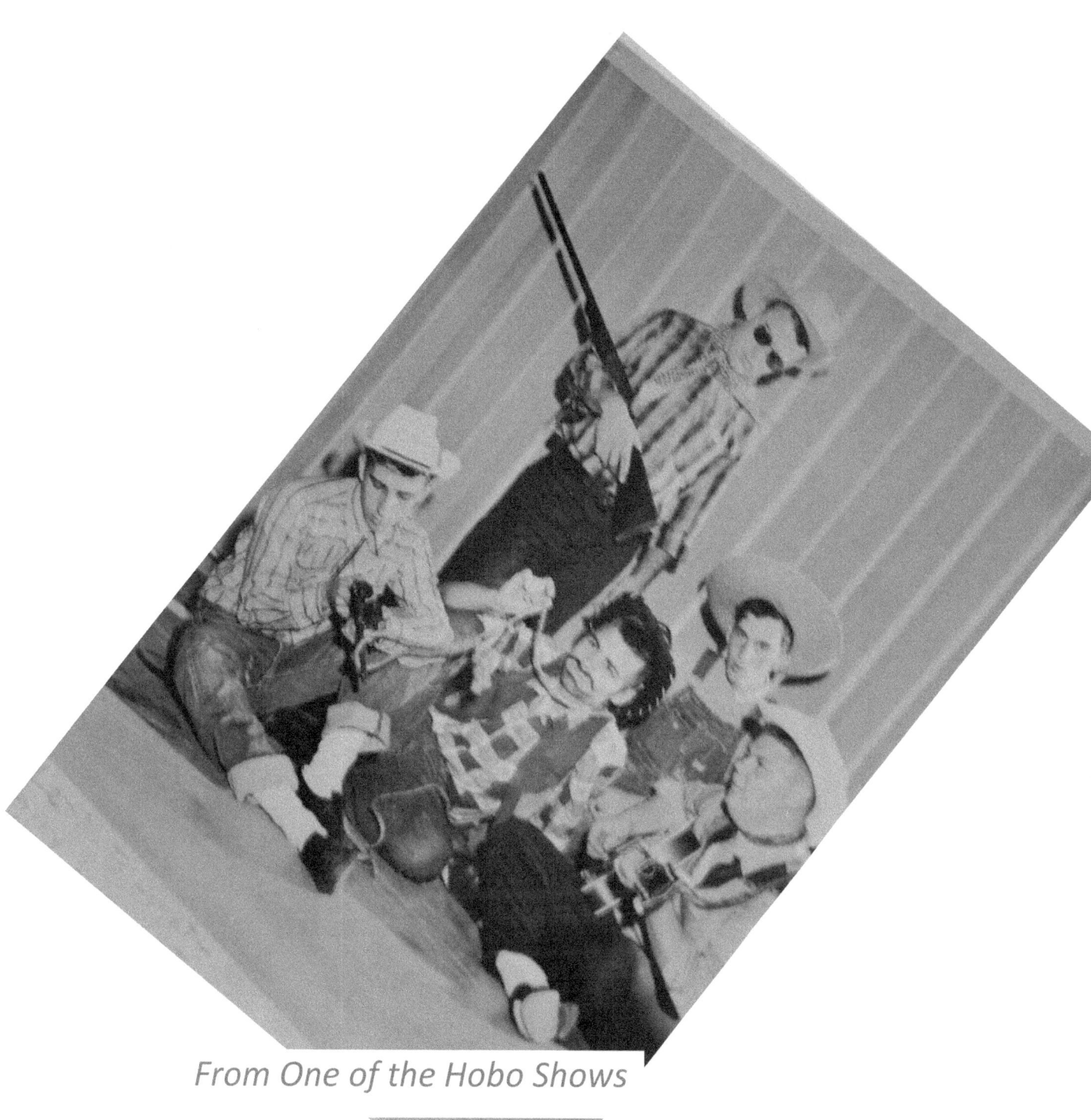

From One of the Hobo Shows

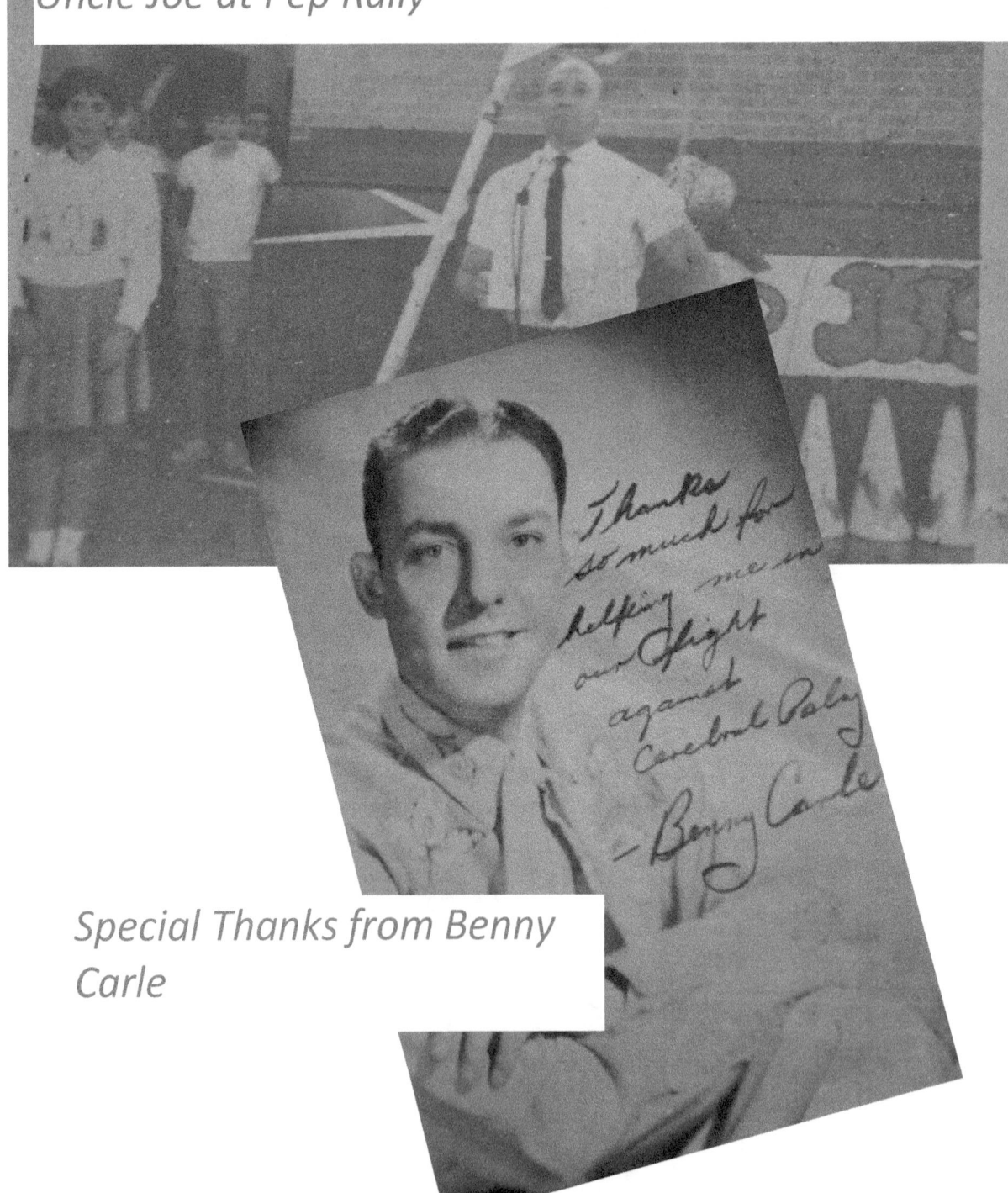

Uncle Joe at Pep Rally

Special Thanks from Benny Carle

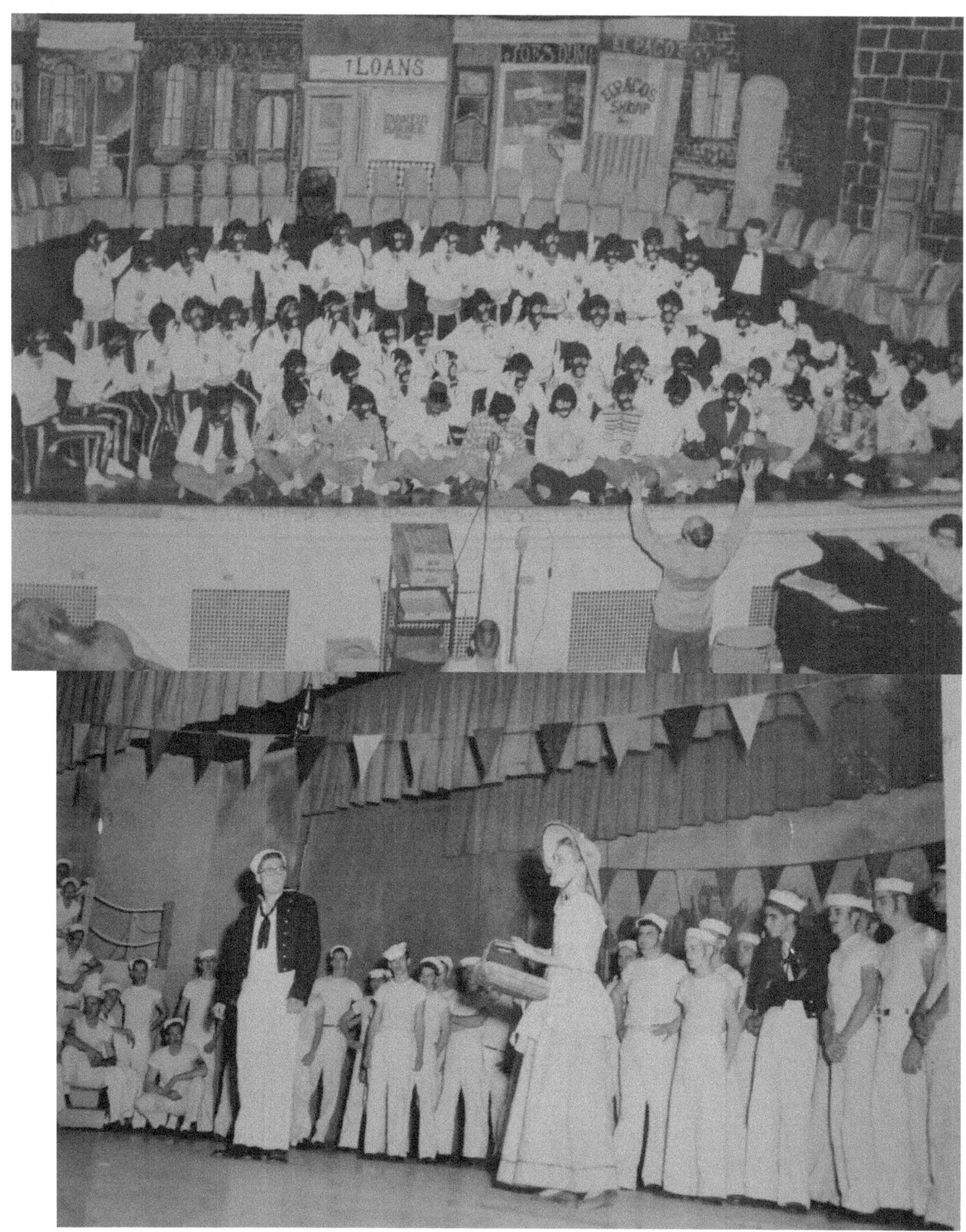

Woodlawn High School Music Department

Presents

The Choir

In

Spring Concert

Friday Evening   May 13, 1949   8:15 P. M.

Woodlawn High School Auditorium

Directors

Claude Dowling	William Amos Hudson
Mrs. H. E. Kirk, Miss Doris Bohannan	Accompanists
Susie A. Pomeroy	Solo Instructor
Reuben A. Martinson	Supervisor of Music
Ralph Martin	Principal

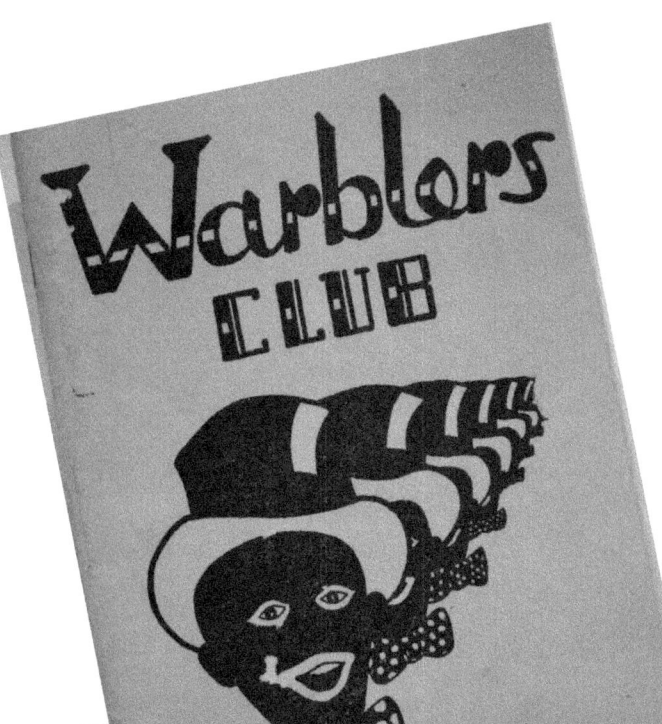

49

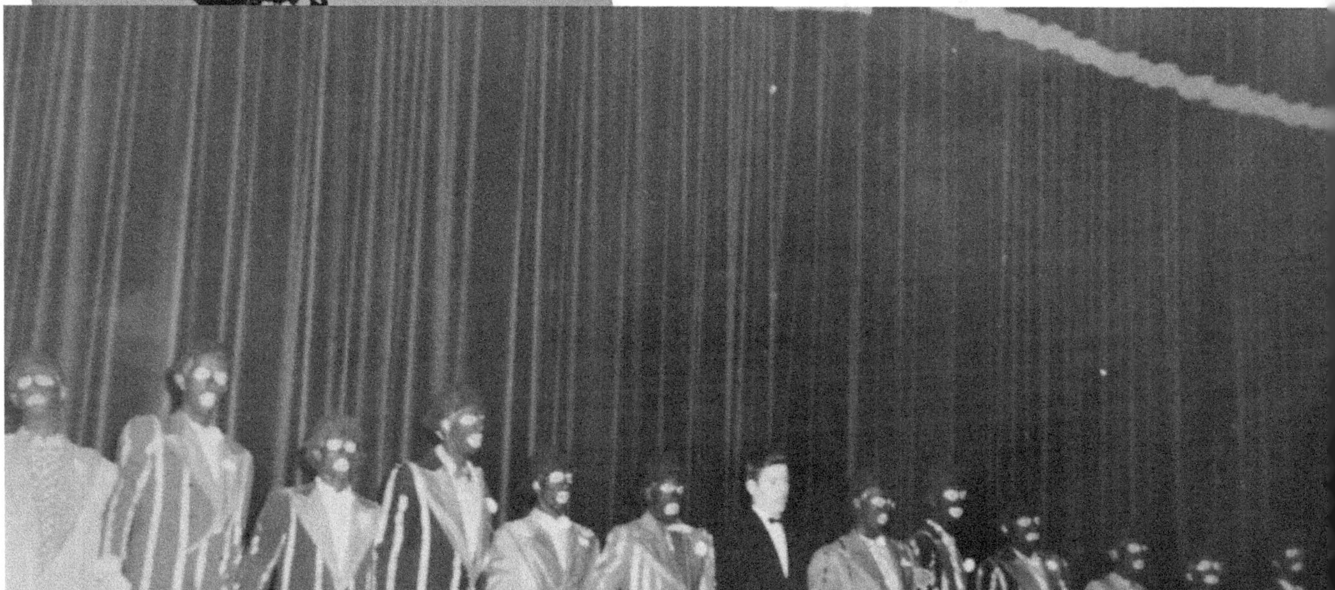

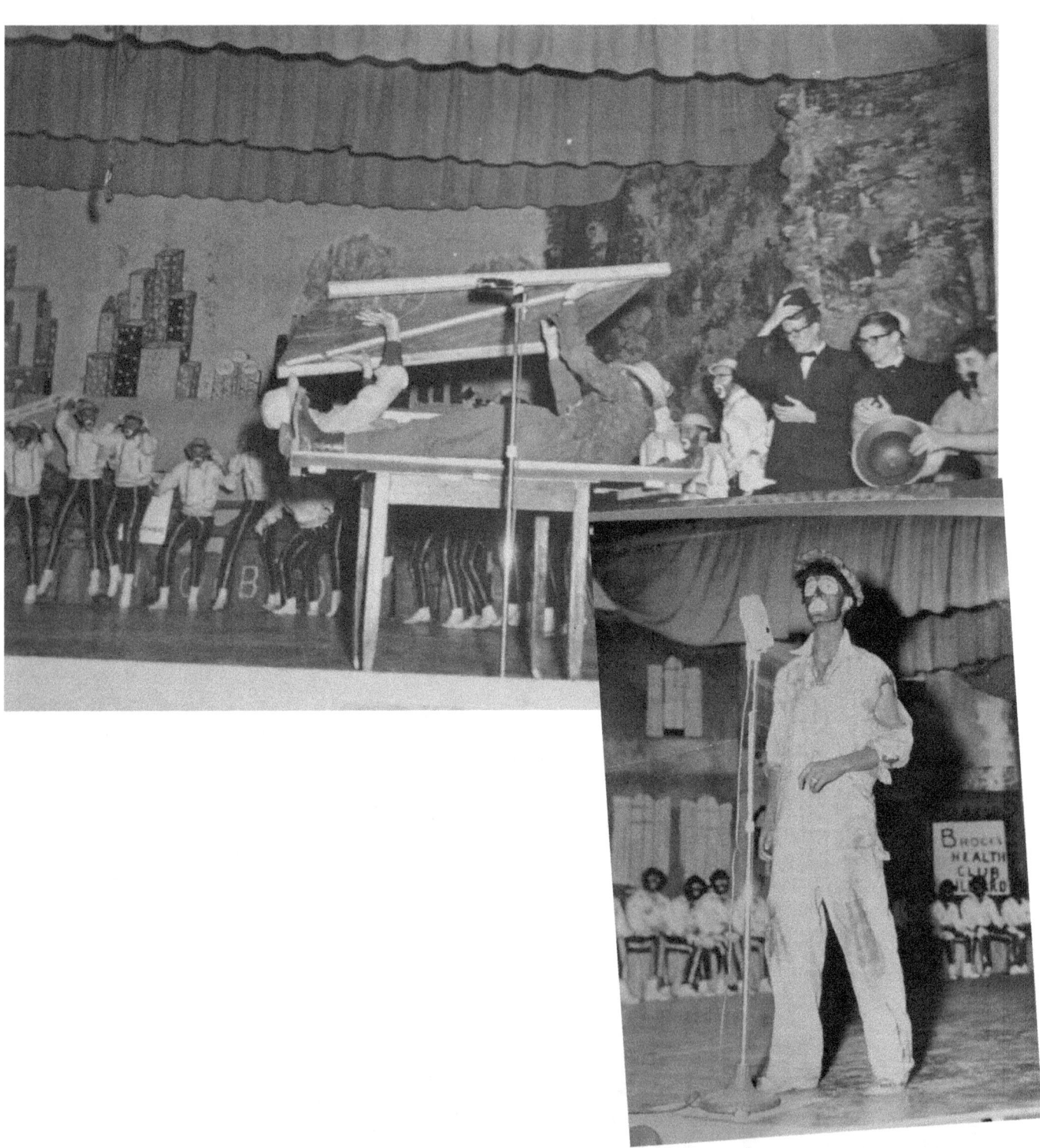

The Apollo Club

Presents

The Warblers Club

in a

Matinee Recital

March, 1933

Woodlawn High School Auditorium

Marc...

John West
Harold Williams
First Bass
Alfred Bivins
Earl Broxton
Henry Lee Greer
Philip Musso
Ed Powell
Philip Walkley

Ben McClosky
Robert McClosky
Second Bass
John Maroney
Tom Ringo
William Scarbrough
Grady Sharp

ASSOCIATE MEMBERS
Malcolm Hornbuckle Hurston Simpson

Club Sponsor and Director

JOHN A. LIGHT

Warblers Doo Wop

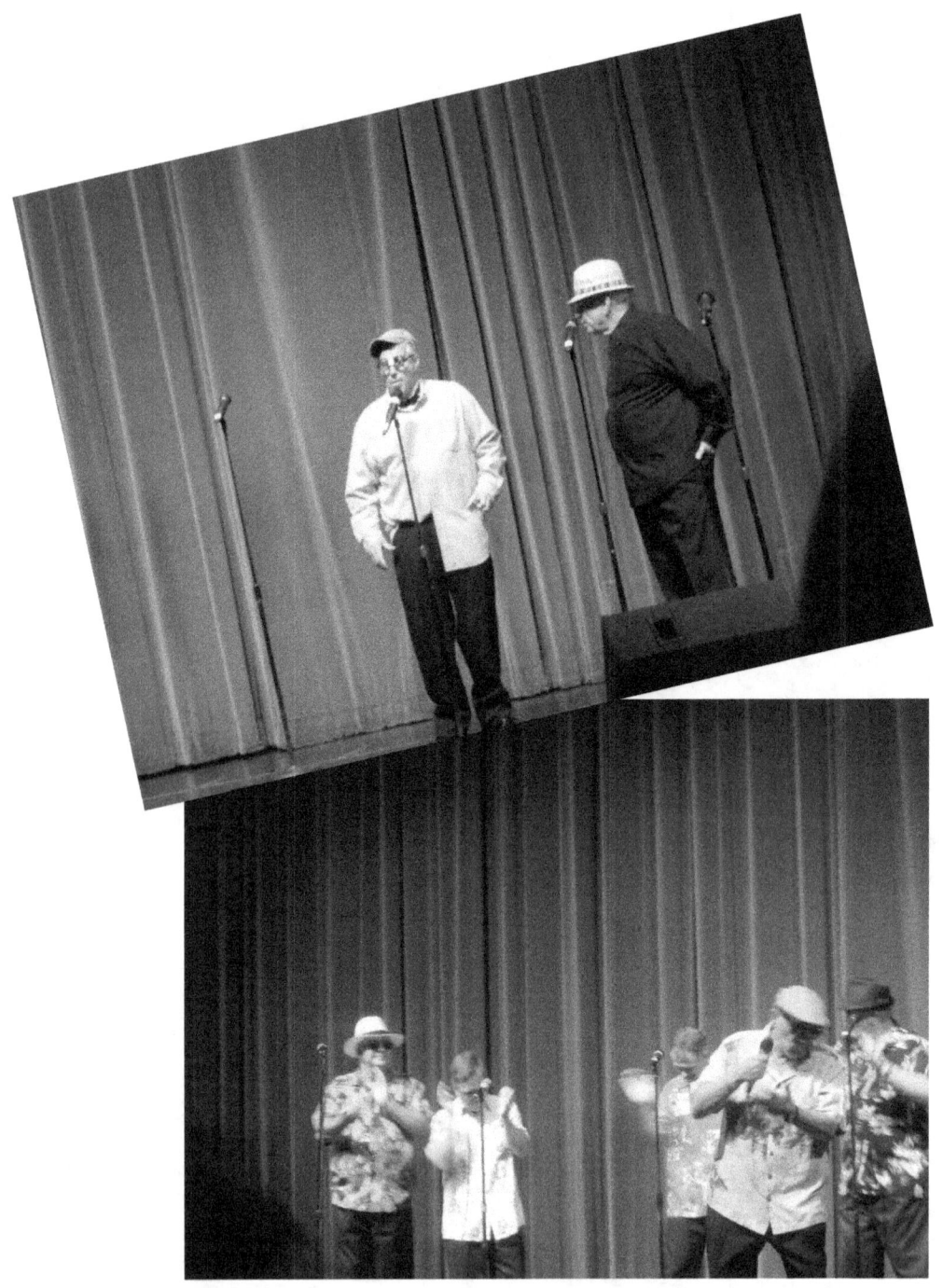

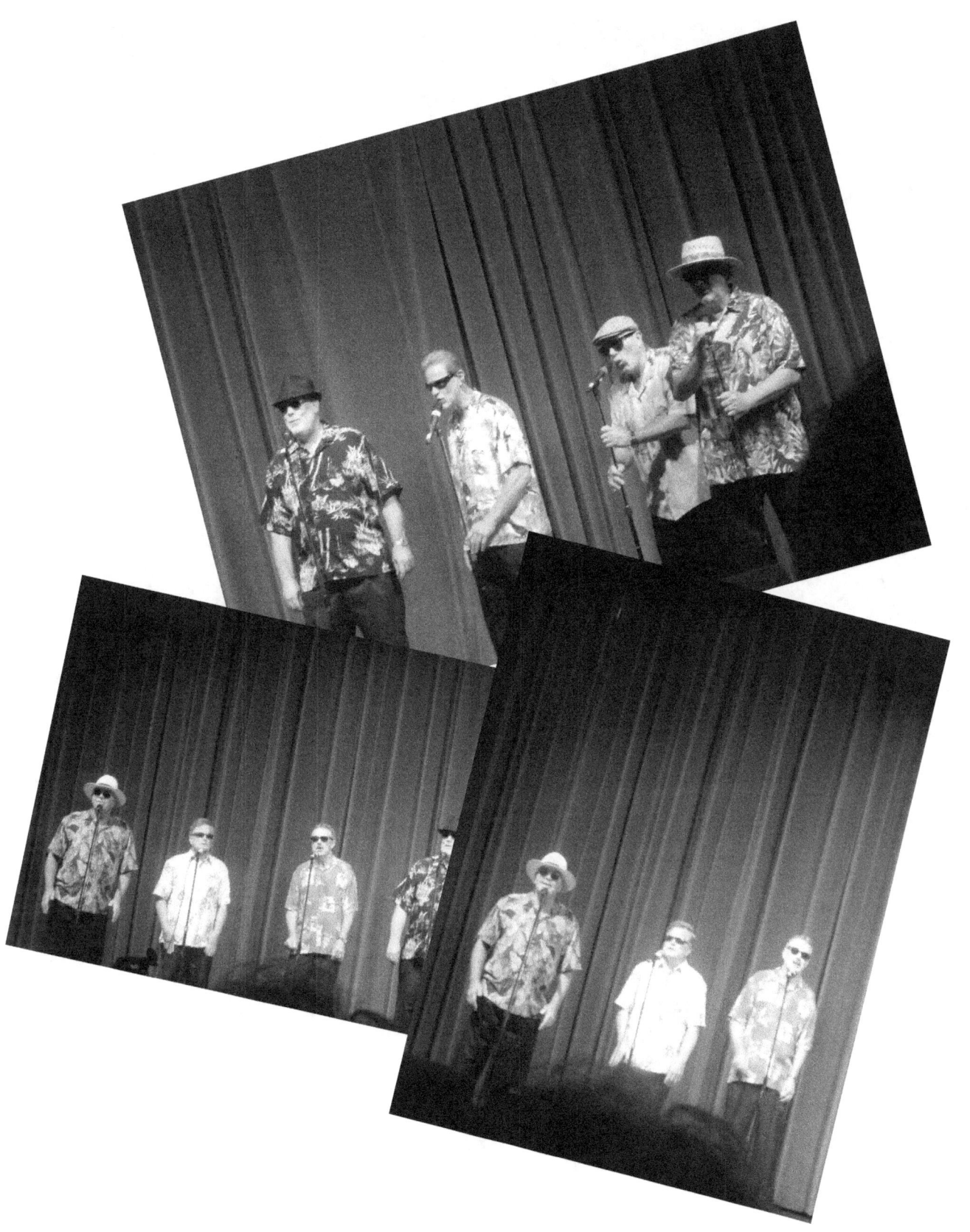

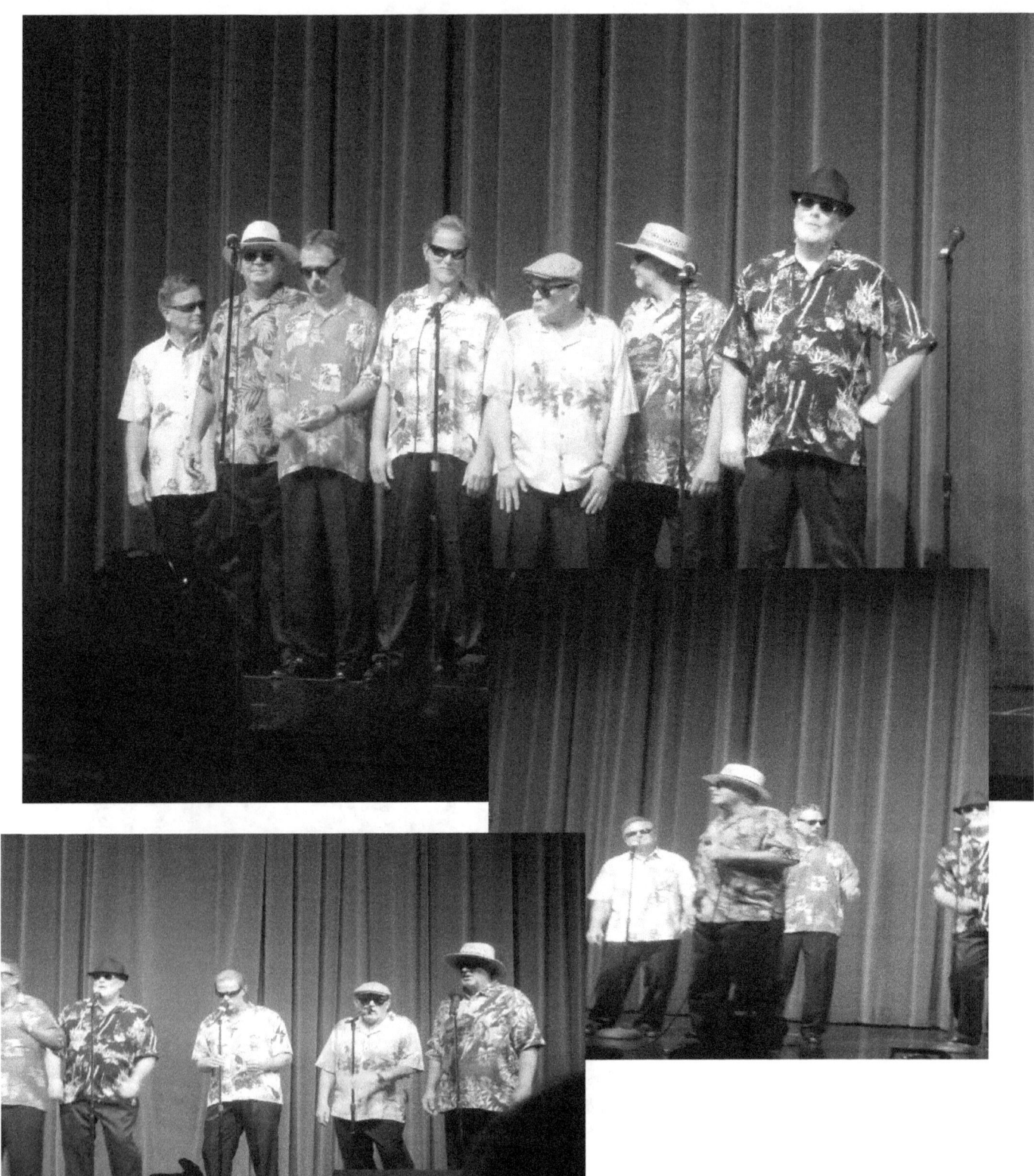

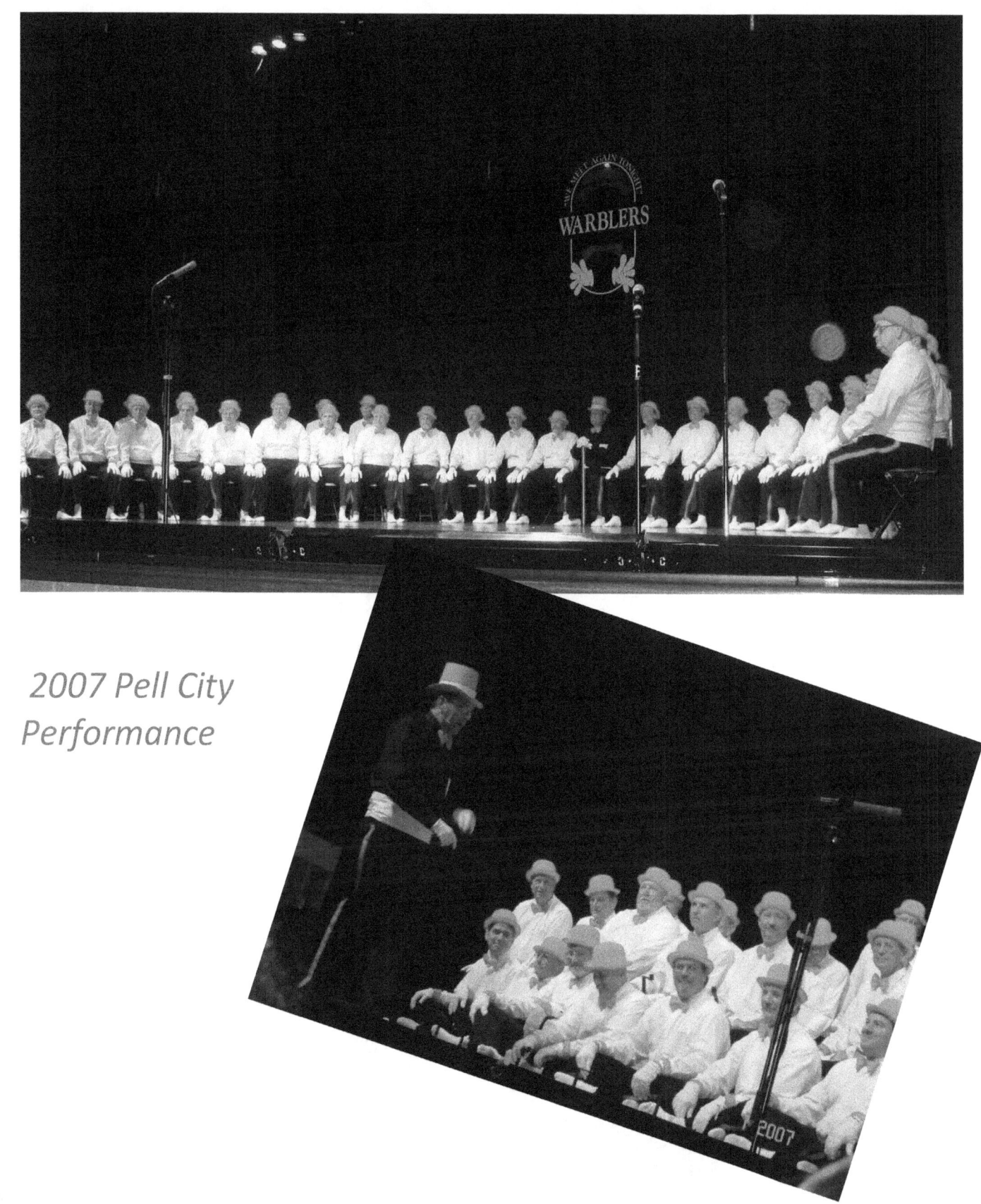

*2007 Pell City
Performance*

55

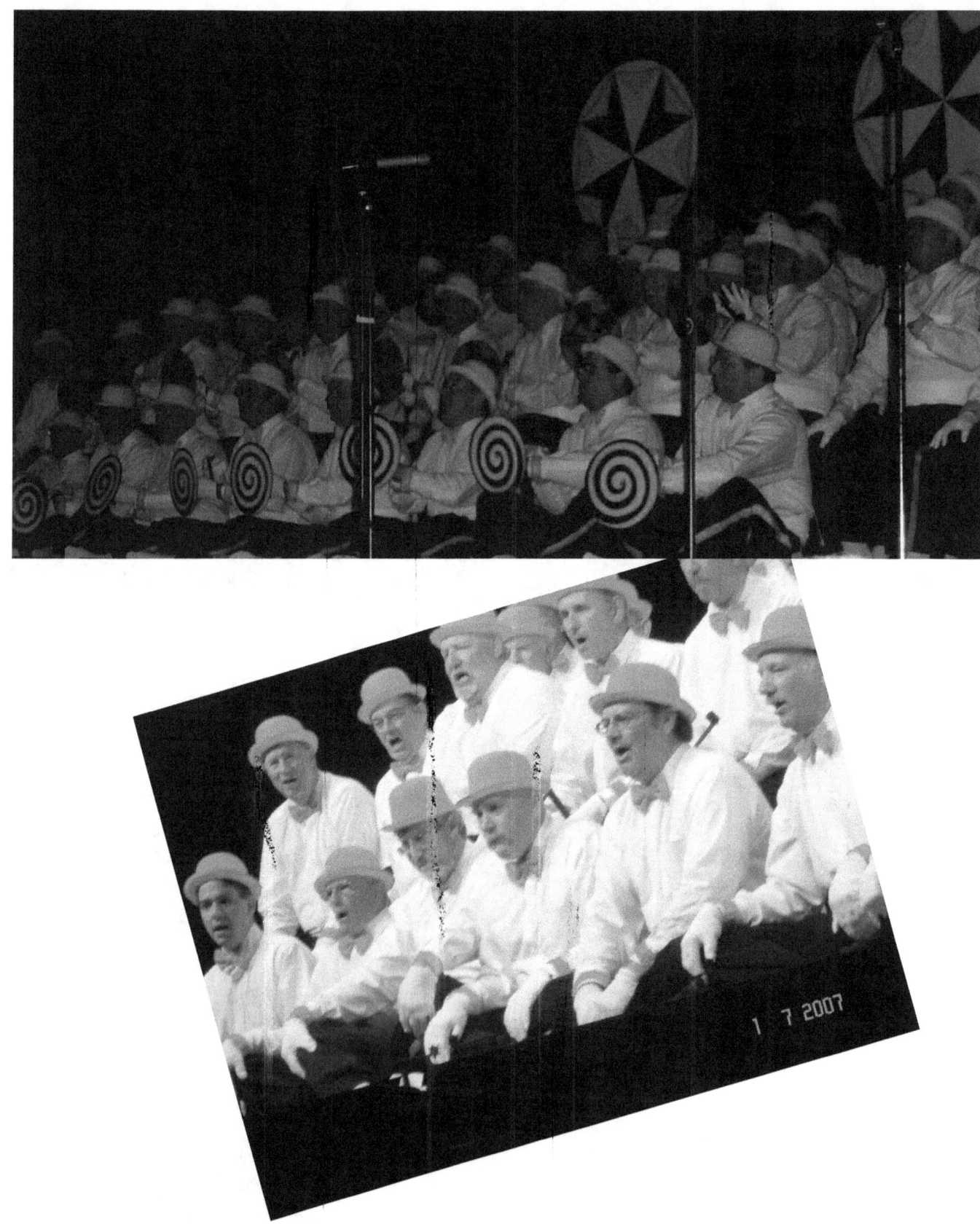

1962 Warblers Minstrel

1. We Meet Again Tonight Boys
2. Opening Chorus
3. Introducing Mr. I.W. Stein.....Yessick
4. Moonlight Bay
5. Introducing "Senator Phil E. Buster....Yessick and John Sanders....
6. Didn't My Lord Deliver Daniel....———— *Bancroft*
7. Tribute to Irving Berlin.
8. Introducing Mr. Ray L. Road....Calfee and John Sanders
9. I Got Shoes
10. Introducting Mr. N. D. House....Yessick and Harold Morgan
    ~~I Ain't Got Time To Die~~ *Meet Me Tonight In Dreamland* ————
11. Hunting & Fishing Dialogue....J. T. Calfee and Inter.
12. Porgy & Bess ......
    A. Summertime
    B. I Got Plenty of Nothin.
    C. It Ain't Necessarily So.

INTERMISSION.

13. Broadway Fantasy.........Sharon Walsch, The "Jesters" & Circle.
    Alternates Crossfire.......Army Script.
14. ~~The Four Kings Minus One.......Yessick, Calfee and Henely~~
    ~~Crossfire........Girls....Harold and John~~
15. ~~Honor.....Homer.~~
    ~~Crossfire Hollywood....Yessick & J.T.~~
16. Barbershop Jamborees...... (2 Numbers)
    Telephone Gag....Yessick, Inter. and all.   *Harold Morgan*
17. Wandering.
    ~~Crossfire...Cockroach Script....Harold & John.~~
18. Lonesome Road.....
    ~~Inter. J.T. and Mr. Morgan~~ *GIRLS CROSSFIRE — HAROLD & JOHN*
19. Down In La.
20. Oh Mona.
21. Closing Chorus.

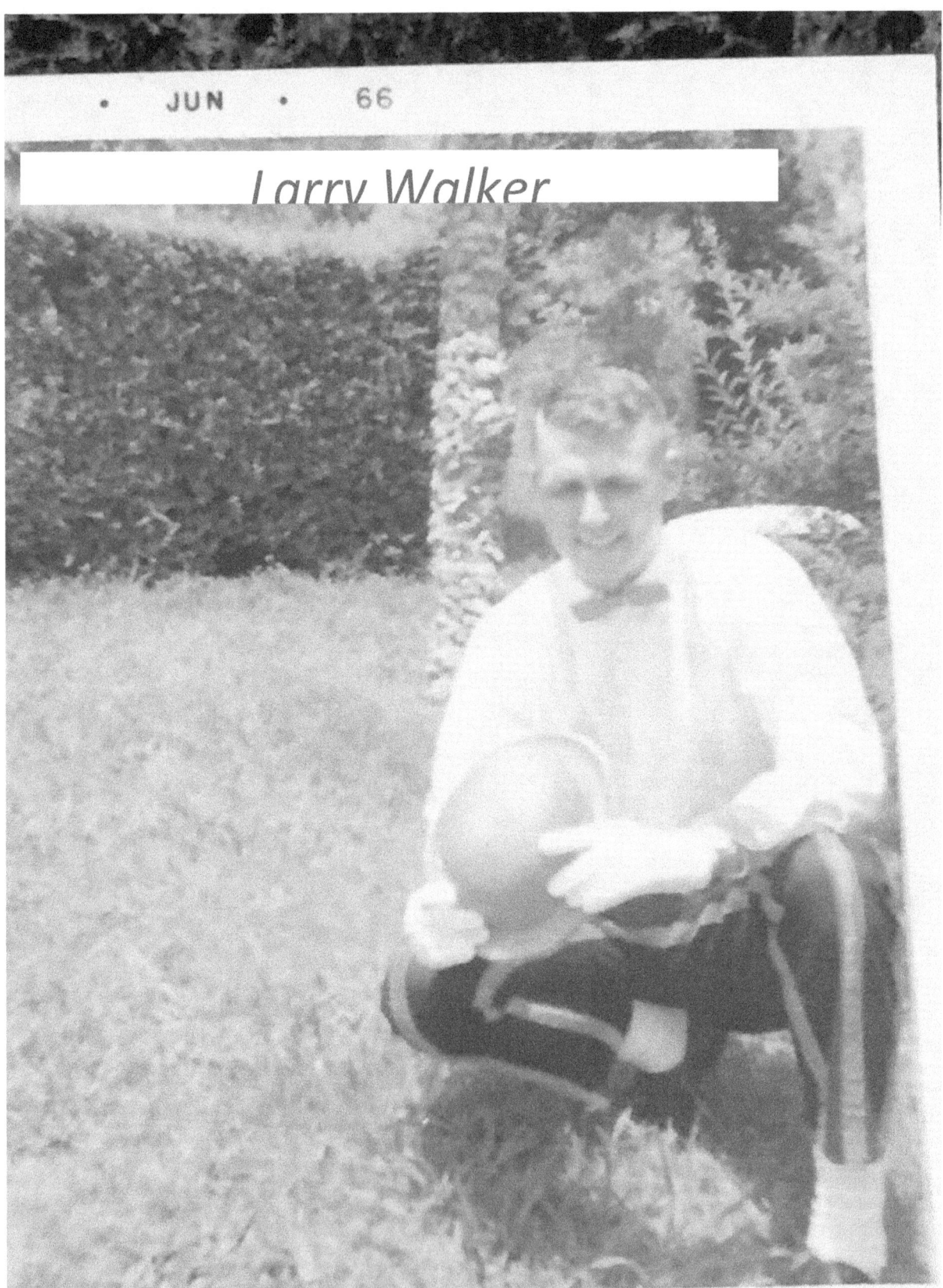

JUN · 66

Larry Walker

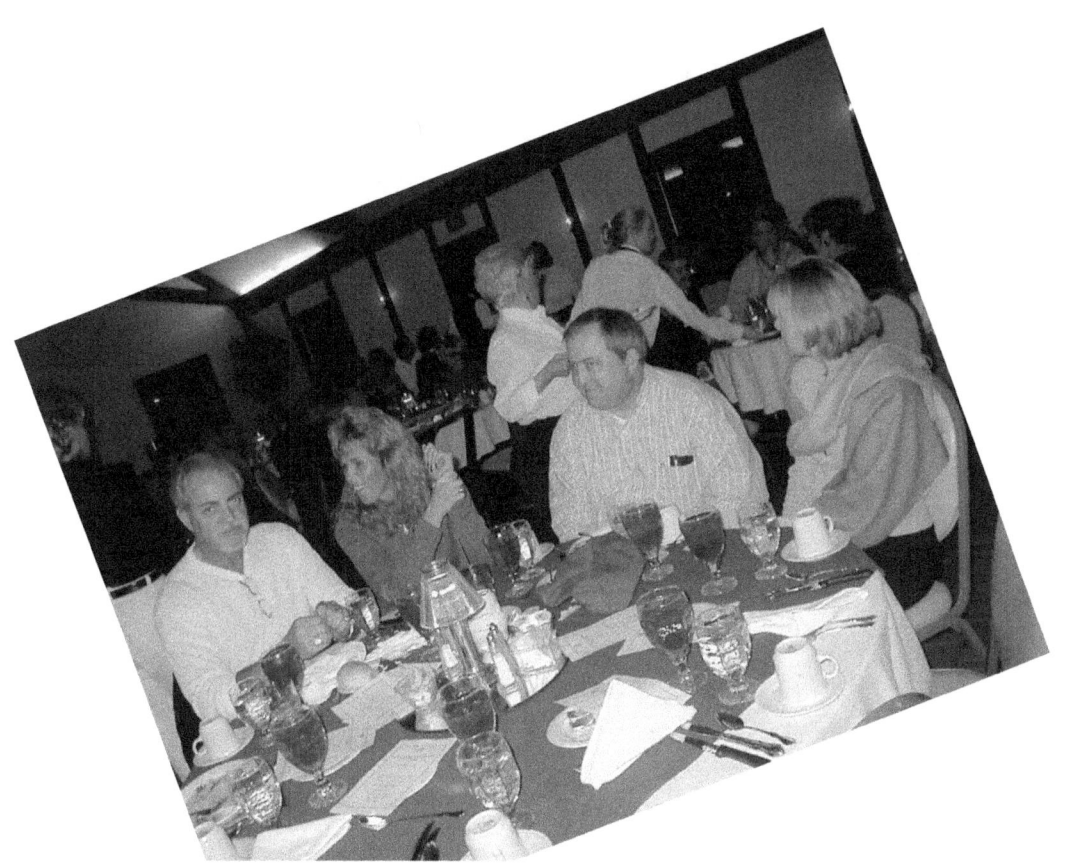

2001 Awards Program

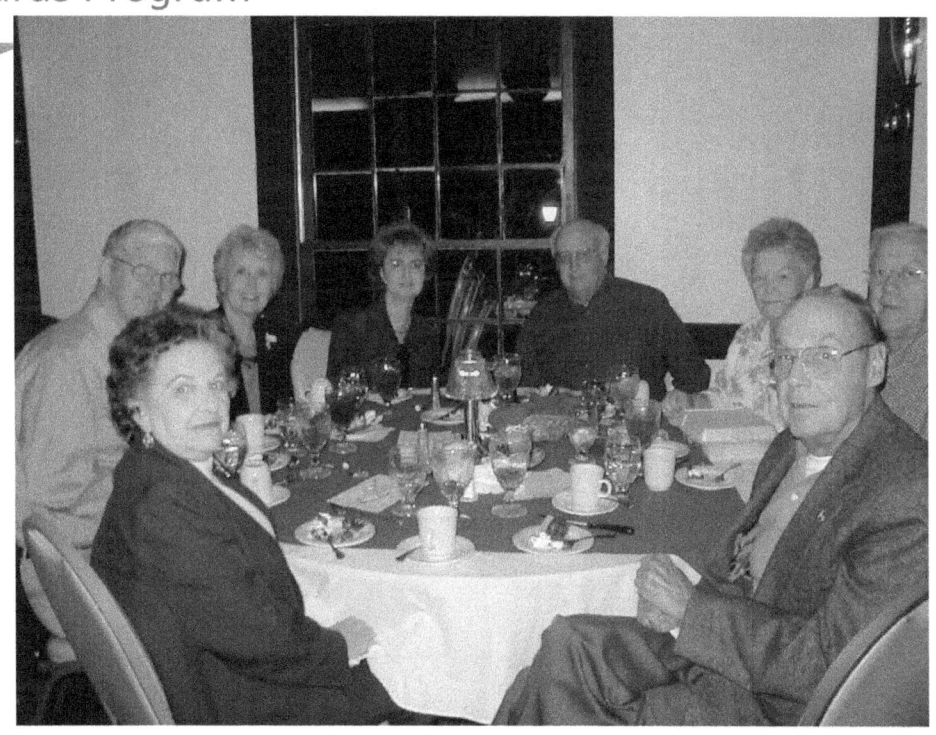

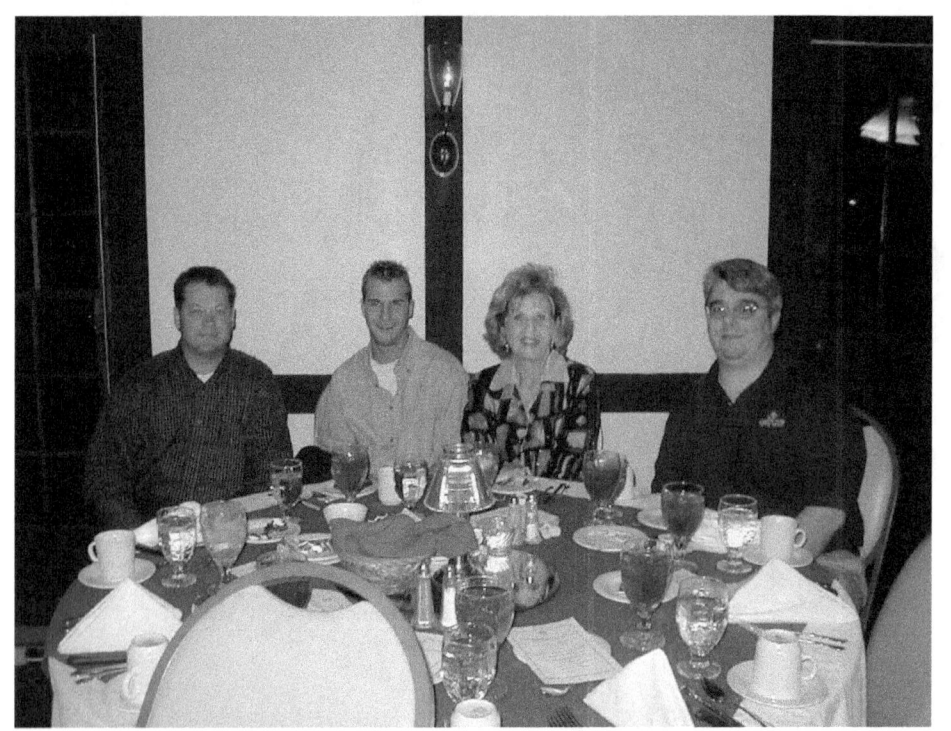

2001 Awards Program

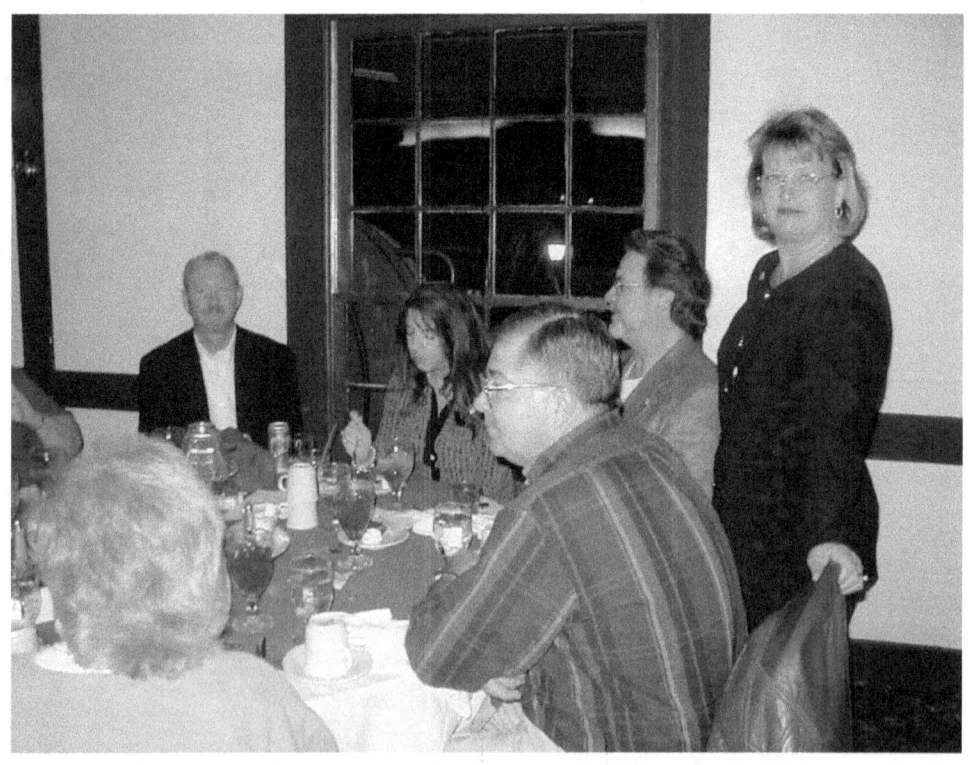

Safe Harbor - Valleydale Baptist

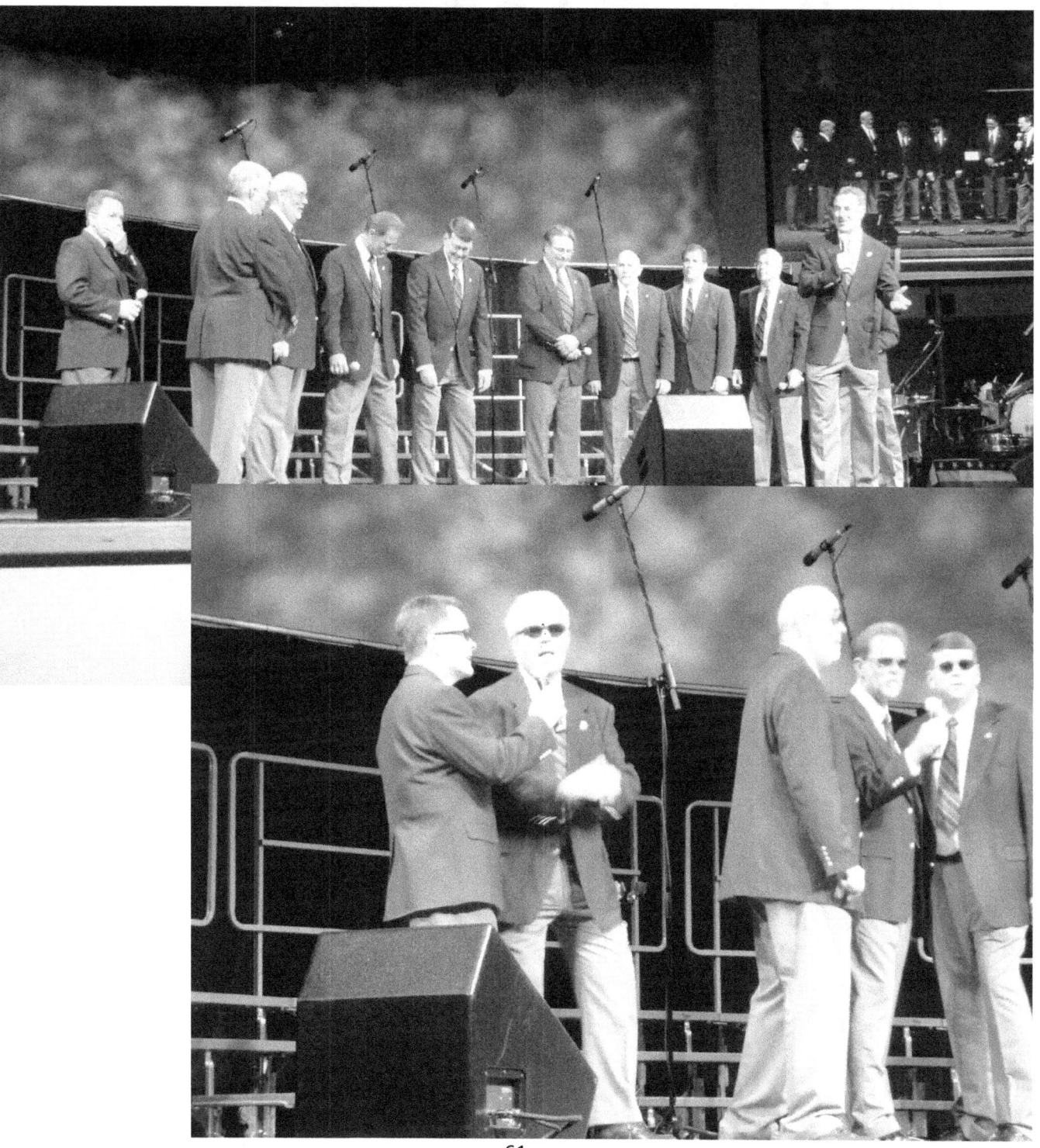

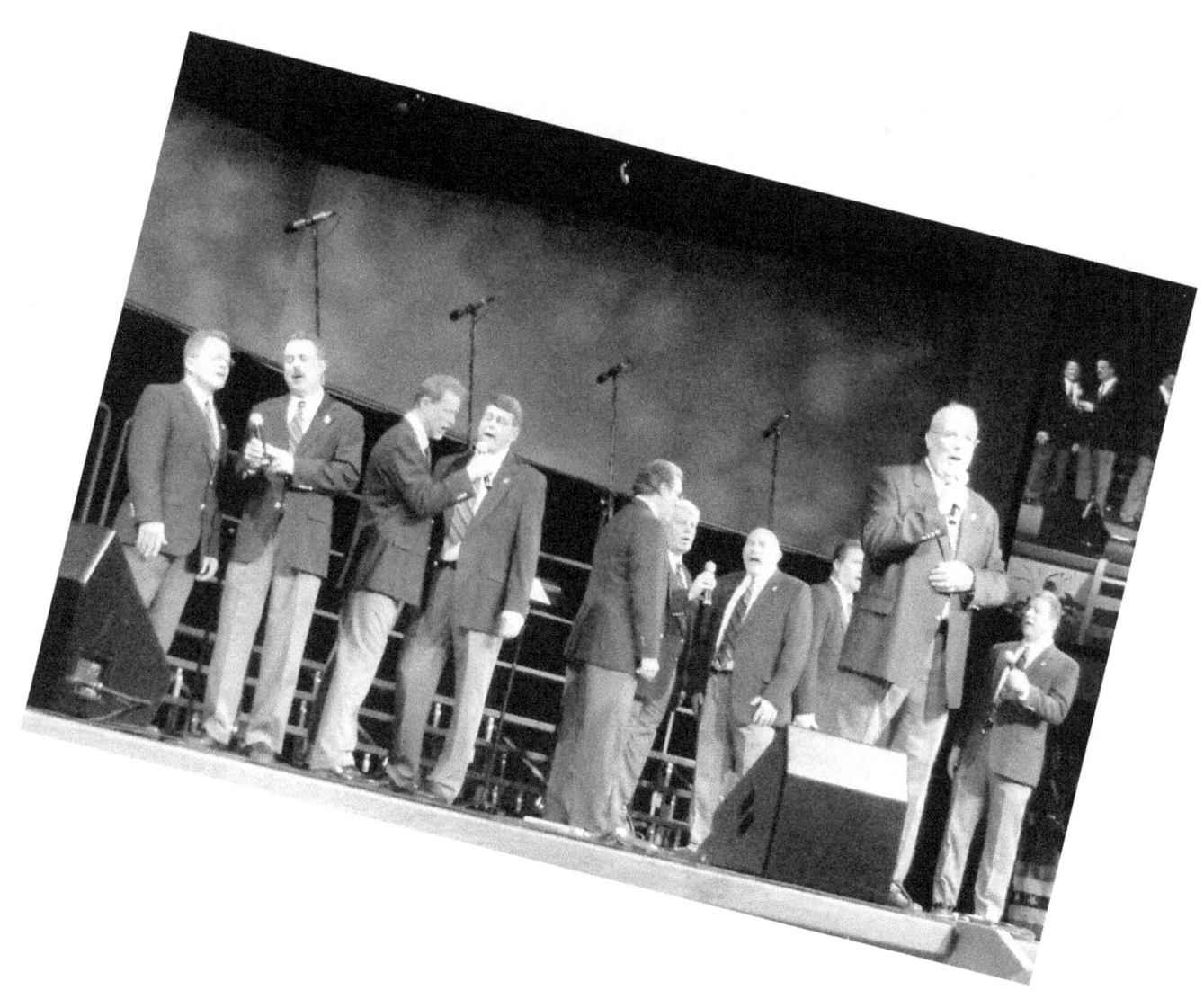

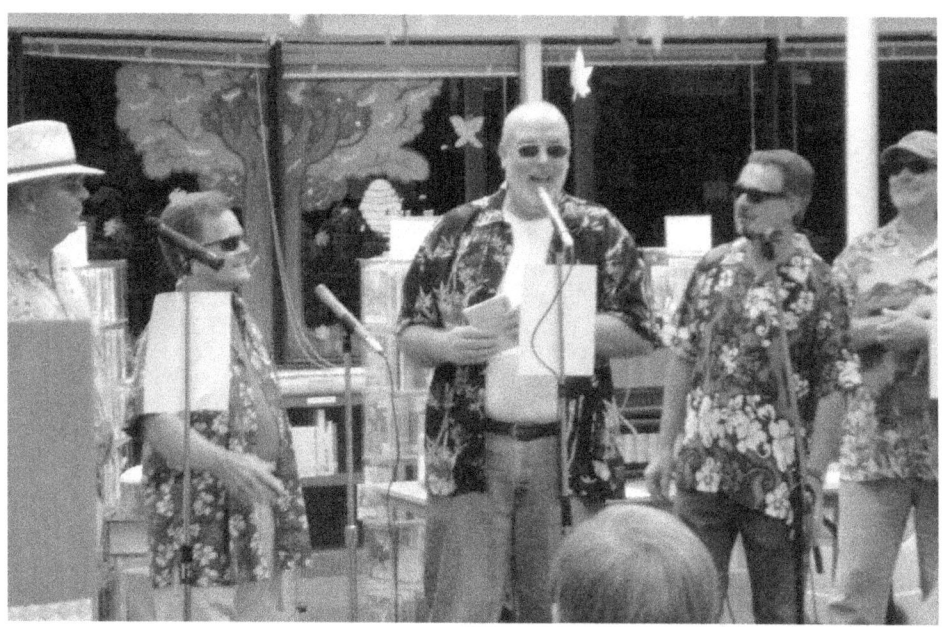

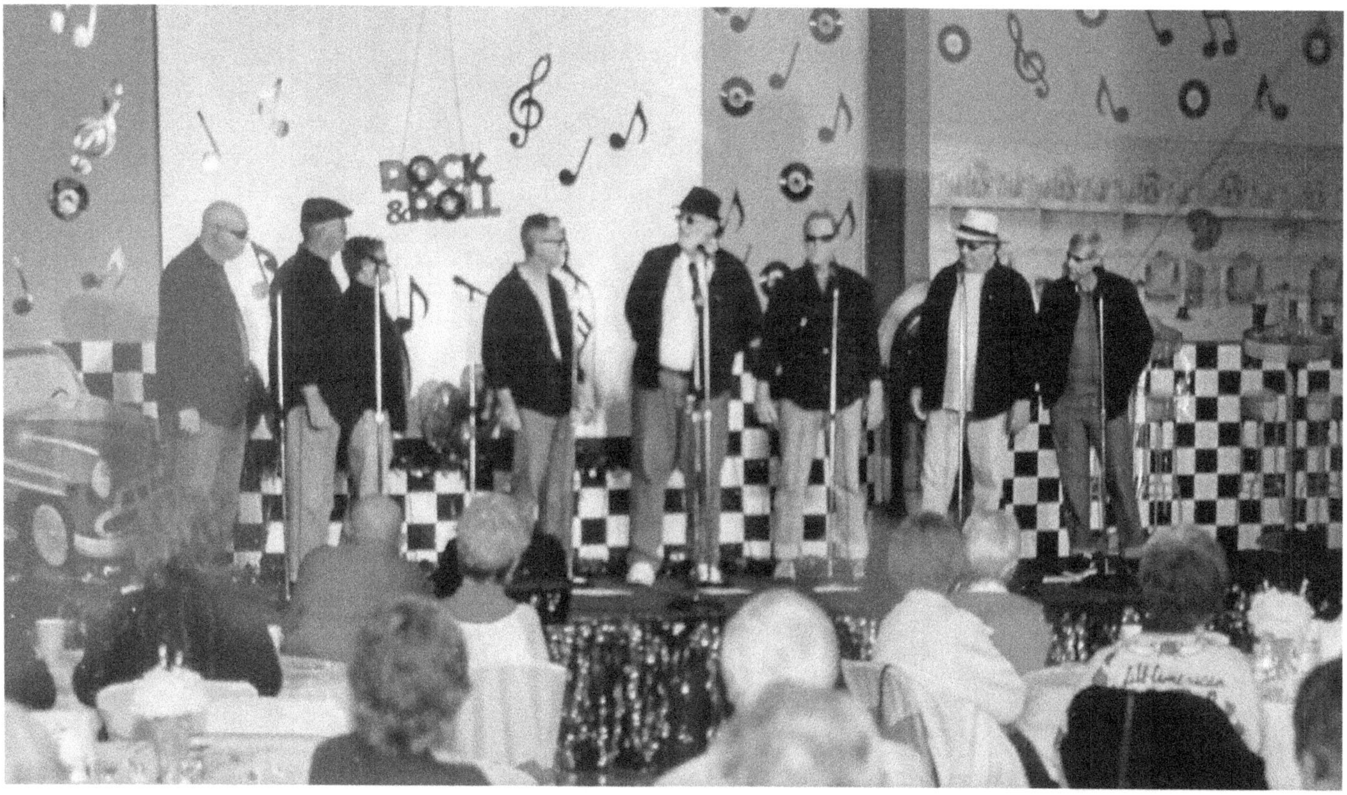

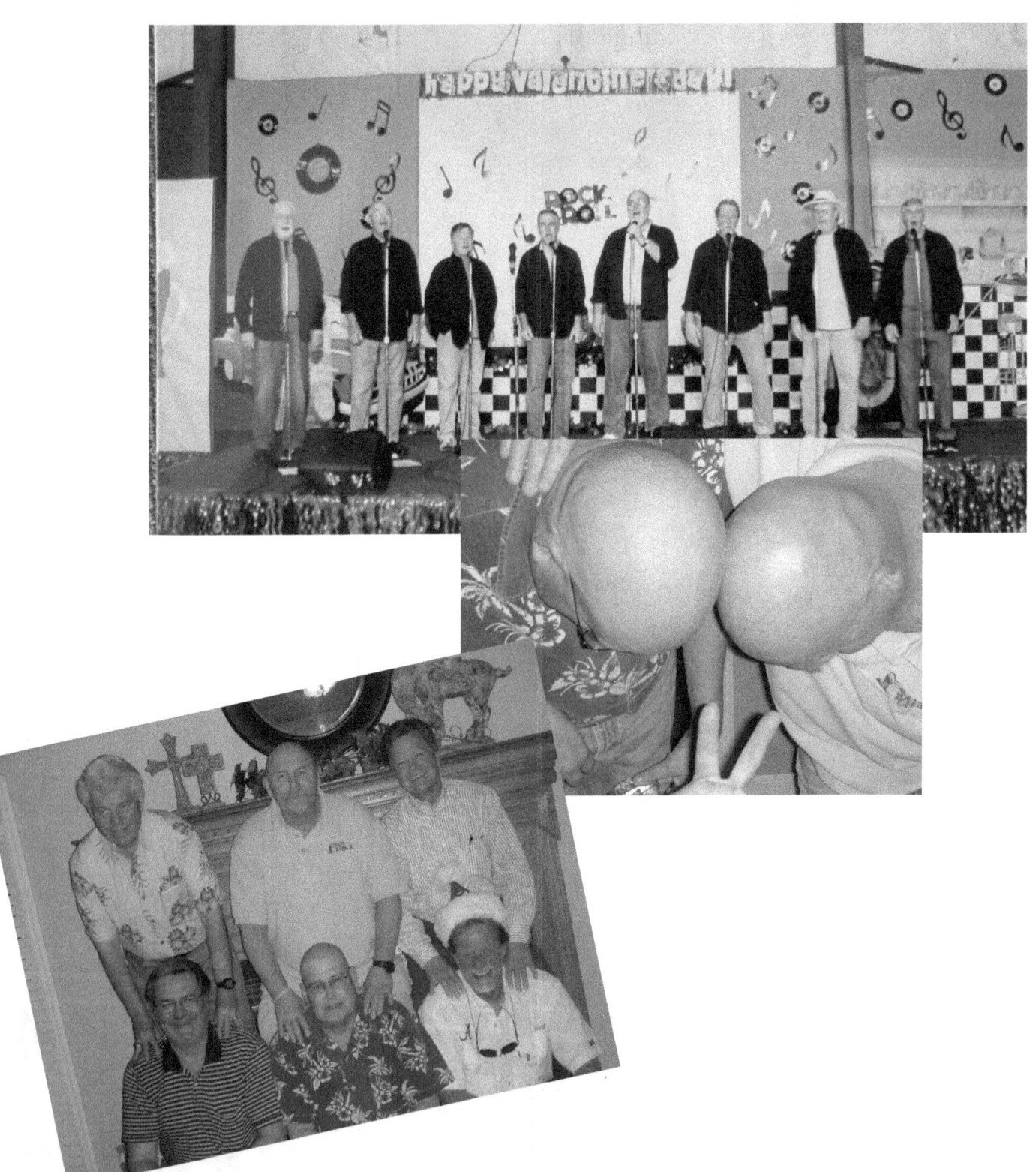

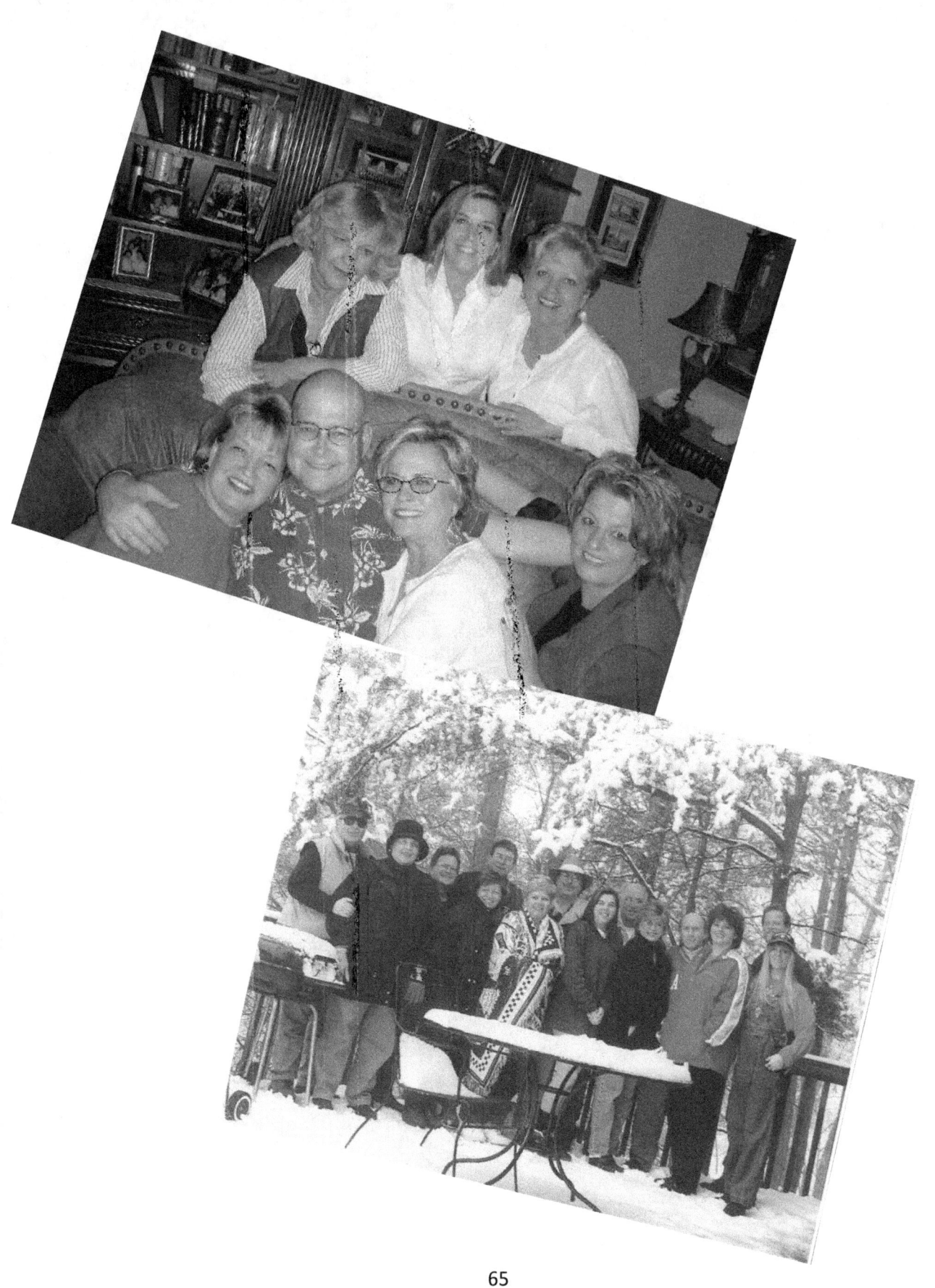

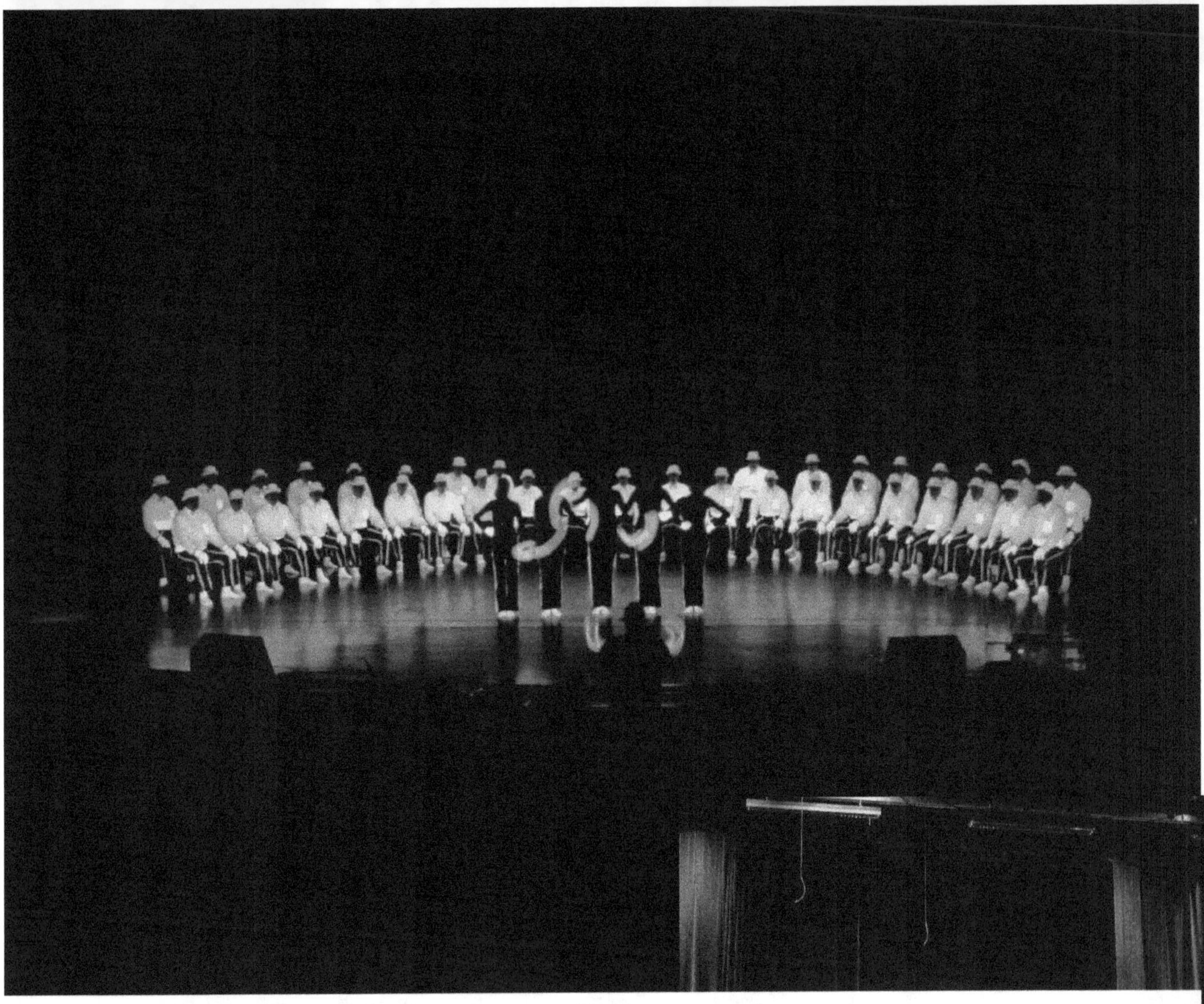

80th Anniversary Show Dress Rehearsal

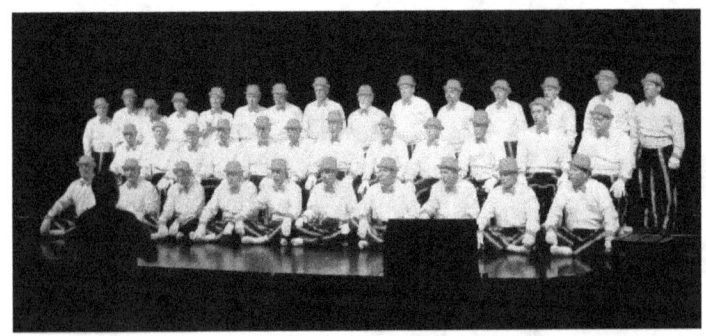

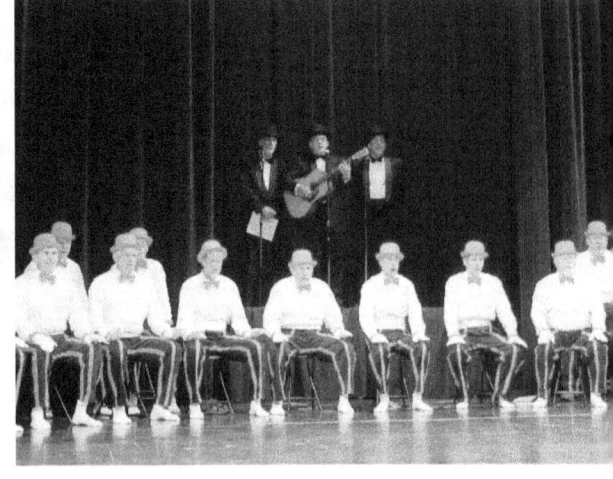

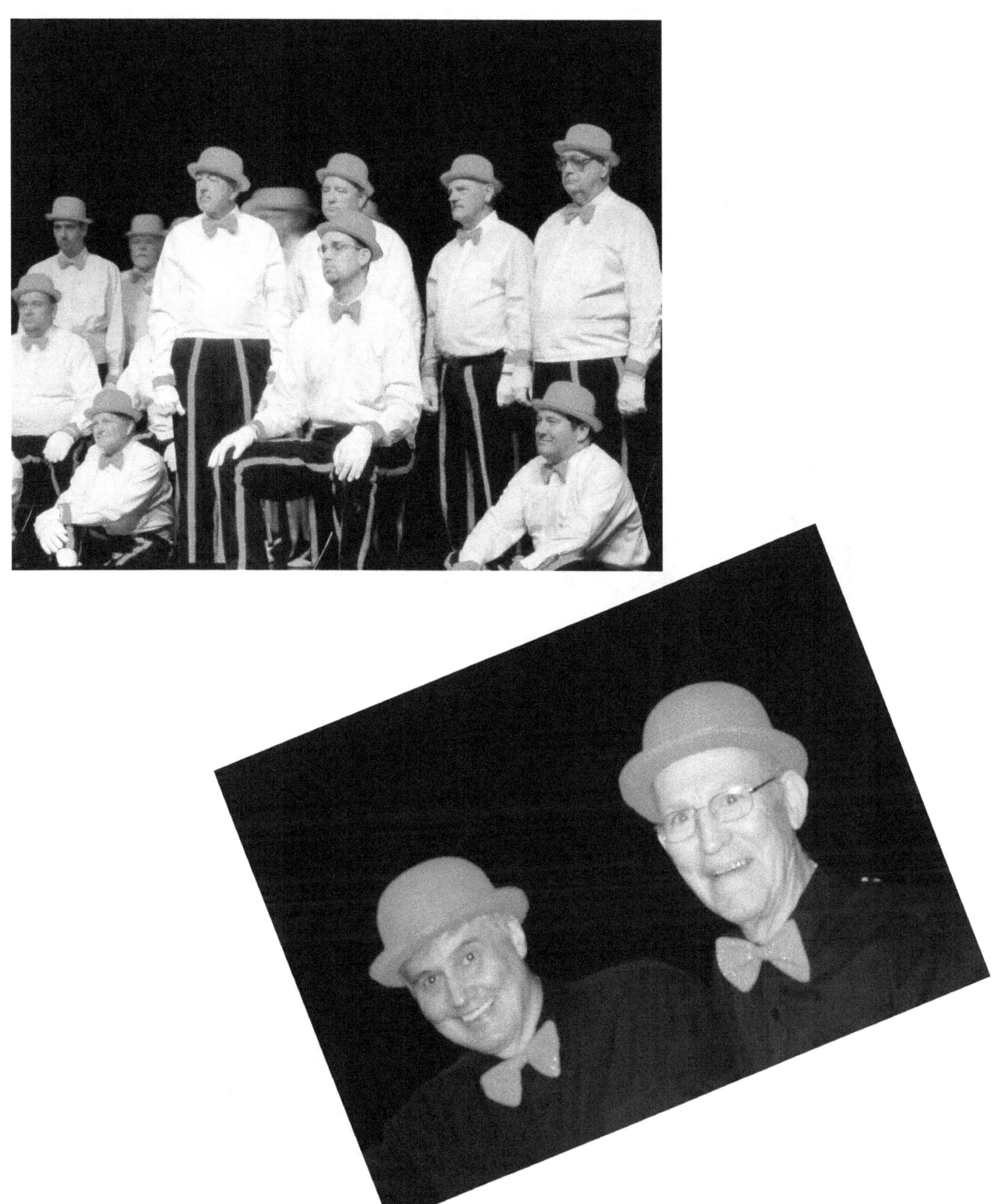

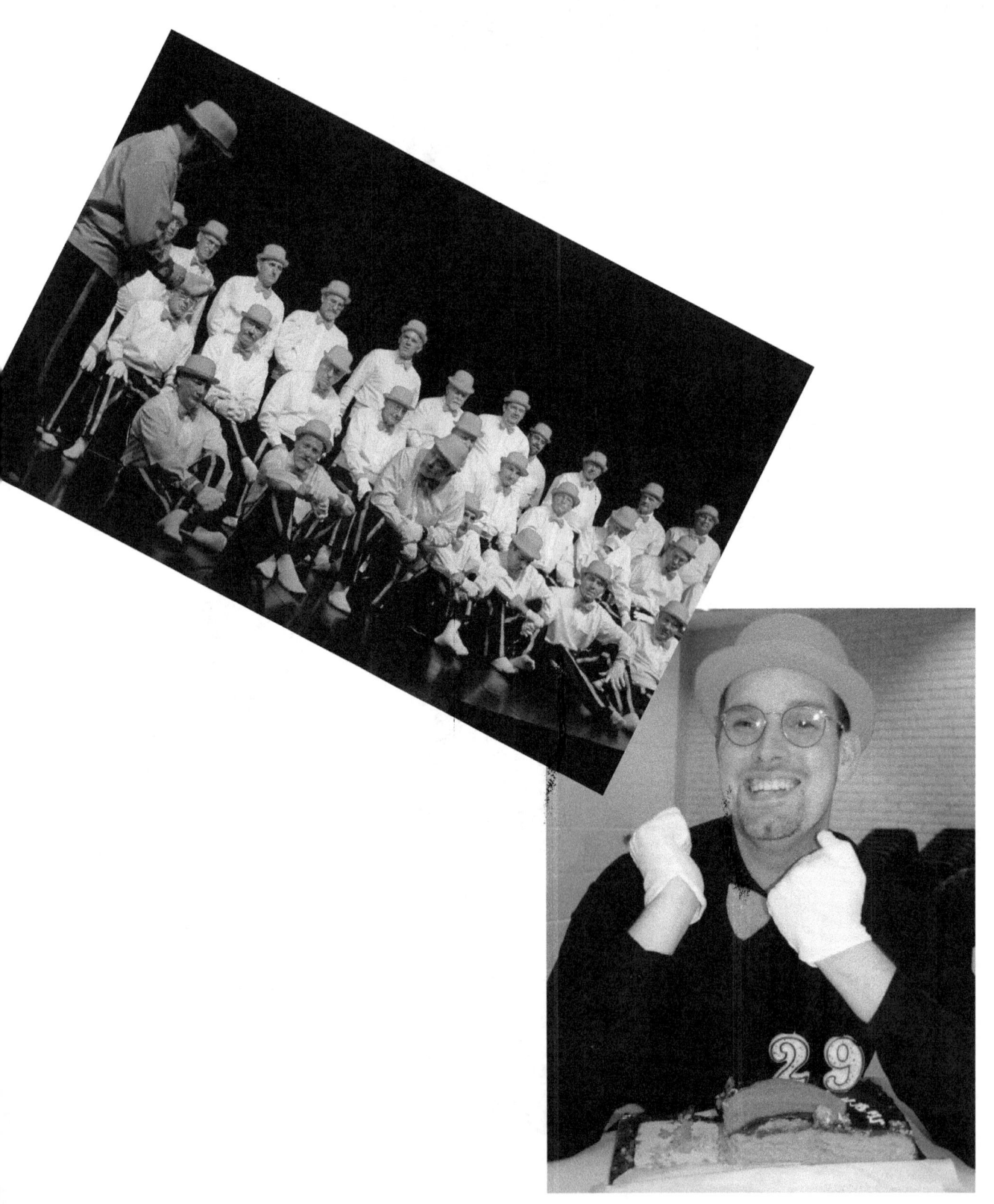

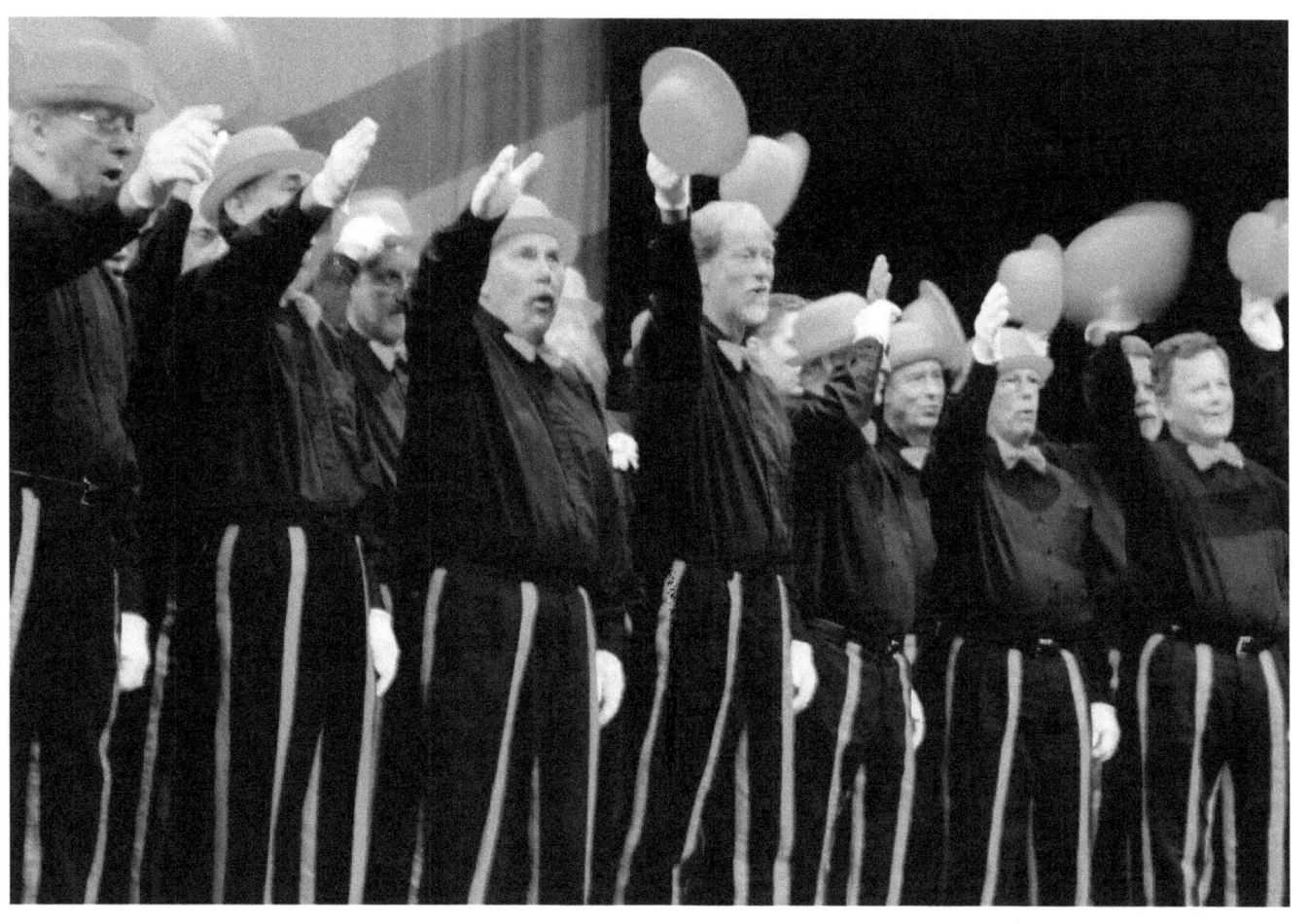

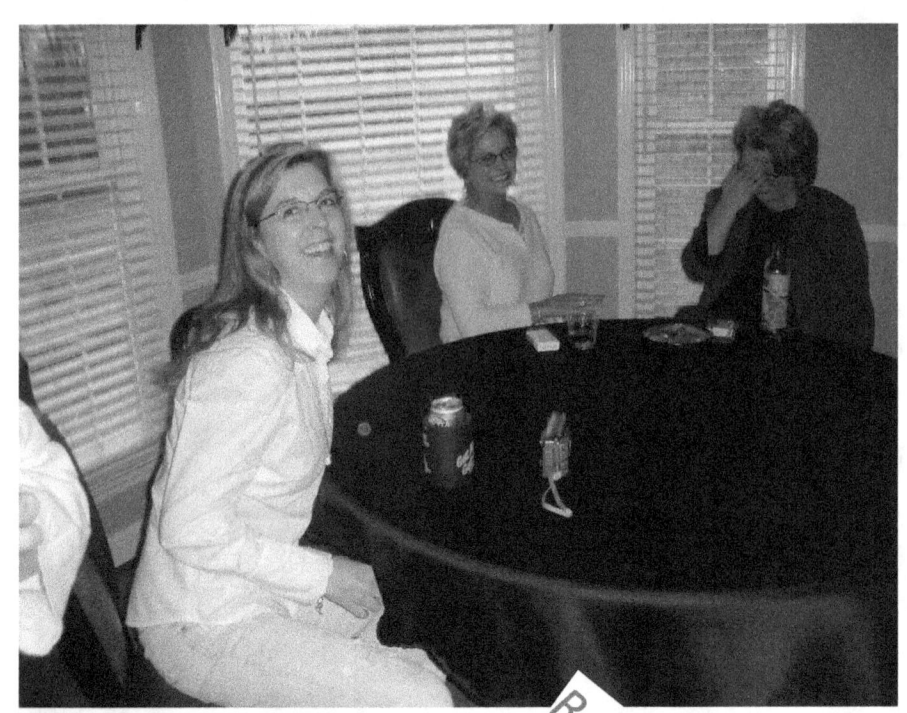

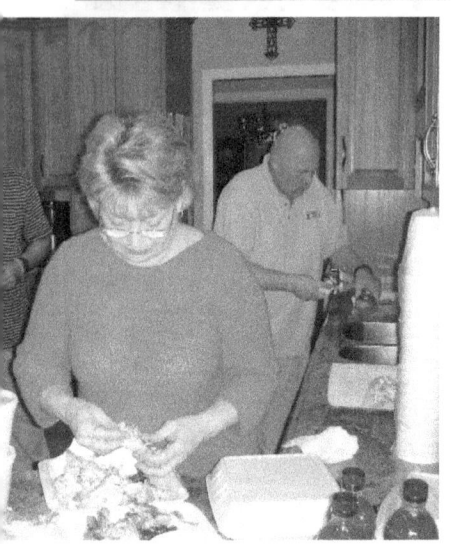

Random Shots from Walter Whited's Birthday Party

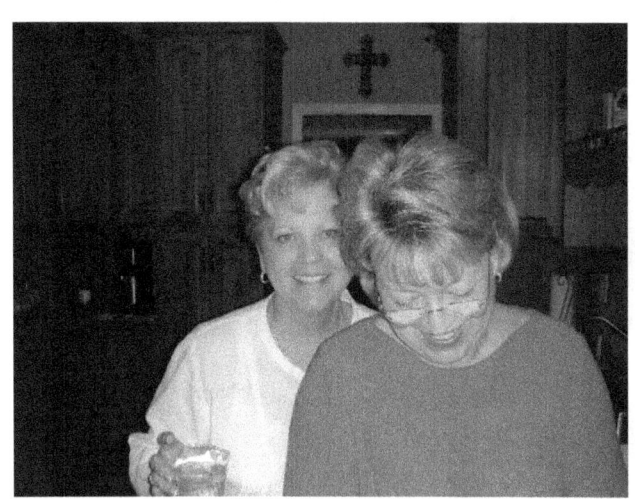

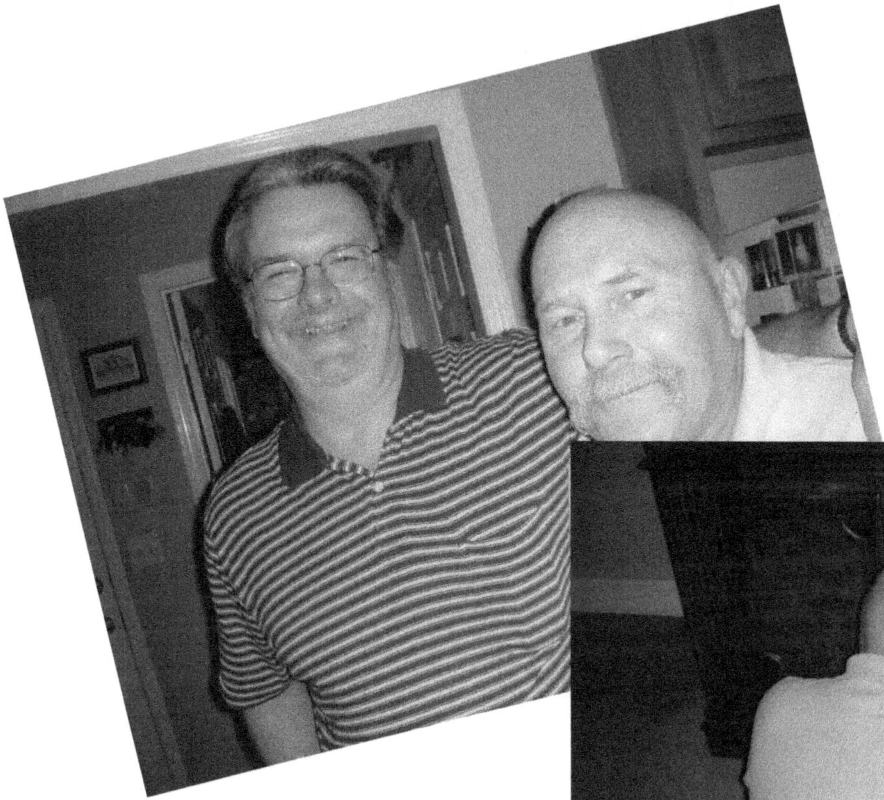

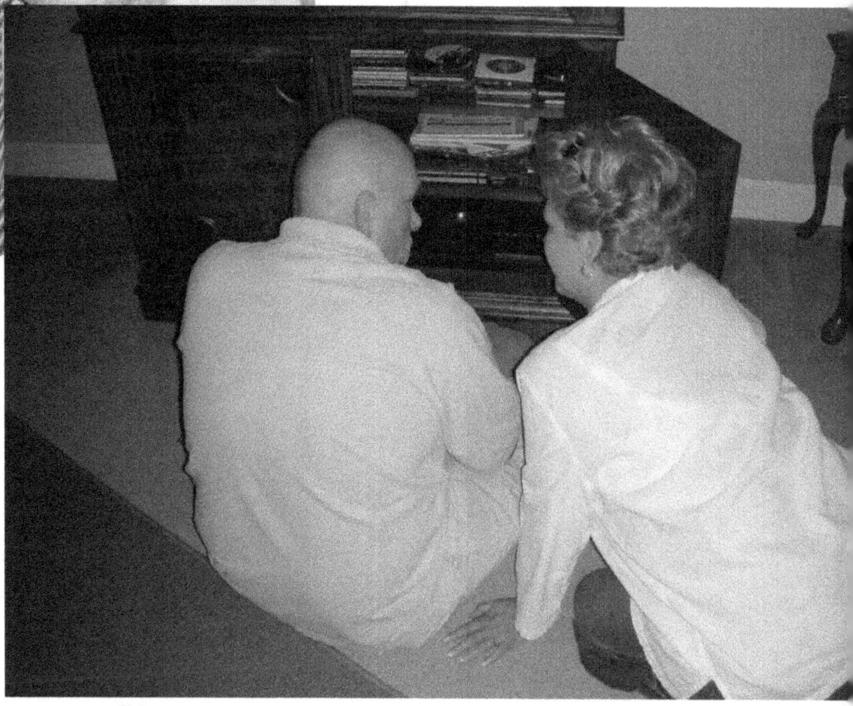

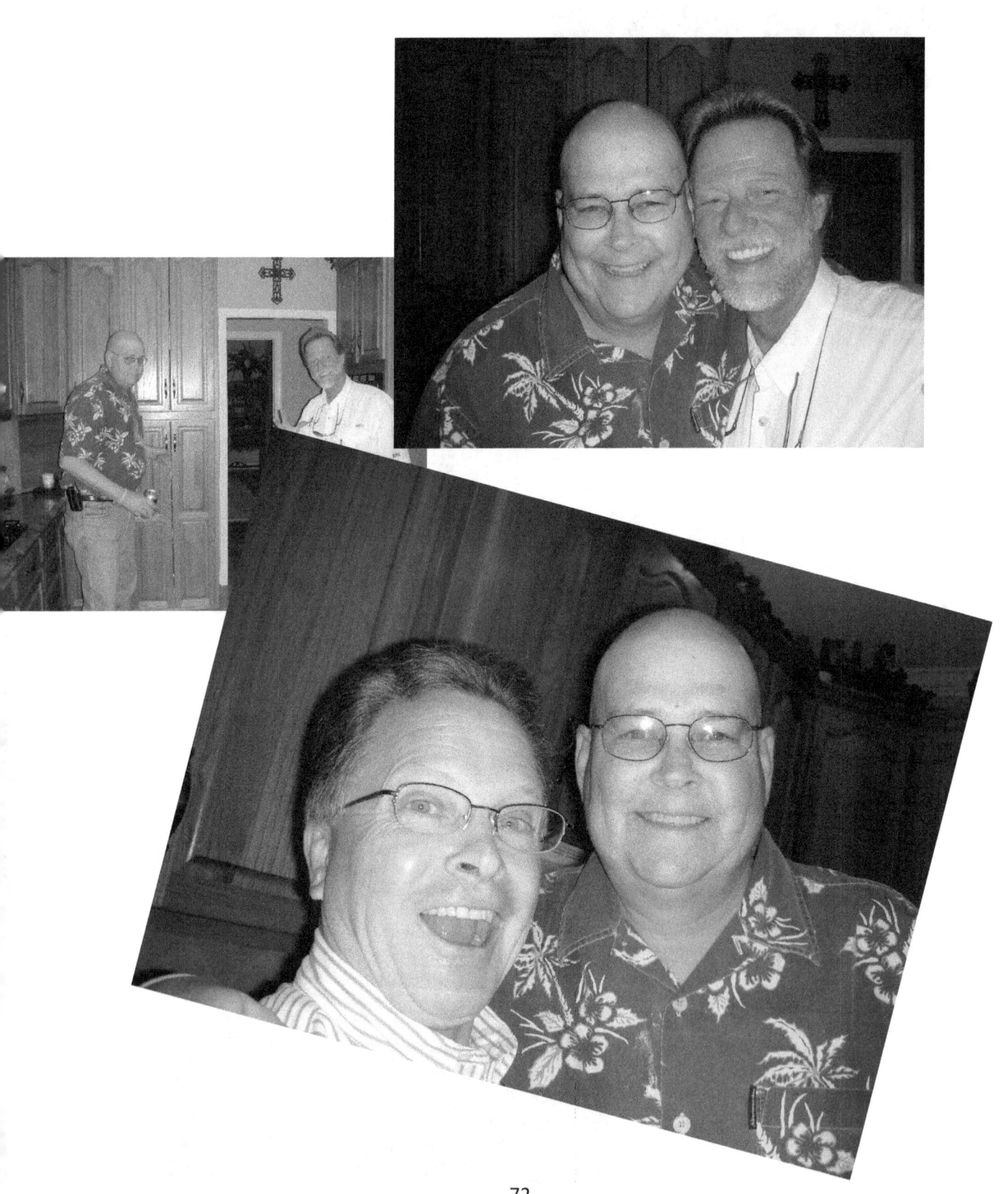

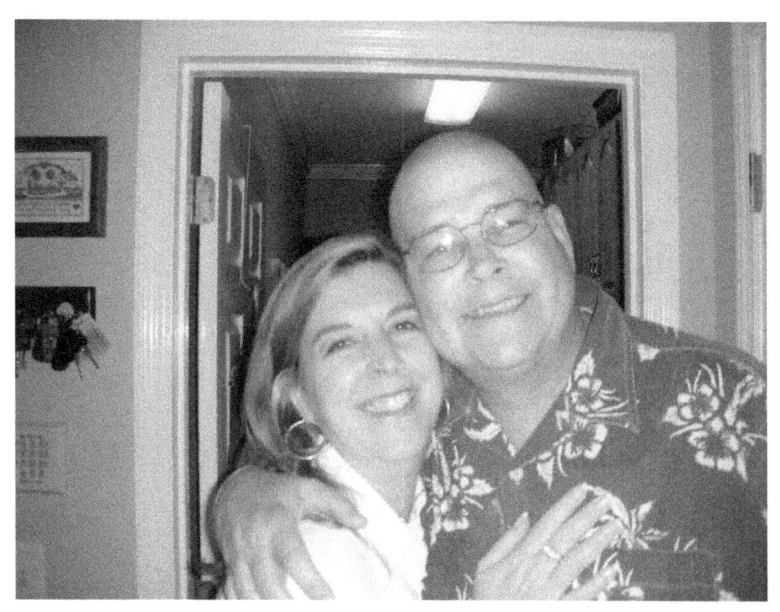

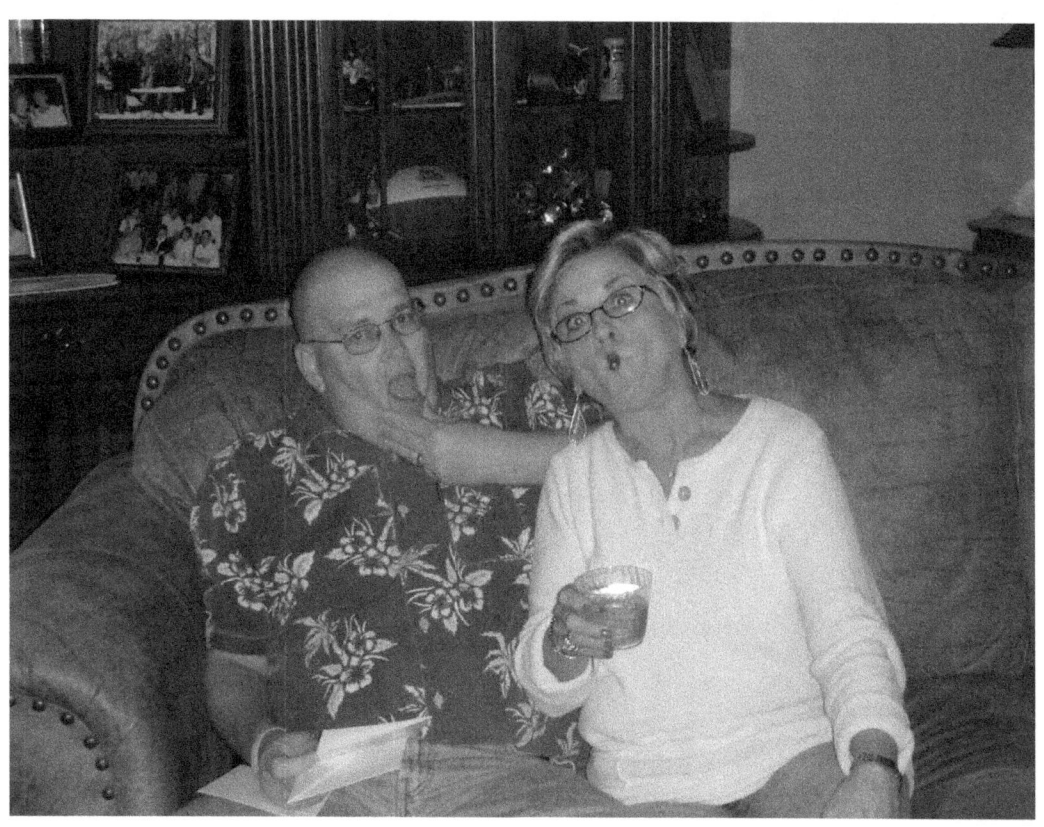

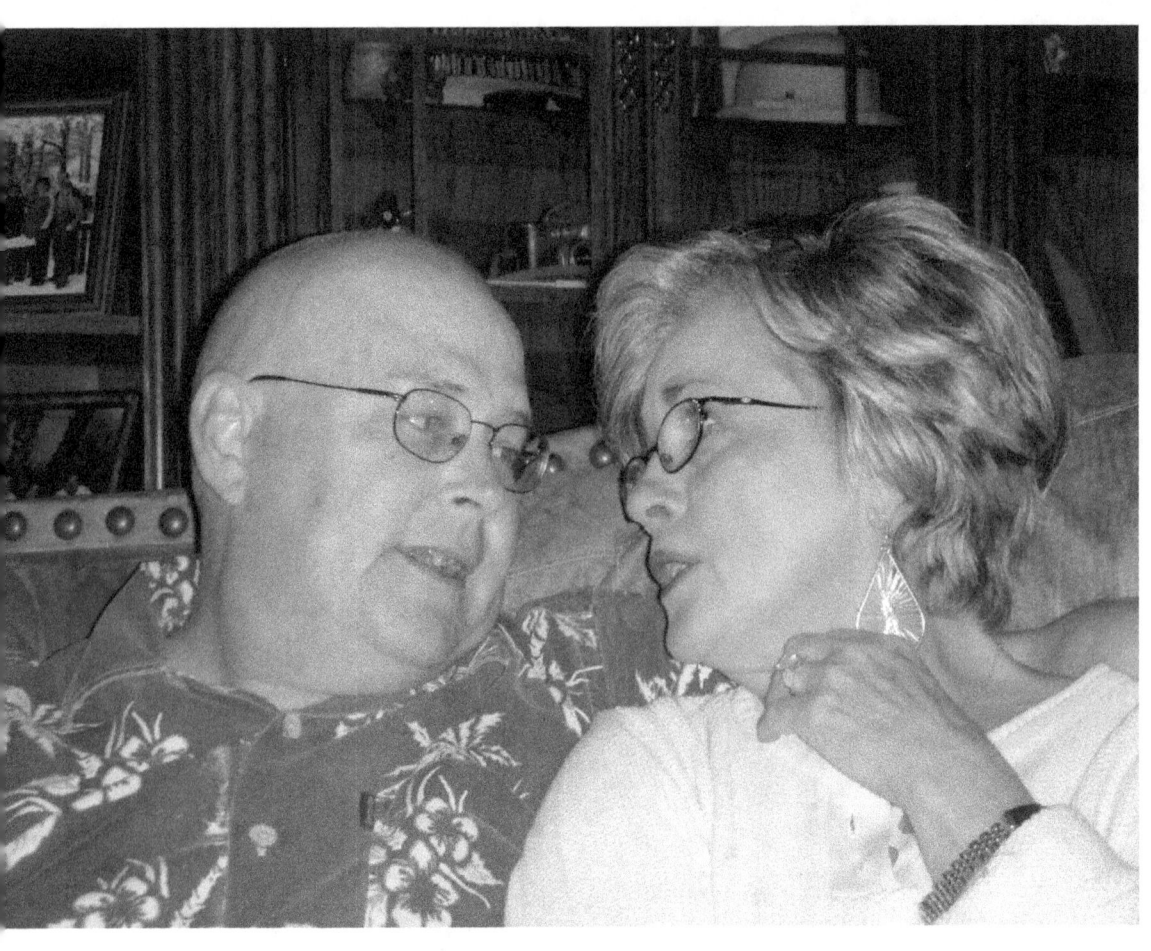

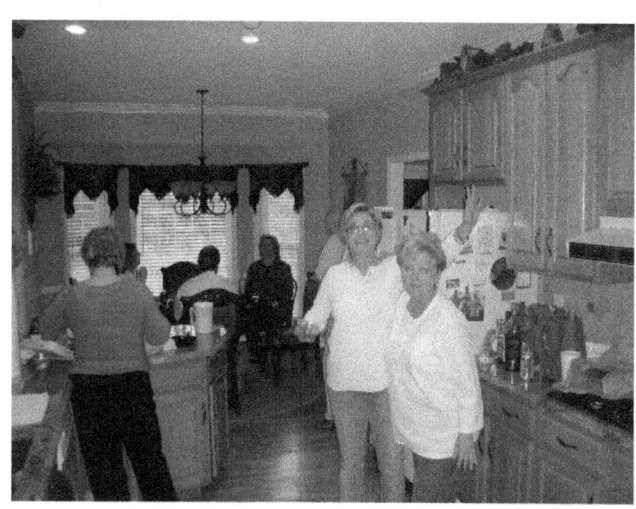

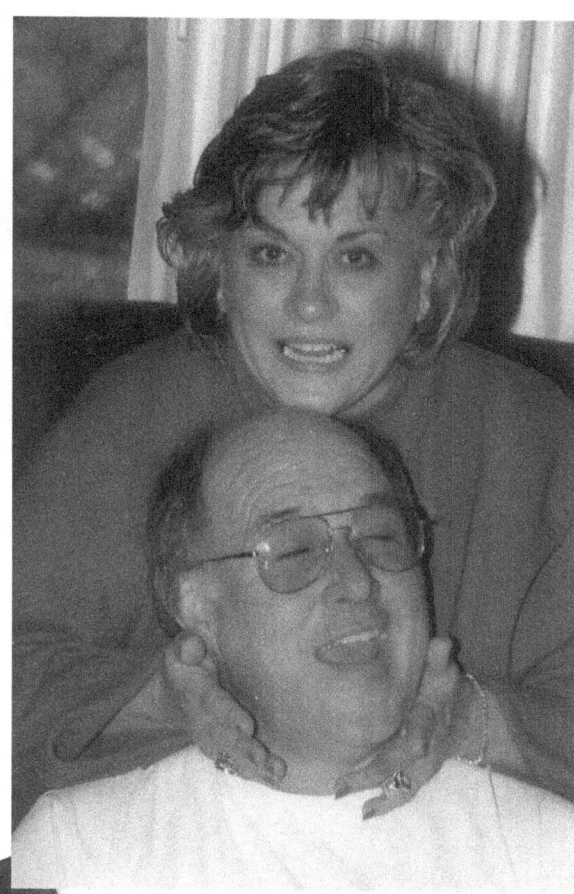

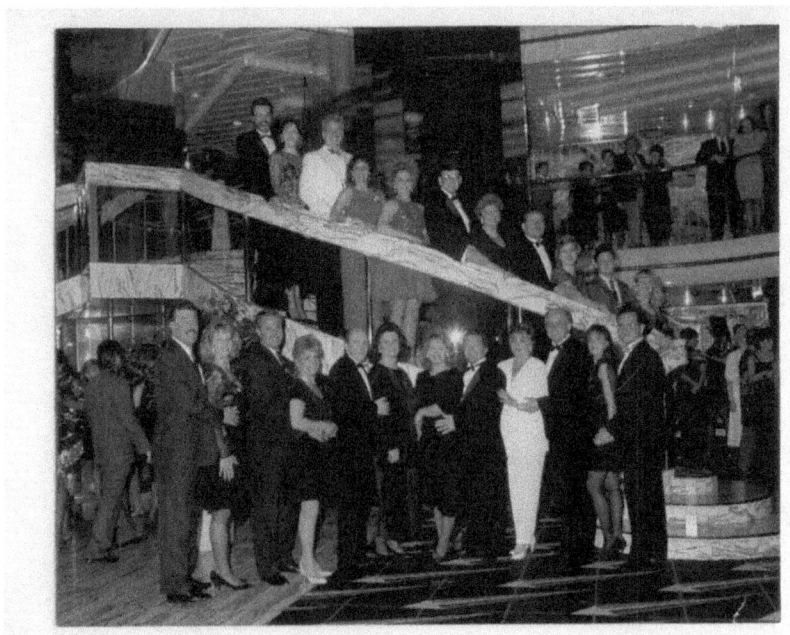

Wayne Brand

*Benefit
Show*

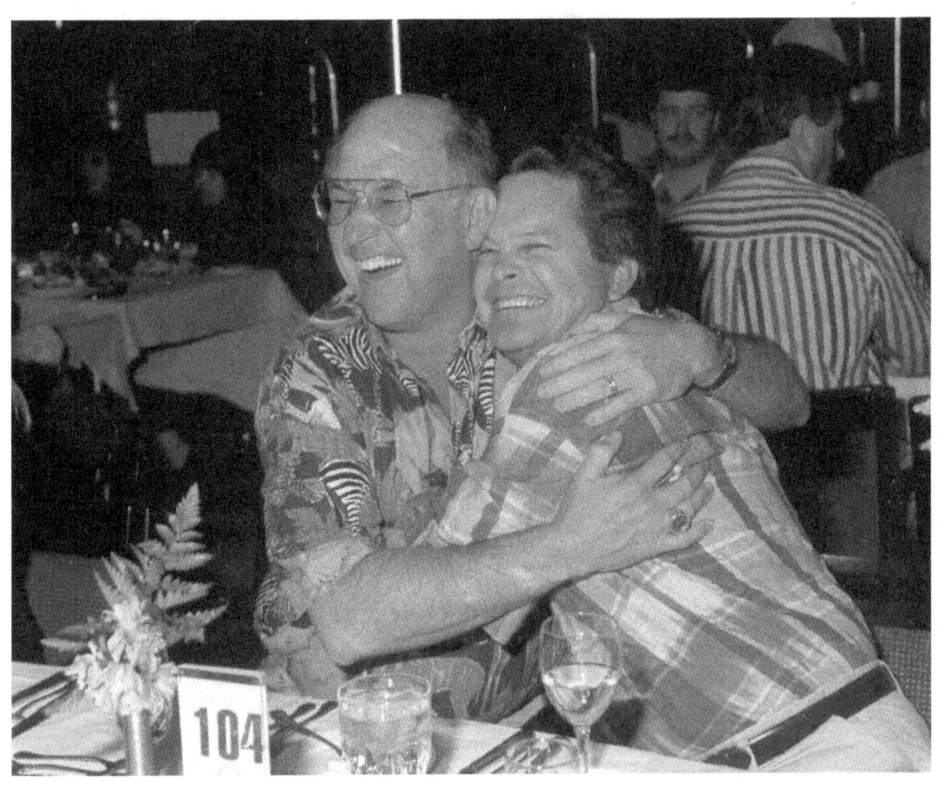

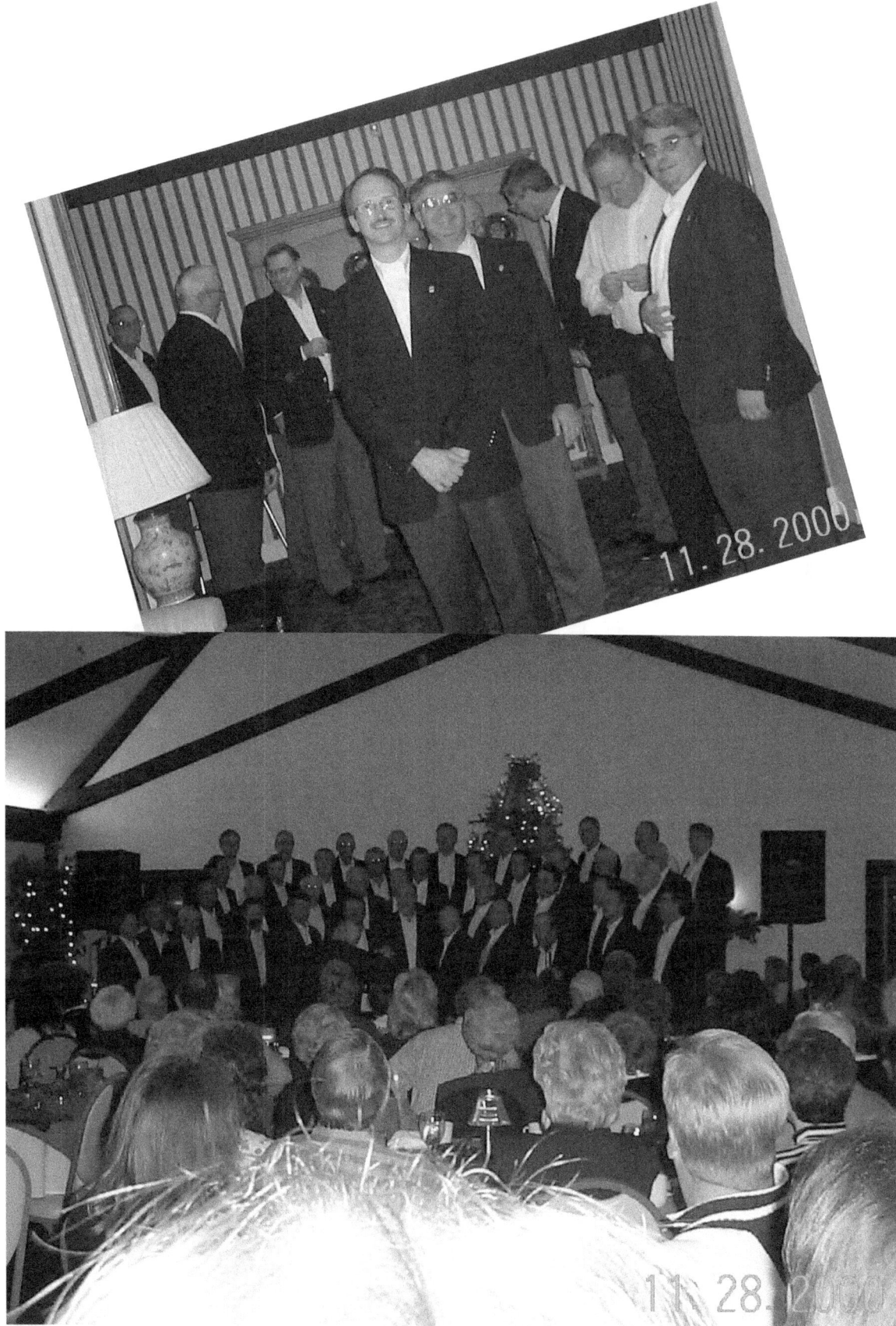

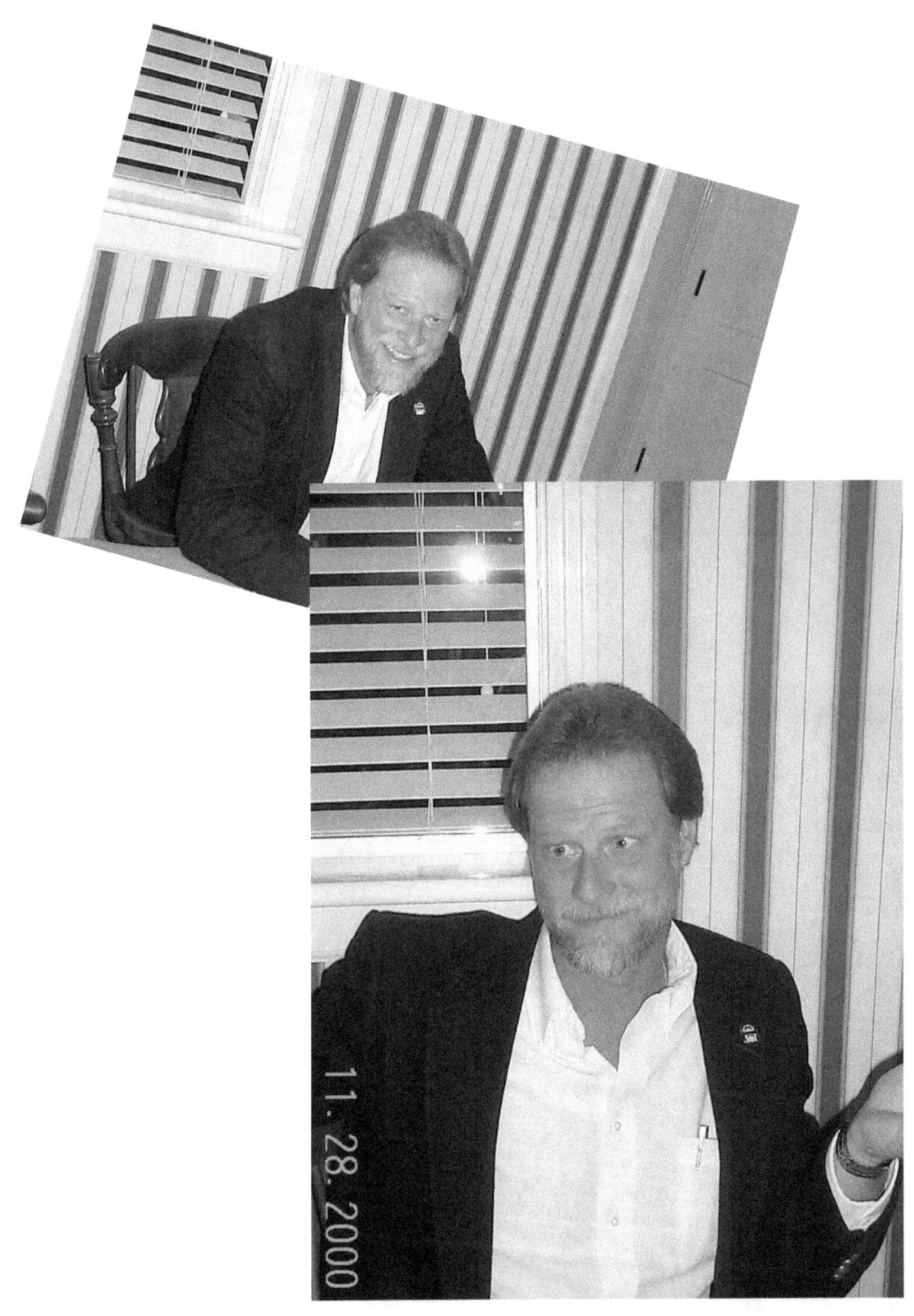

From Wayne Brand's Funeral

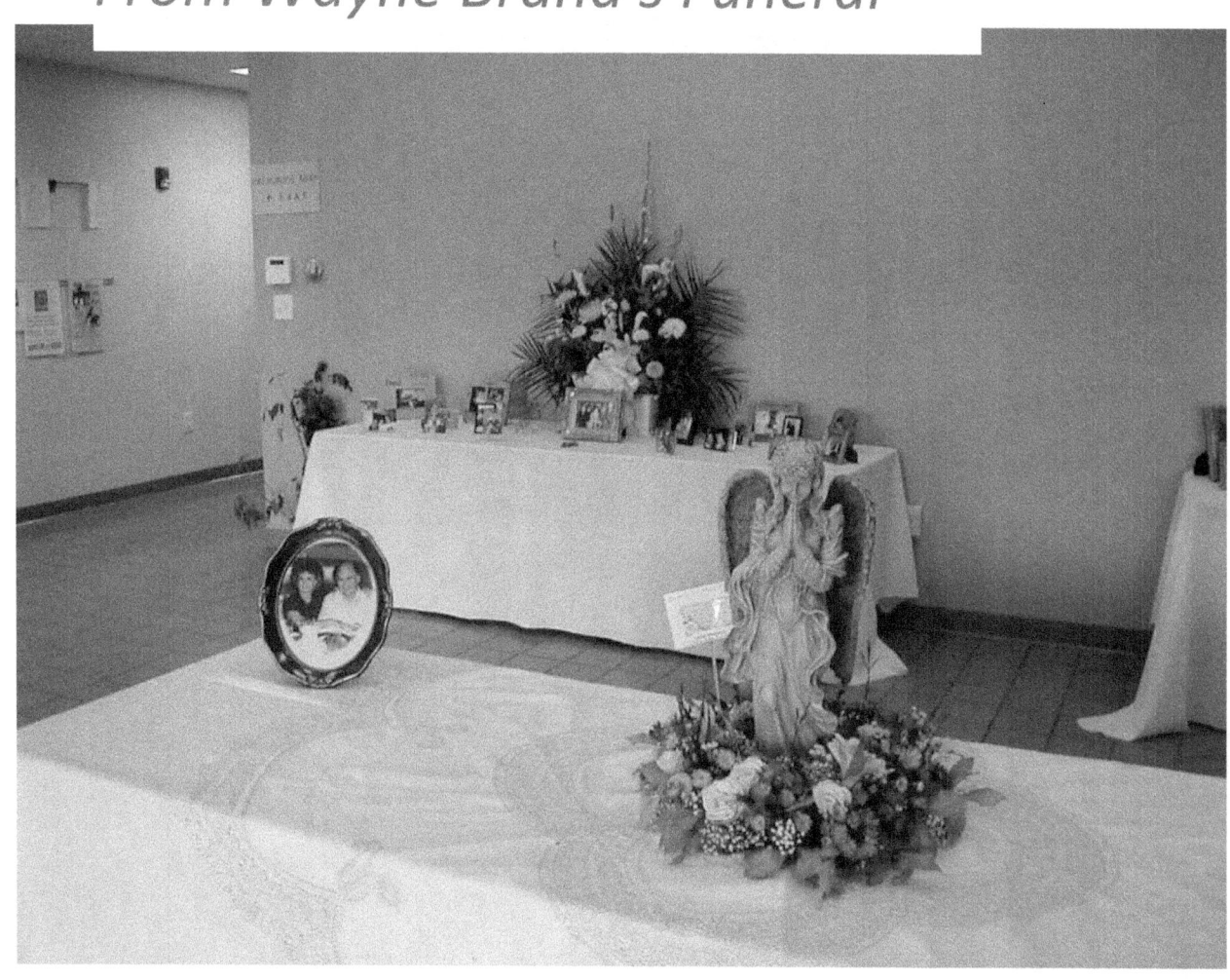

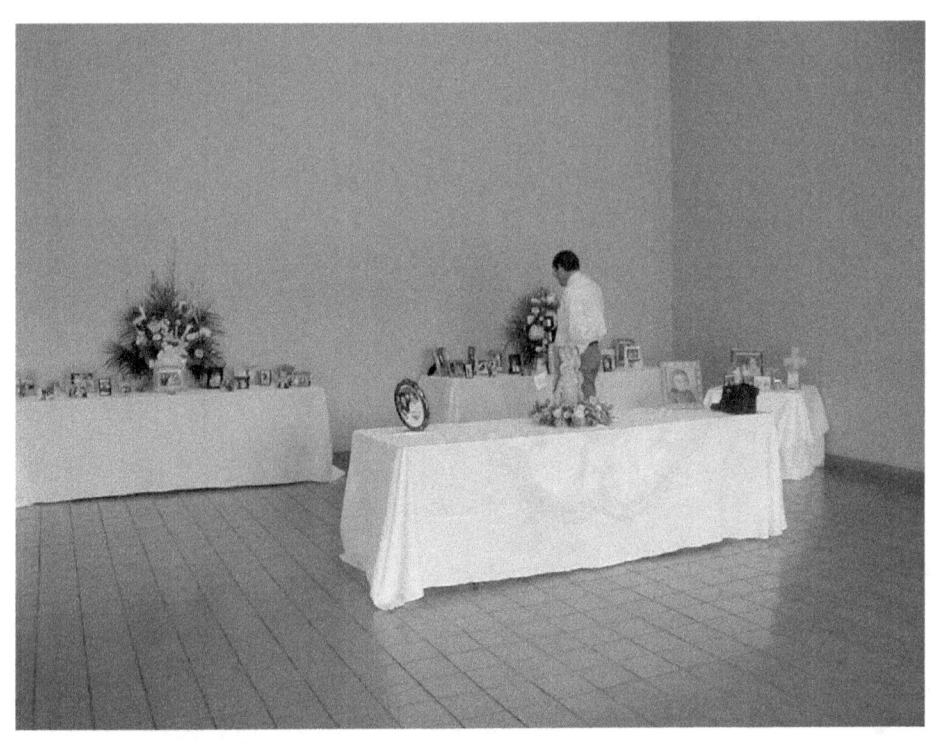

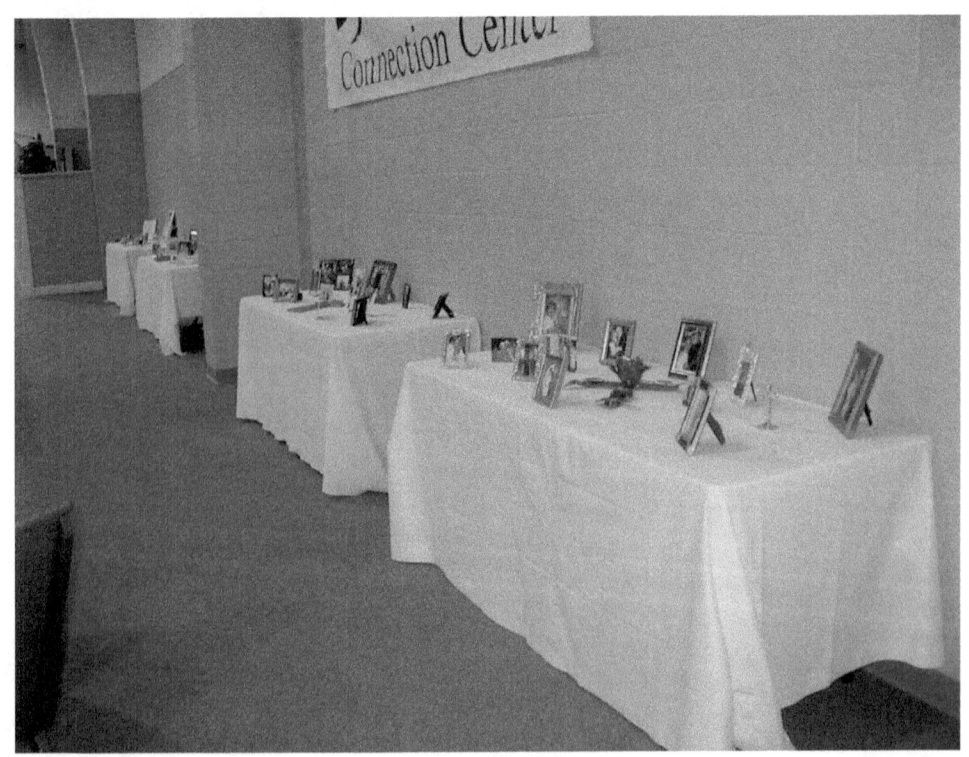

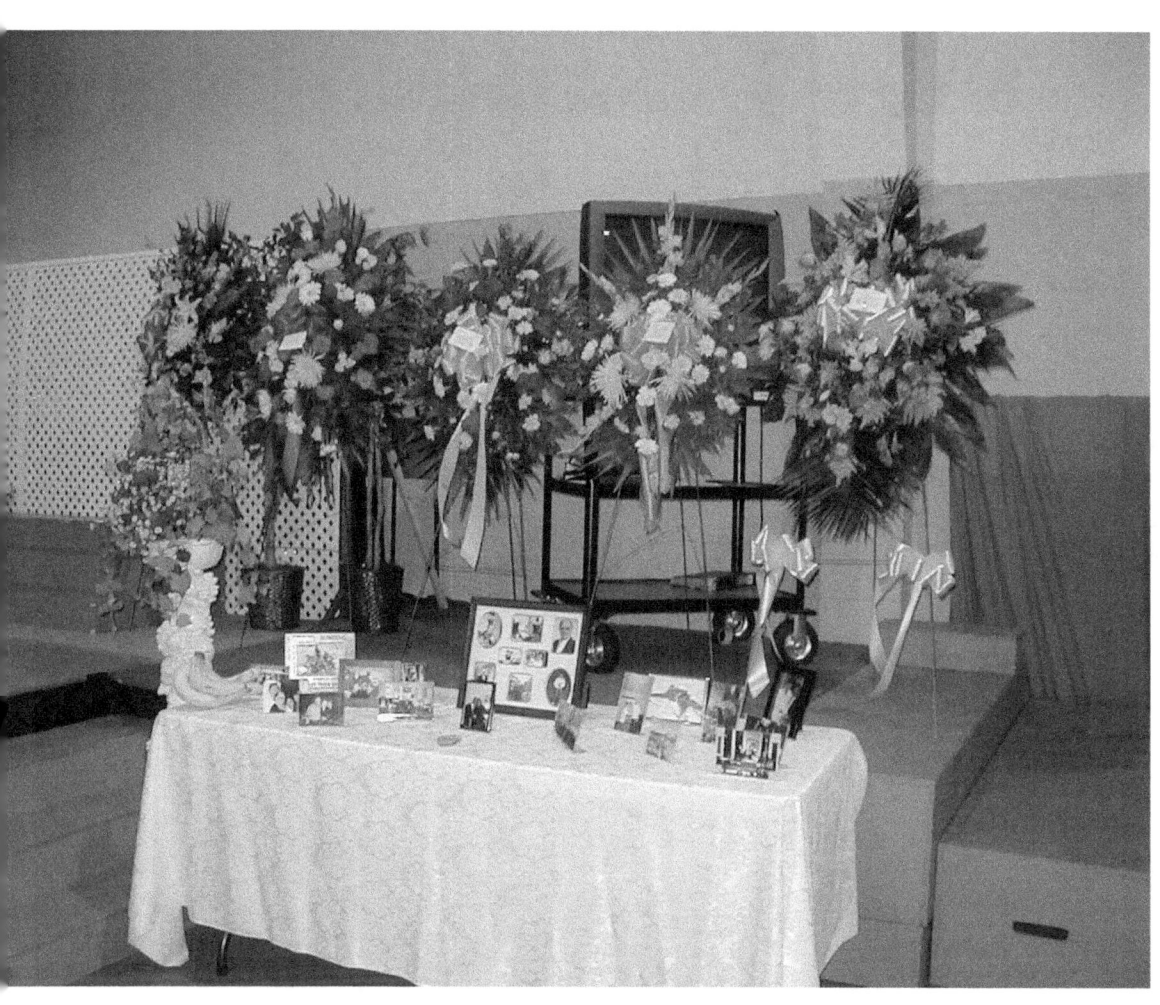

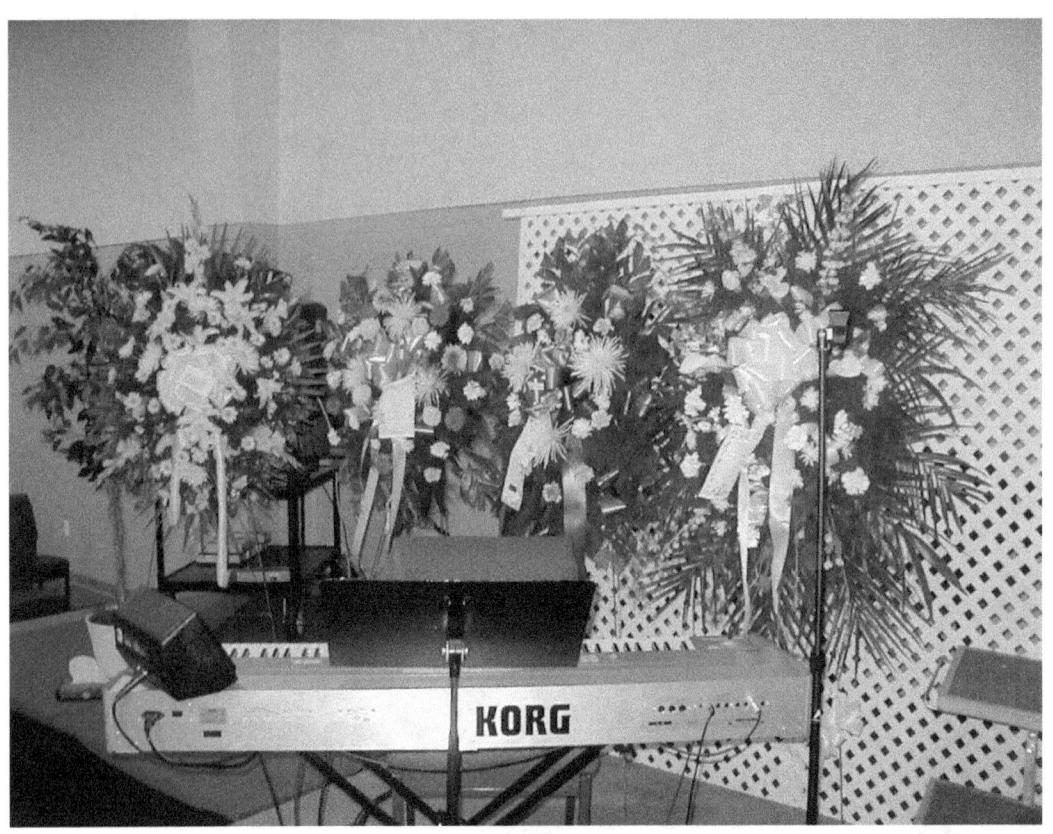

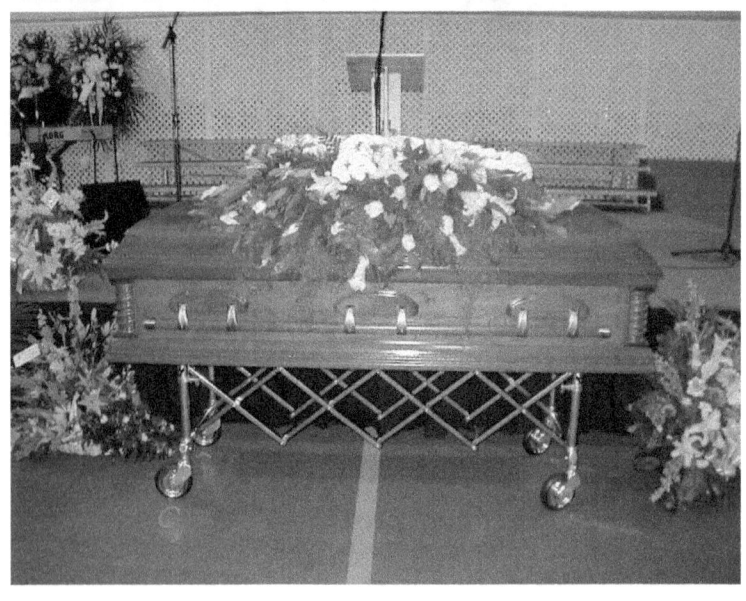

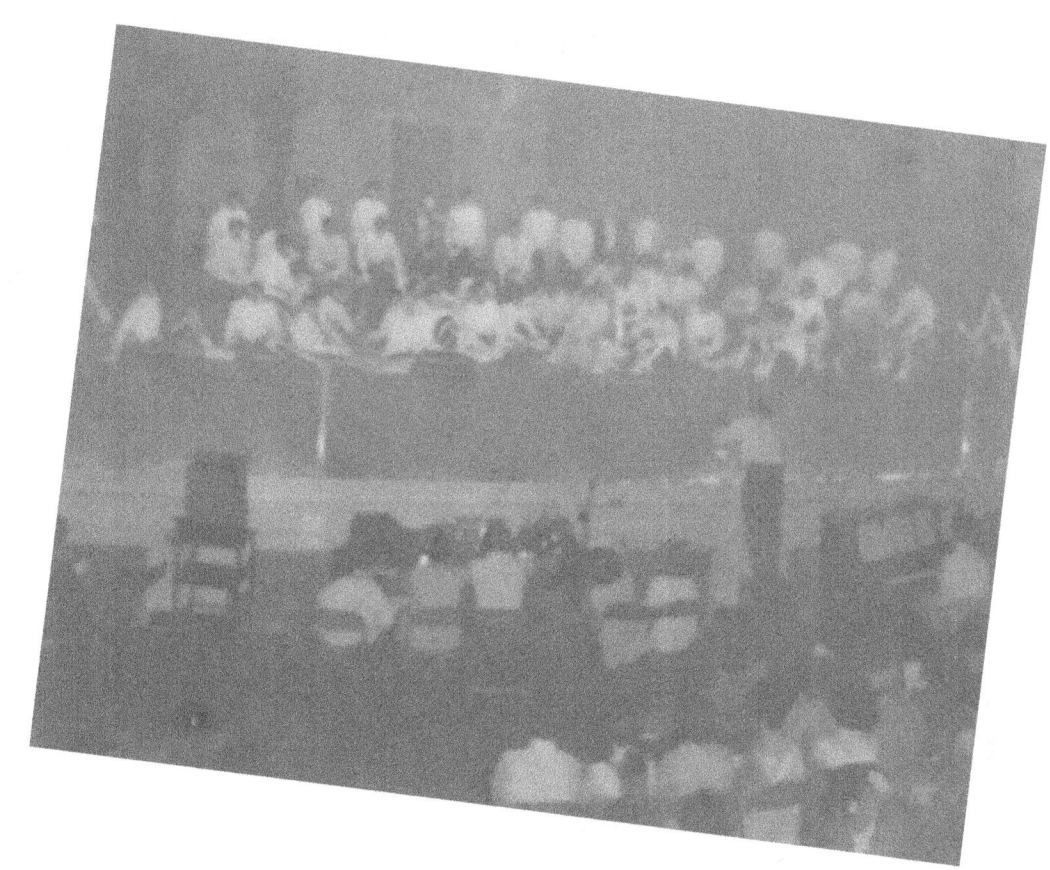

Preparation for "Big Show"

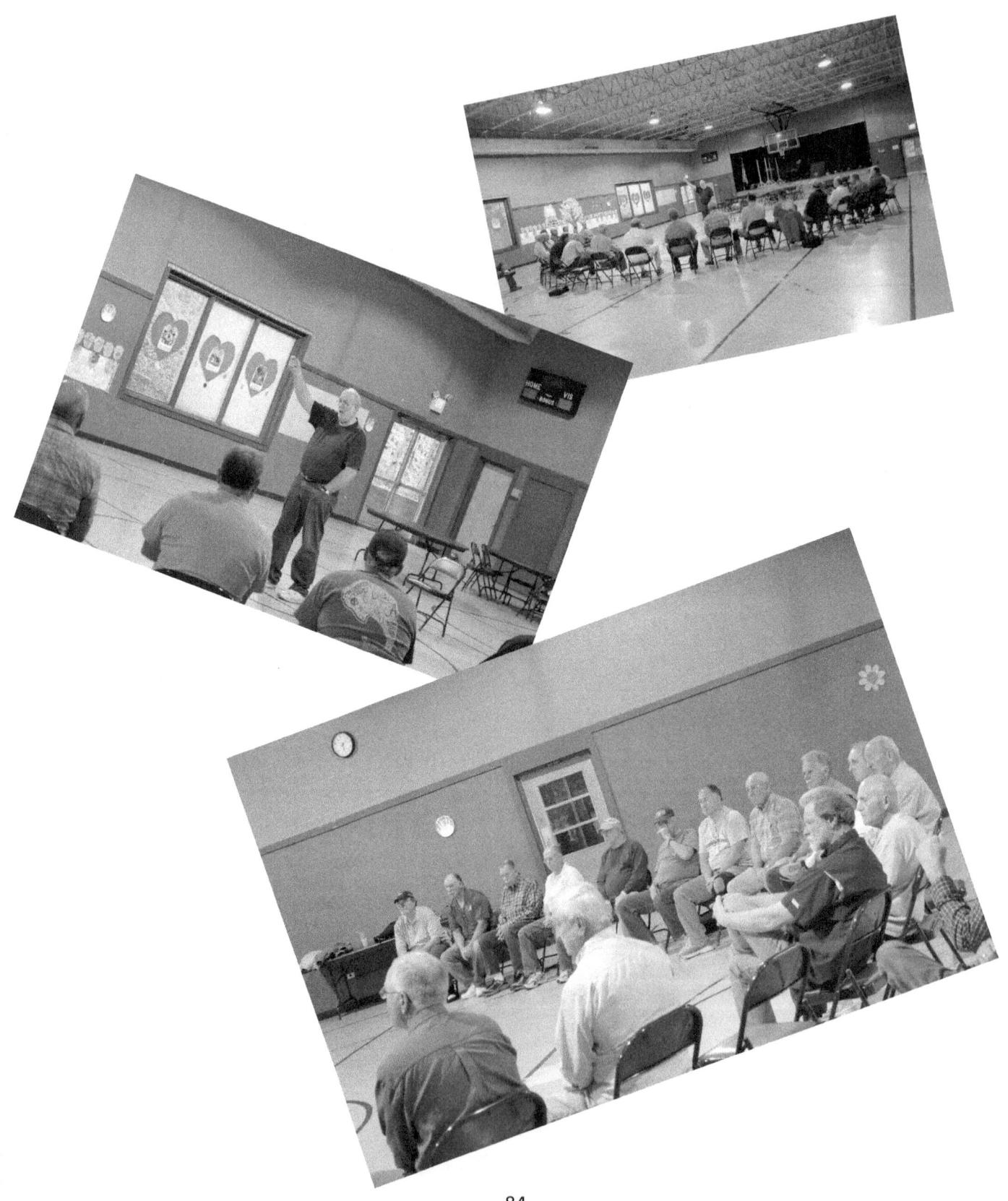

84

WARBLER PERSONNEL
(Arranged Alphabetically)

Wayne Atkinson, Roy Attison, Steve Baldis, Ken Bannister, Charlie Boone, Larry Bowman, Bobby Bradley, Bill Brewer, John Broussard, Glenn Bryan, Jeff Burkett, John Butler, Frank Butler, Phil Cain, Robert Corfielter, Terry Collier, Bob Collins, Tom Corley, Mike Crawford, Leslie Culpepper, Reginald Davis, Danny Douglas, Sammy Doyle, Gil Franks, Robert Frew, Kenneth Graham, Mike Graval, Tony Henderson, Stephen Heneger, Bruce Hill, Byron Hill, Steve Hopkins, Jim Huling, Walter Hunter, Jonny Jordan, Chris Lewis, Steve Loggins, Roger Lucas, David McAfee, Randy McArthur, Randy McBrayer, Mark McElroy, Louis McKnight, Donny Mills, Sam Mitchell, Kent Moa, Randy Morrison, Bill Overstreet, Tommy Reynolds, Steve Spencer, Gary Spears, John Suddeath, Tammy Tuggle, Larry Watts, Bill White, Chris Wilson, Reddy Williams, Larry York.

PRINCIPALS

Mr. "Interlocutor"	Jim Huling
Endmen (in order of appearance)	Jeff Burkett, Danny Douglas, Randy McBrayer, Bruce Hill, Mark McElroy, Tom Corley, and Roy Attison.
Alternate Endmen	Randy Morrison, Charlie Boone, Glenn Bryan, and Ken Bannister
Accompanists	Julee Knox and Lyn Funderburke
Understudy to Interlocutor	Randy Morrison
Warblers Club Sponsor and Director	Joseph D. Turner
Principal of Woodlawn High School	E. E. Moree

PRODUCTION STAFF

Ticket Distribution	Bill Lee
Ushers	Ushers Club
Backstage Crew	Cavaliers Club
Lighting and Sound Crew	Stage Crew Club
	Sullivan, King, Knight, Marshall, Harris, Dobbs, Nolan, Spivey, Deccardi, Towers and Carpenter
Make up	Girls Glee Club
Walk On Parts	Cavaliers Club
Set	Patsy Williams, Christy Oglethee, Sharon Freeman, Valerie Ligon and Warblers Club
Properties	Warblers Club

The Warblers Club
of
Woodlawn High School

Presents

THE RETURN OF THE HOBOS

✳ ✳ ✳

March 23, 24, 25, & 27   8:00 P.M.

Woodlawn High School Auditorium

E. E. MOREE, Principal

PROGRAM
•

We Meet Again Tonight Boys	Circle
Opening Chorus	Circle
Introducing "Mr. E. S. Cape"	Jeff Burkett
Rogers and Hammerstein	
Everybody's Got a Home But Me	Randy Morrison
Introducing "Mr. Y. L. Life"	Danny Douglas
Hobo Convention Fever—Piano Solo	Chris Lewis
Introducing "Festus" and "W. C. Fields"	Randy McBrayer and Bruce Hill
Plenty Good Room—Arr. Turner	Circle
Introducing "Mr. Rav E. Olley" and "Mr. Elwood P. Suggins"	Mark Elroy and Tom Corley
The New Ashmolian Marching Society and Students Conservatory Band	Circle
Introducing "Mr. Al A. Gator"	Roy Attison
Mood Indigo—Duke Ellington	Circle
Soon-A-Will-Be-Done—Arr. Dawson	Circle
Introducing "Nashville Fugitive"	Gil Franks
Cotton Fields—Arr. Turner	Circle

INTERMISSION

(Intermission will last 15 minutes. Cold drinks are being served in the front halls. Please return to your seats at the dimming of the houselights. No one admitted during first number after intermission since it is a blacklight production number.)

•

Ezekiel Saw De Wheel—Arr. Dawson-Turner	Circle
Ding Dong School	Alternates and Interlocutor
Along Came Jones	Quartet
Gil Franks, Jim Huling, Danny Douglas, Randy McBrayer	
Down in the Valley—Arr. Meade-Turner	Circle
I Got Shoes—Arr. Turner	Circle
Without A Song—Vincent Youmans	Danny Douglas
Walk Together Chillum—Arr. Staff-Turner	Circle
Floatin Down To Cottontown—Arr. Turner	Circle
Ol' Man River—Kern-Hammerstein	Phil Cain
Kentucky Babe—Arr. Turner	Circle
Oh Mona—Hillbilly Folk Song	Endman and Circle
President's Speech	Bruce Hill
Closing Chorus	Alumni and Circle

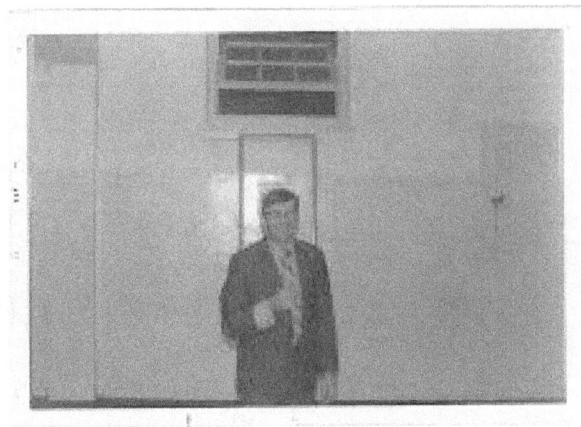

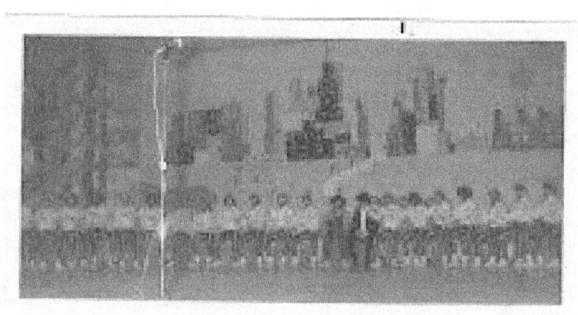

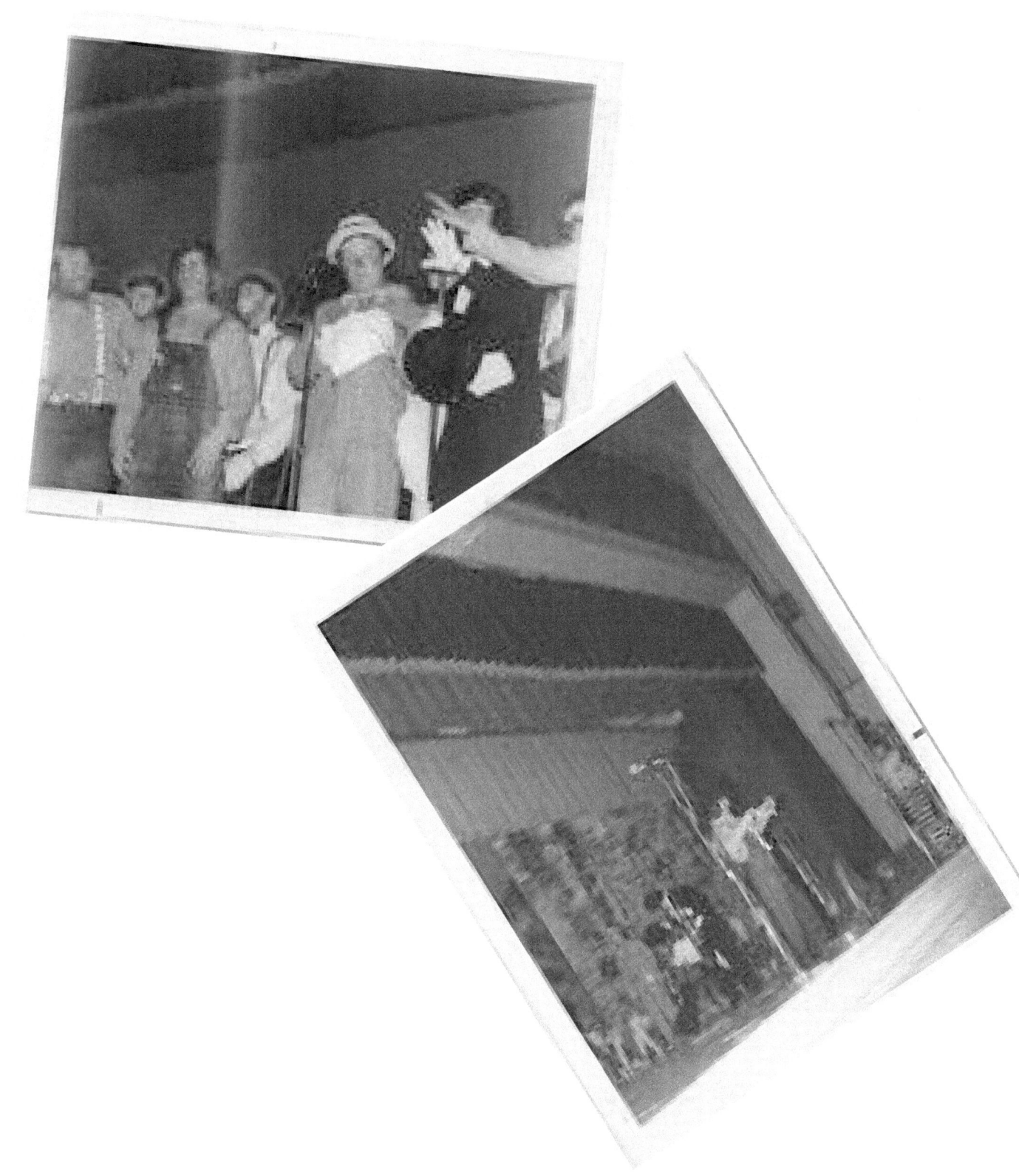

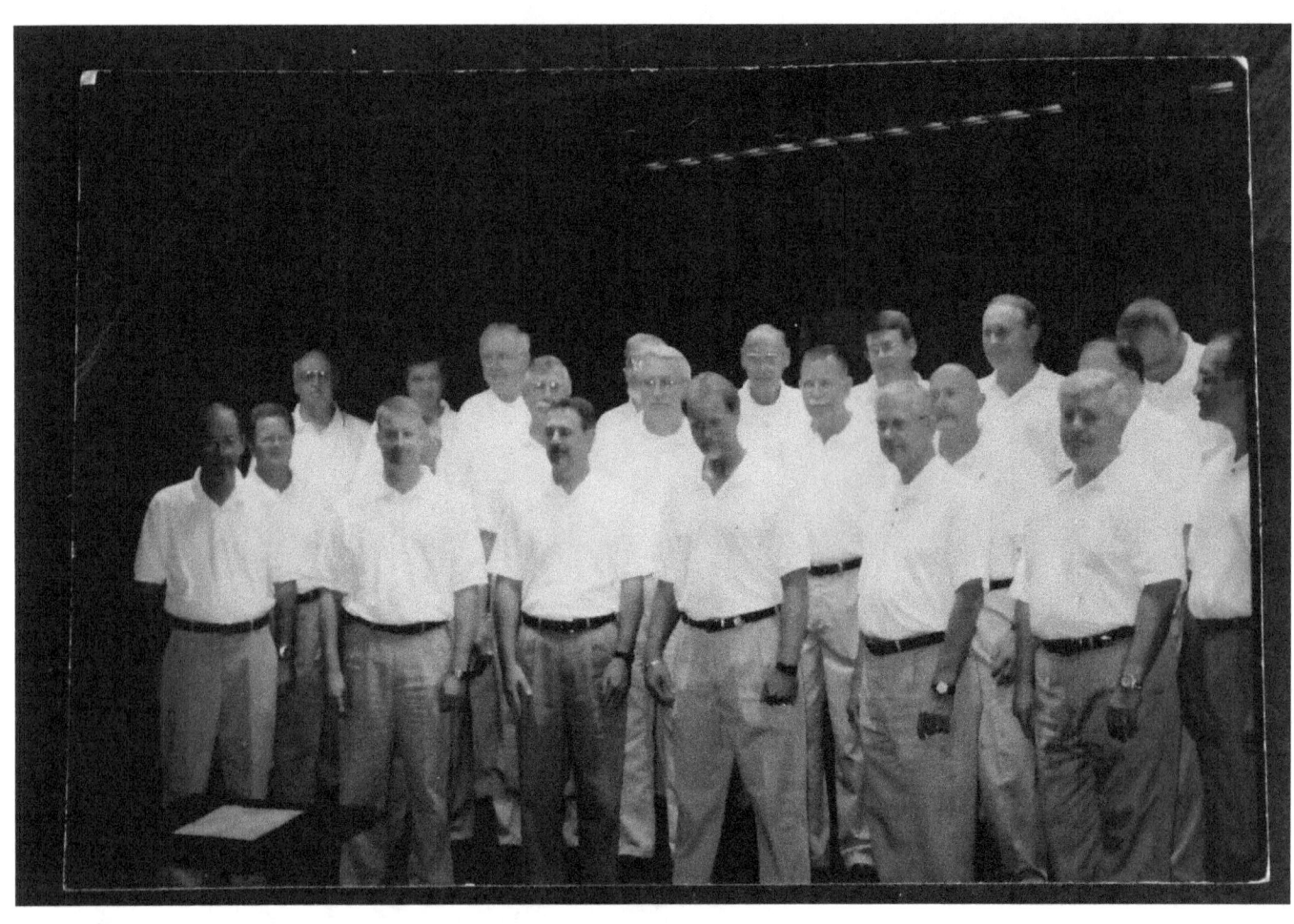

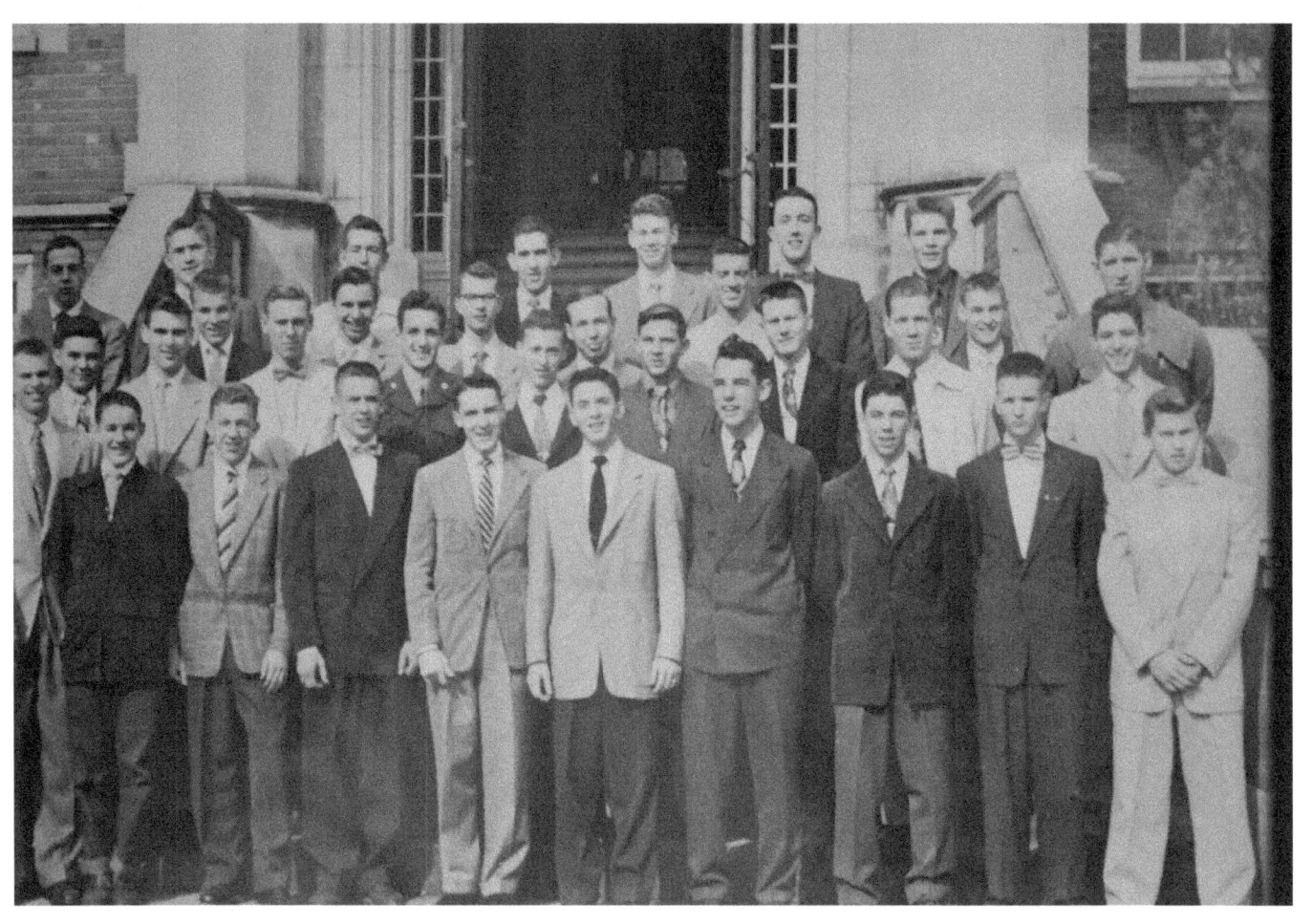

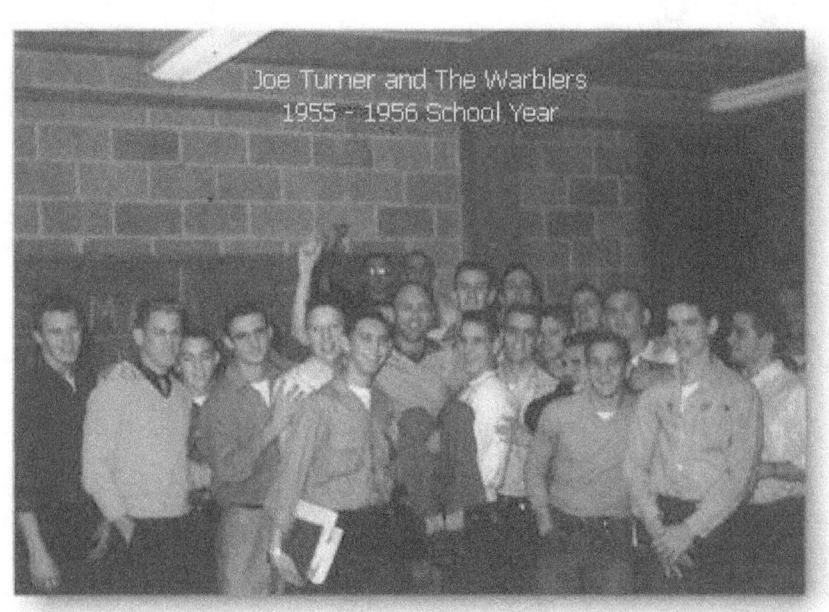

Joe Turner and The Warblers
1955 - 1956 School Year

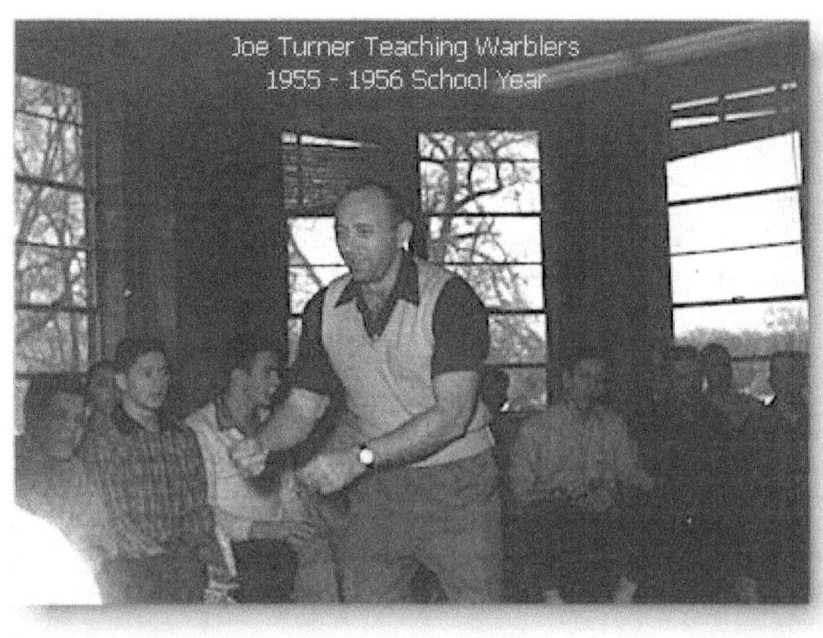

Joe Turner Teaching Warblers
1955 - 1956 School Year

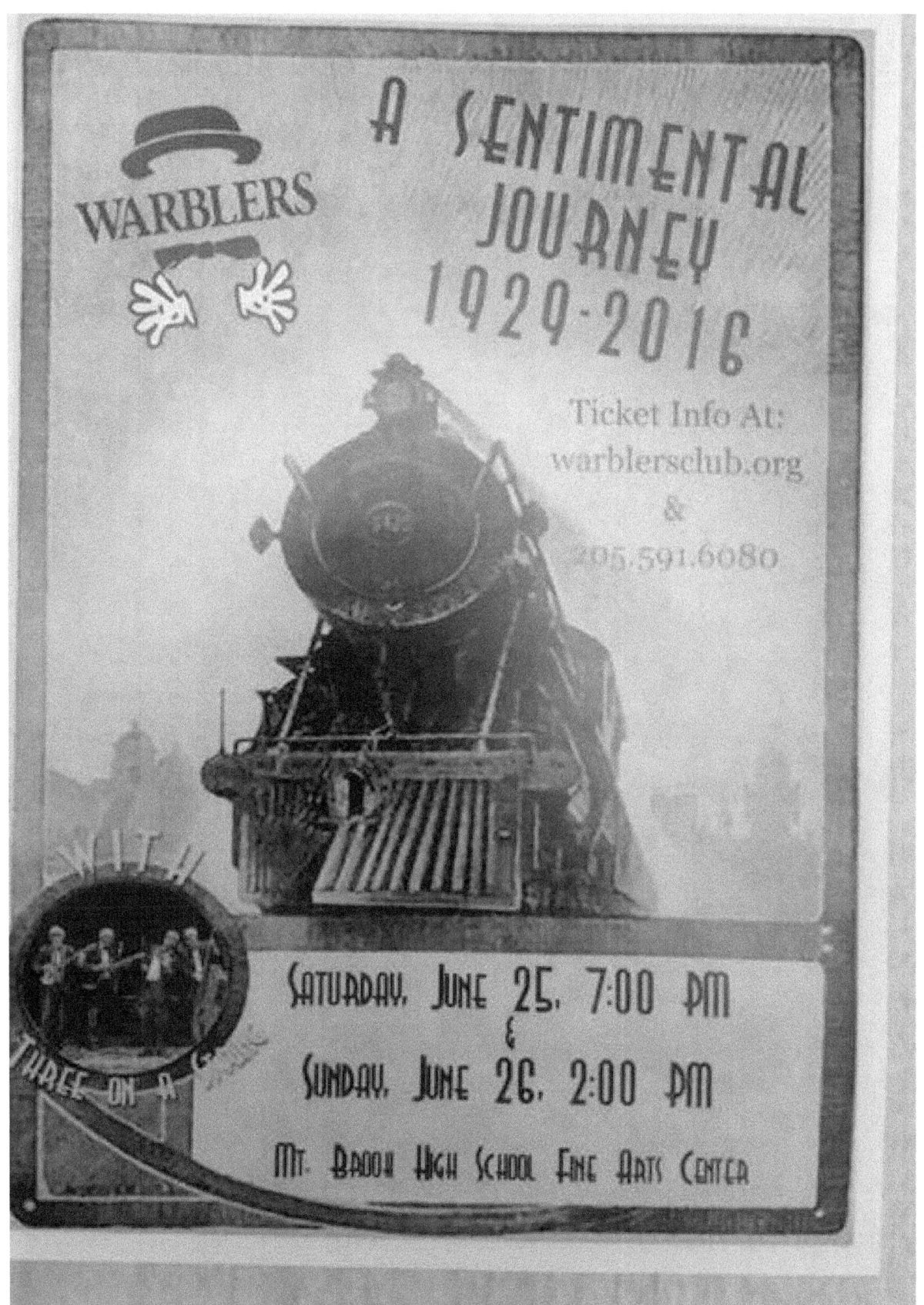

DANNY SMITH BEFORE STUNT NIGHT IN 1967

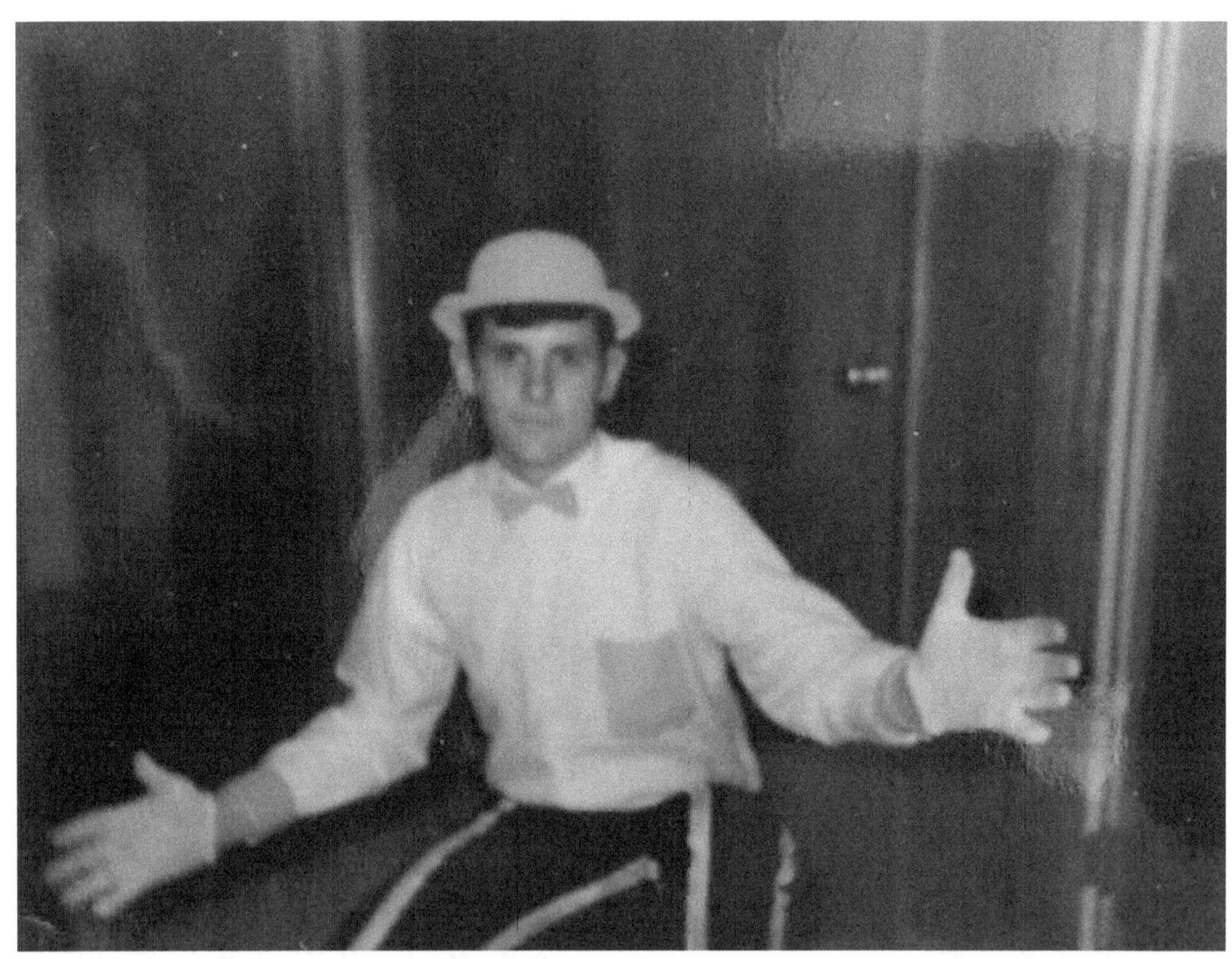

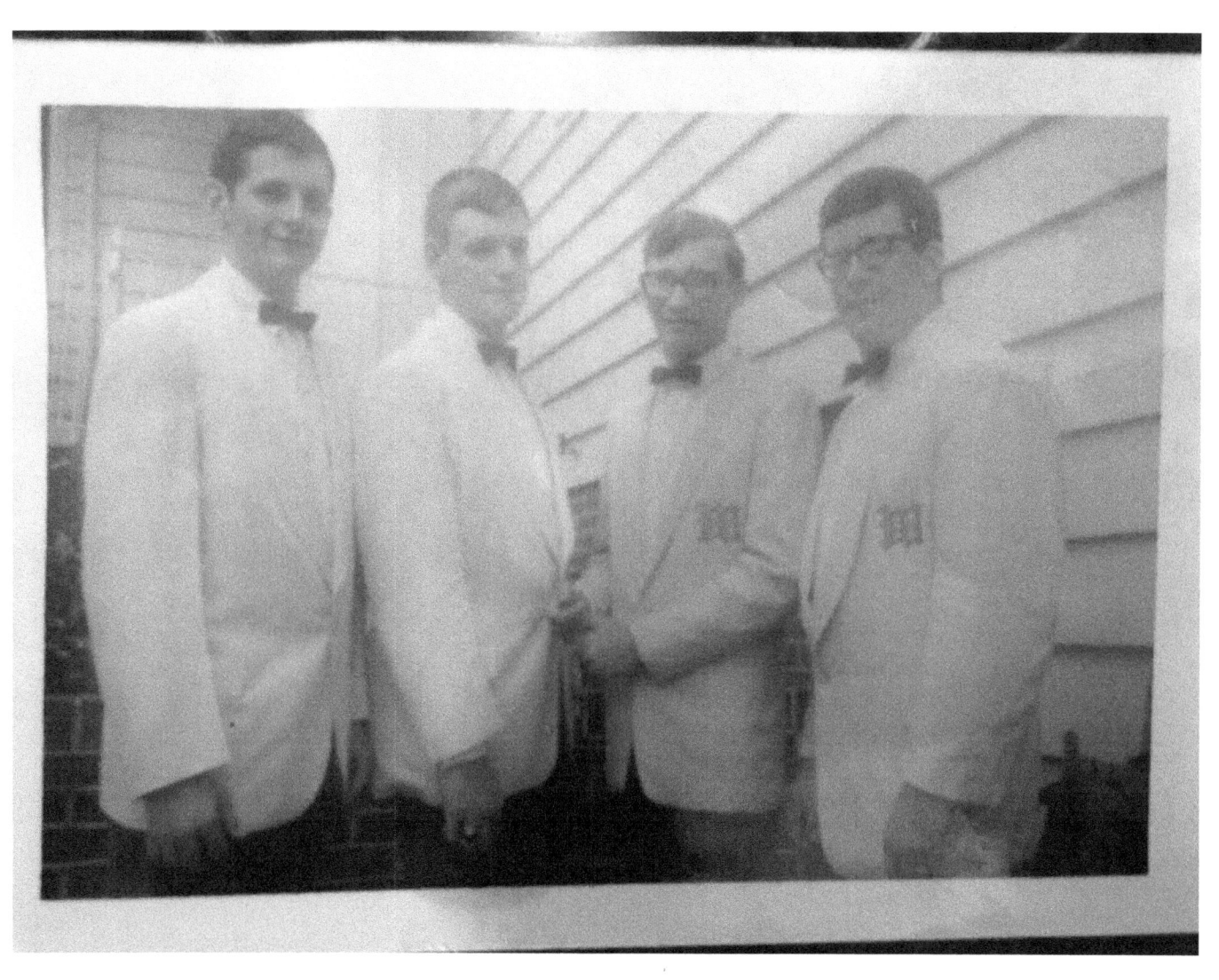

LEFT TO RIGHT: DANNY SMTH, JERRY PITTMAN, MIKE VINSON,
BRUCE SPROULL

Just prior to our quartet performance at a 1967 AEA luncheon.

Warblers present $5,000 to Children's Hospital

Thanks to the Warblers, Children's Hospital has $5,000 more to use in helping sick children get well.

Men who were members of the glee club at Woodlawn High School during the period from about 1930 to 1978 reunited in July and put on three shows at the Alabama Theatre. At the time, organizers said they would give to Children's Hospital any proceeds from ticket sales left after expenses were met.

Sunday, the Warblers did just that.

Warbler Neal Allen said 65 to 70 of the men met at the hospital, sang for children there and presented the $5,000 check.

Then on Tuesday, about as many Warblers turned out for a less joyous occasion — the funeral of Warbler **Donald Lawrence "Larry" Cokeroft**. Cokeroft, a Jefferson County sheriff's deputy, was killed Saturday night. On the rainy, foggy night, he and a partner were responding to a call when their patrol car skidded and wrapped around a tree between Brookside and Forestdale.

Allen said the Warblers sang two songs at the funeral, including "Soon Ah Will be Done (With the Troubles of the World)." It was, he said, something Warblers could do for the family of a man they considered their brother.

Warblers plan to keep on singing, too. Allen says that after the July reunion, which packed the Alabama, members of the vocal group realized "nobody wanted to let the spirit die."

Allen said the group plans to sing at the Alabama Theatre at Christmas time and is committed to perform in conjunction with the Alabama Reunion in April. A committee that includes longtime Warblers director **Joe Turner** has been set up to review requests for performances, Allen said.

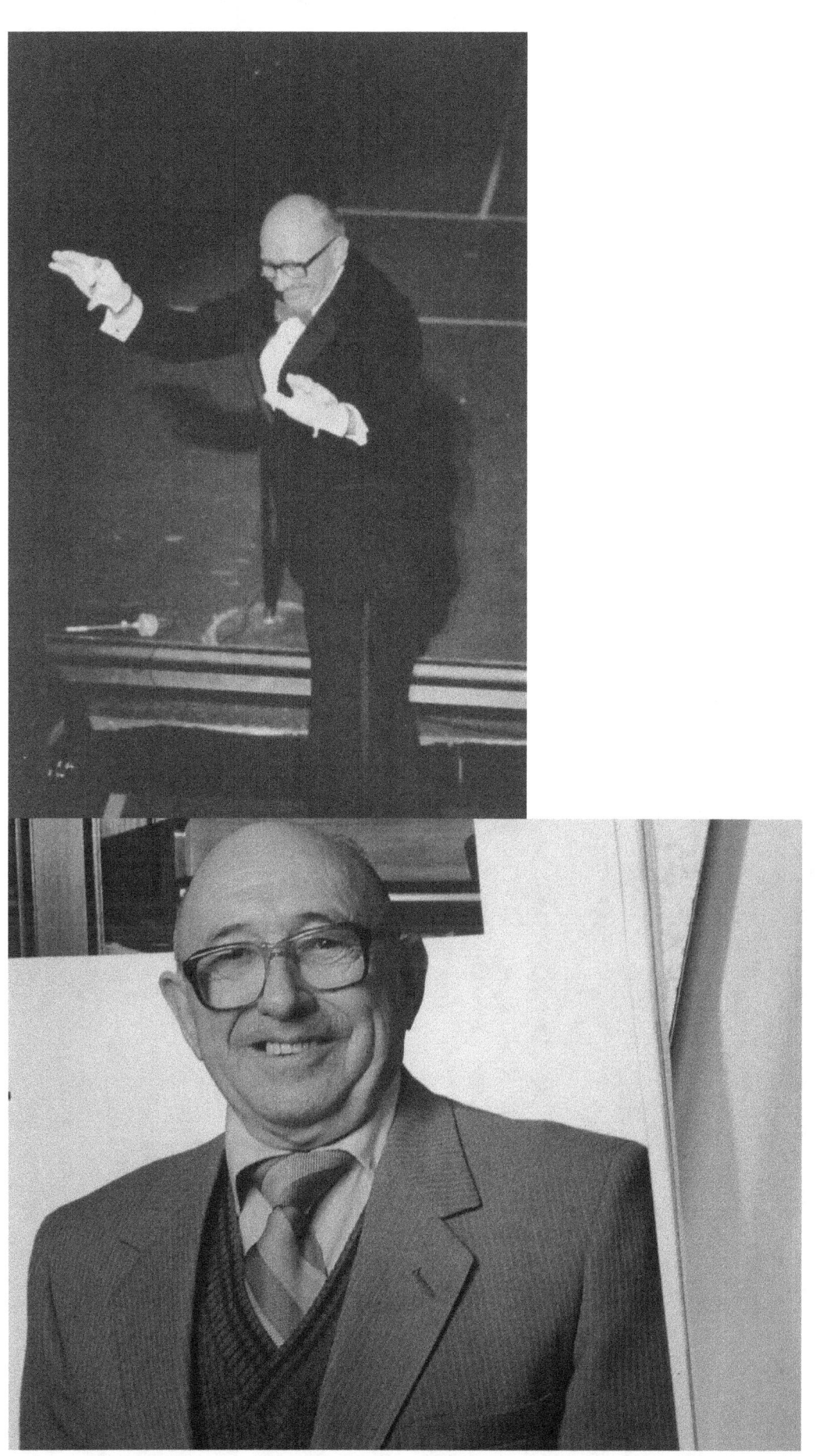

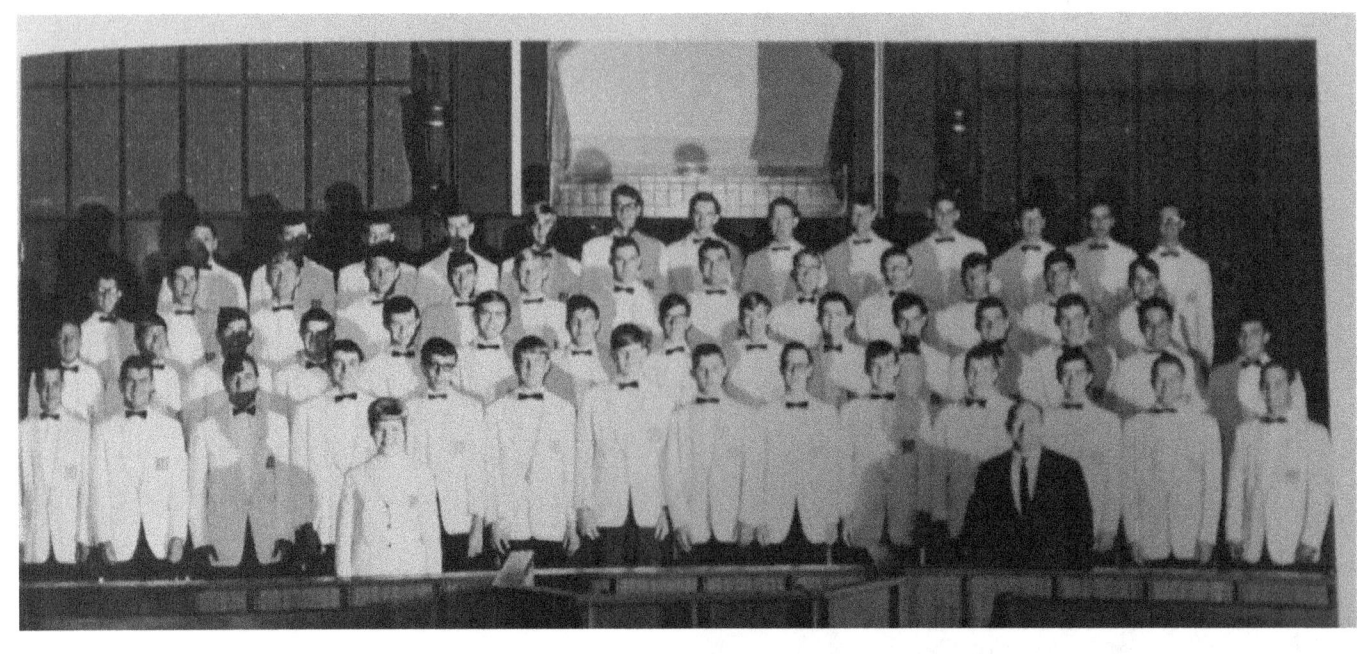

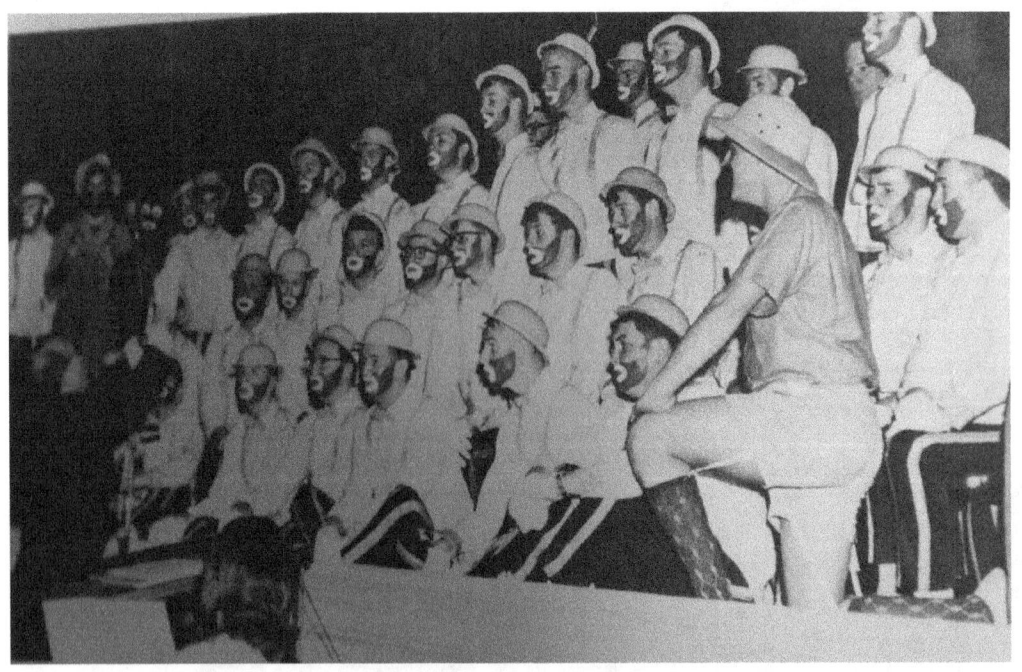

96

Hobo conventions were popular shows for the Warblers in the '60s.

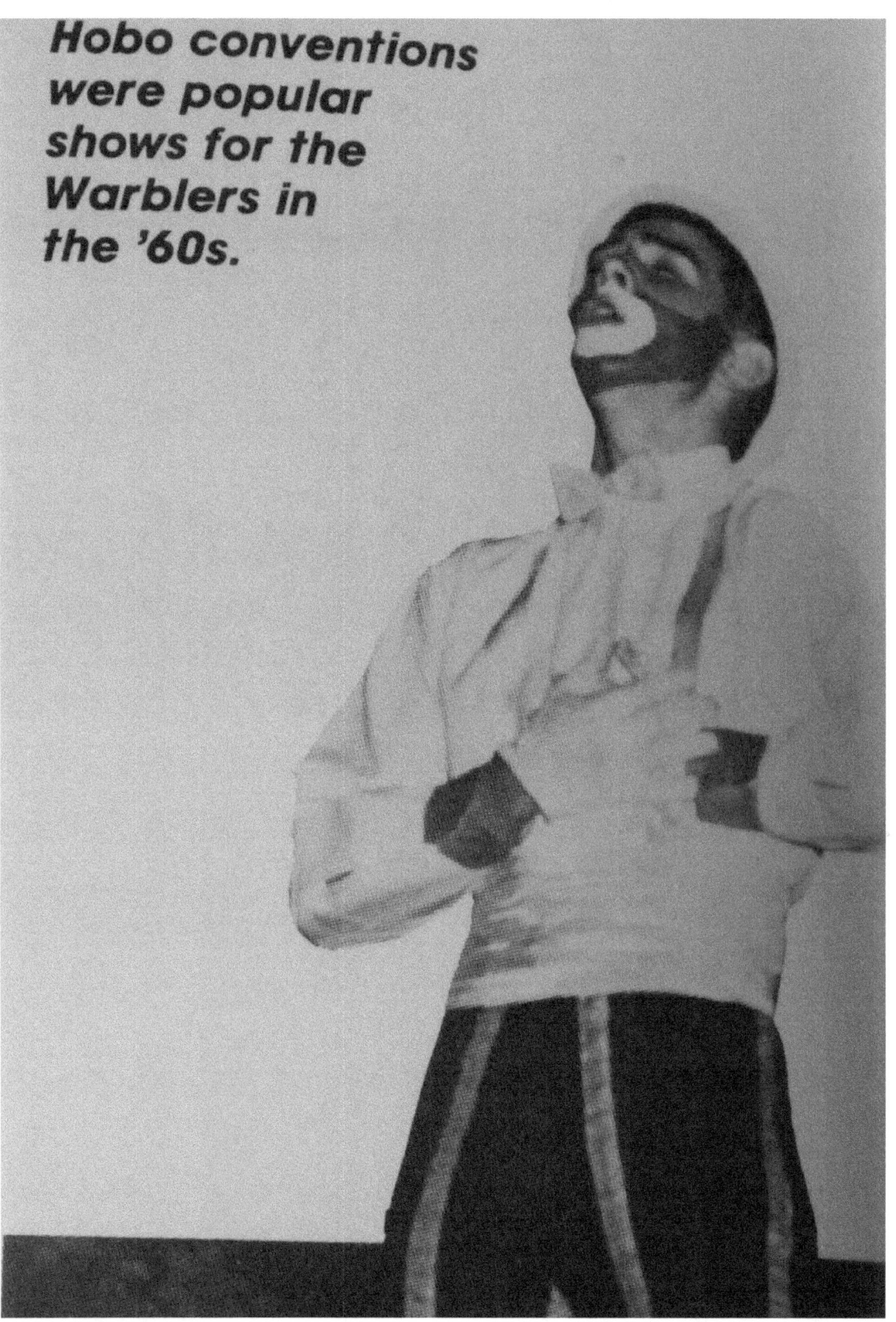

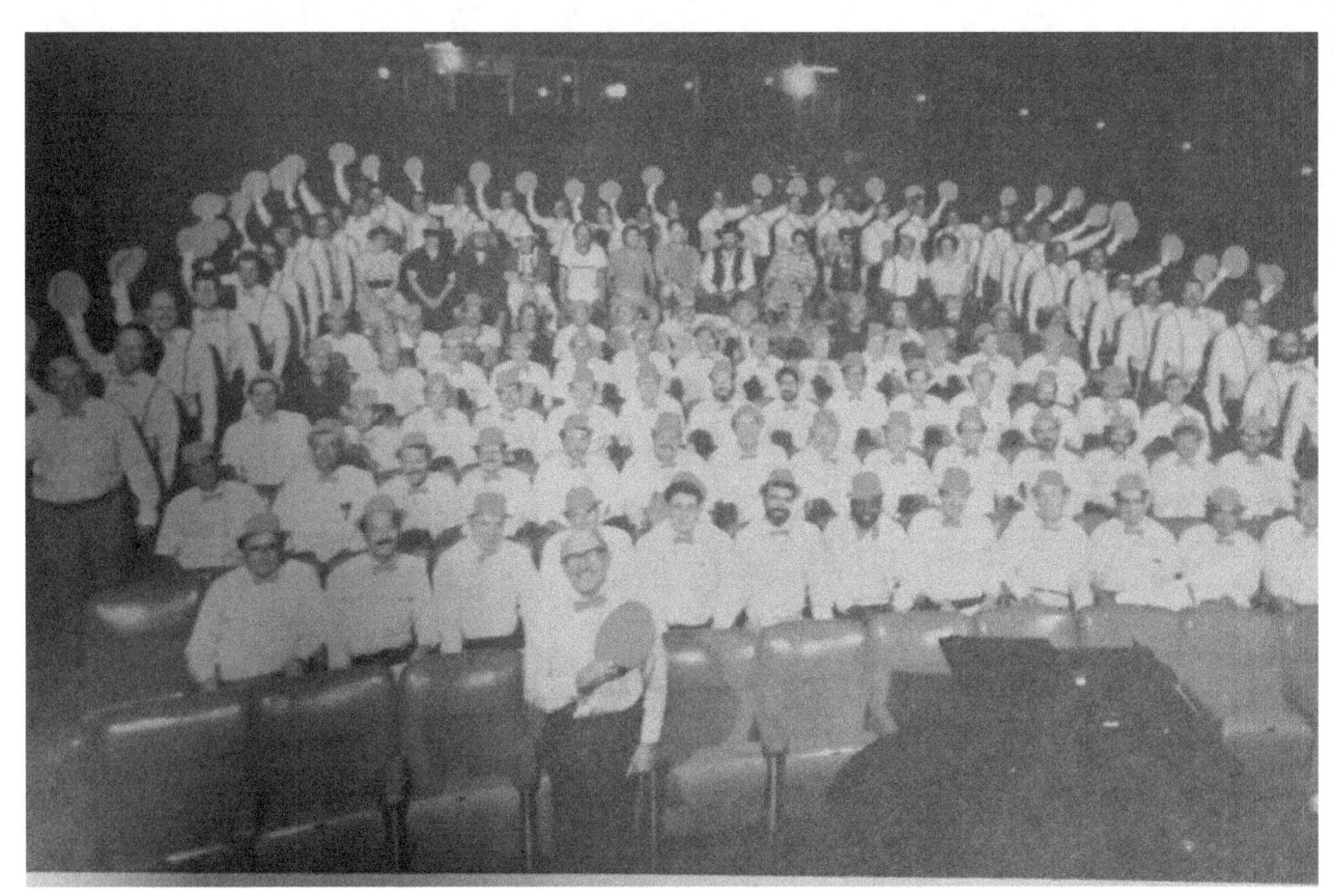

1988 Reunion Show

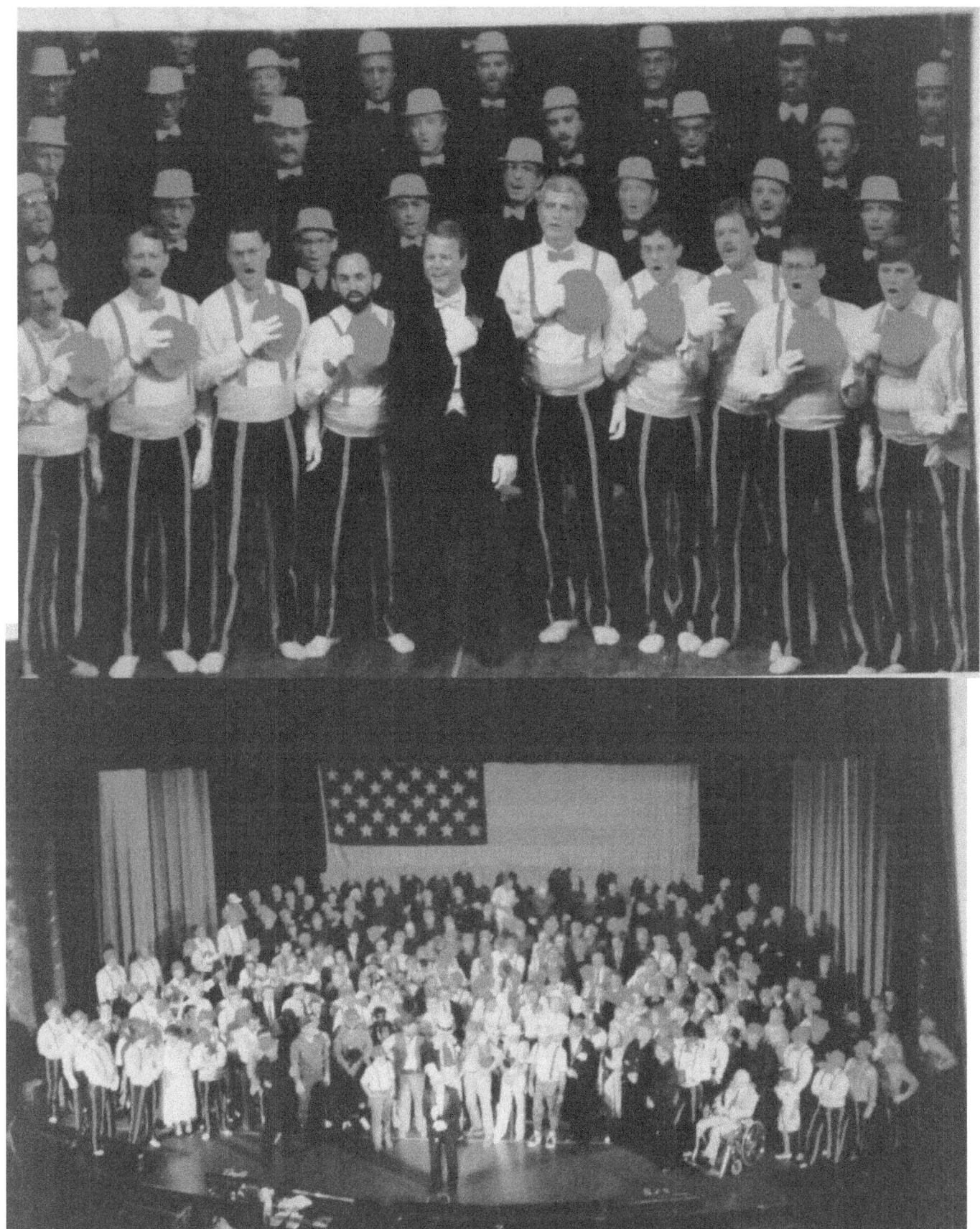

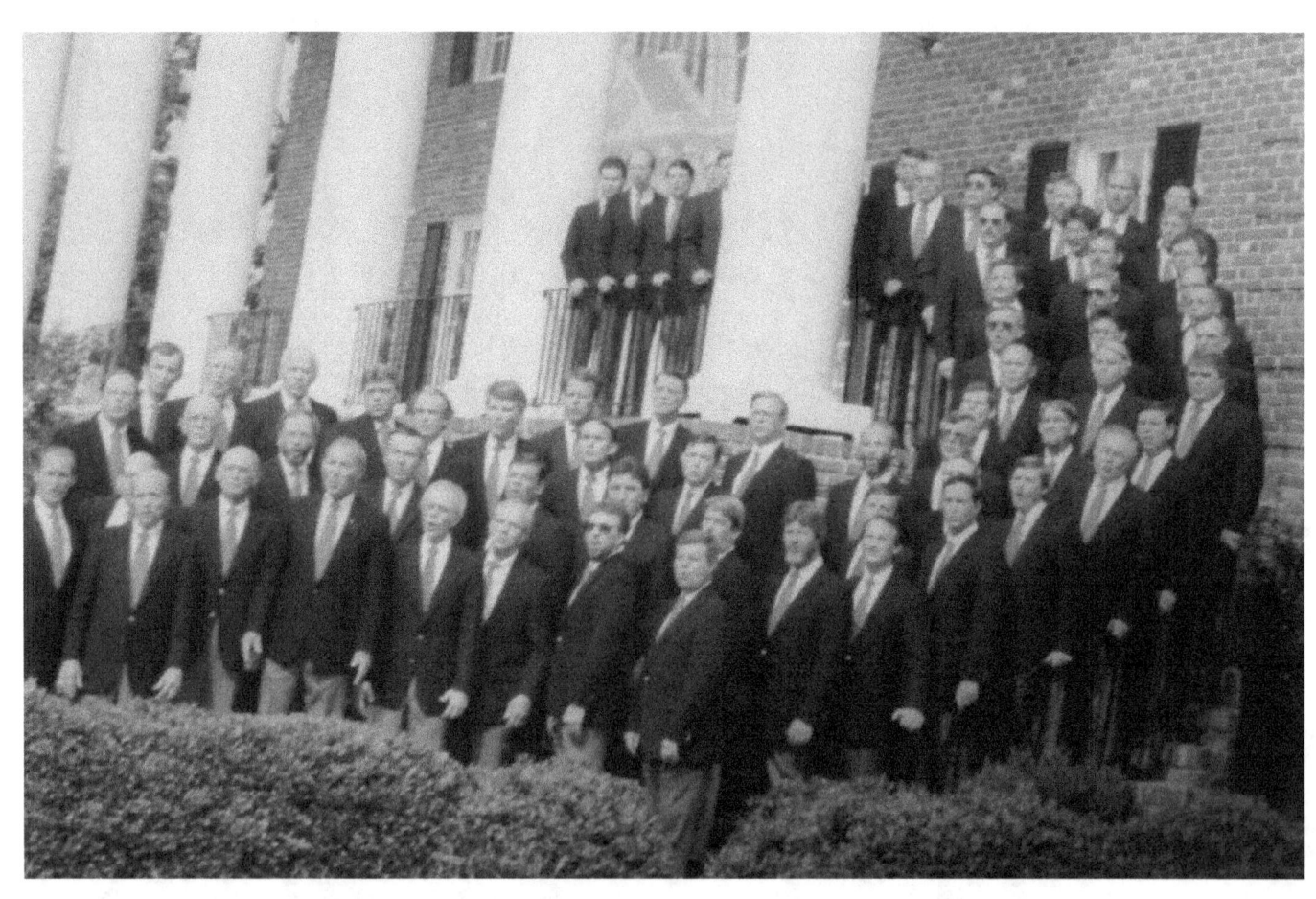

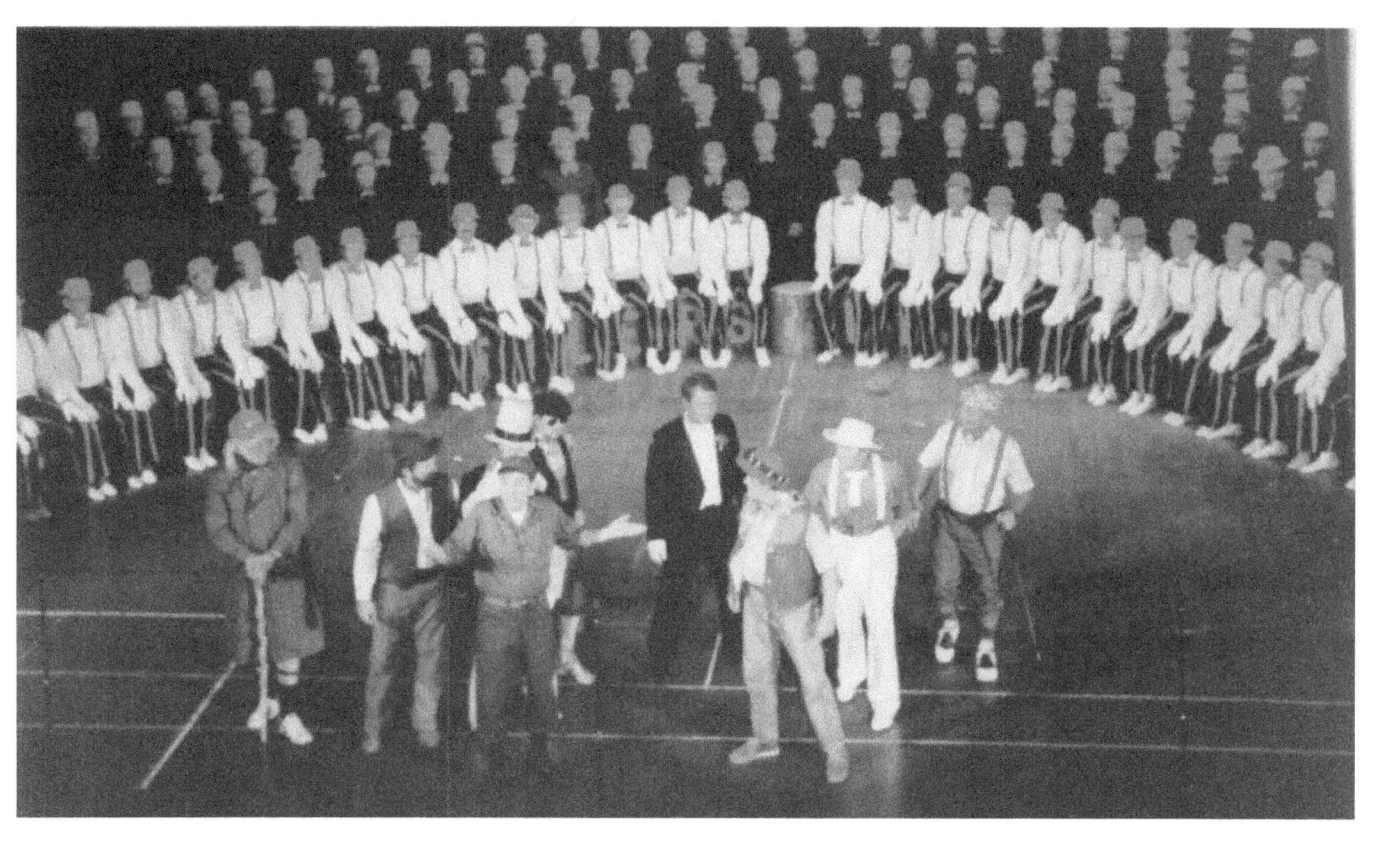

The pictures on the following pages are group pictures from the Woodlog (WHS Yearbook). The quality of the pictures, in some cases, is not very good. Many school years are shown. They are not in any necessary order. Some of them are identified by year and some of them have members name included (if legible). Every decade since the formation of the Warblers Club is represented.

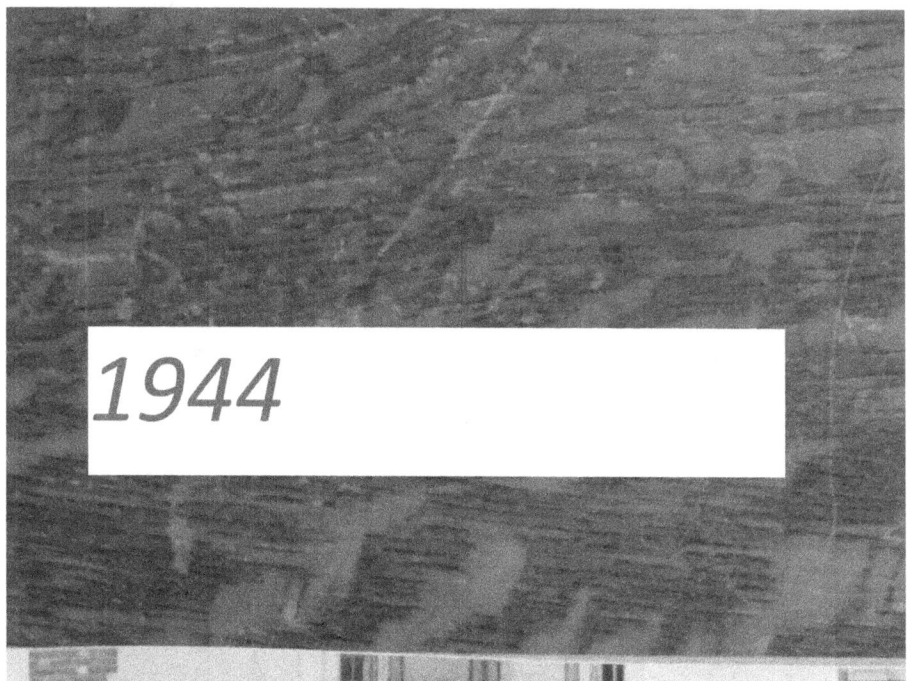

1944

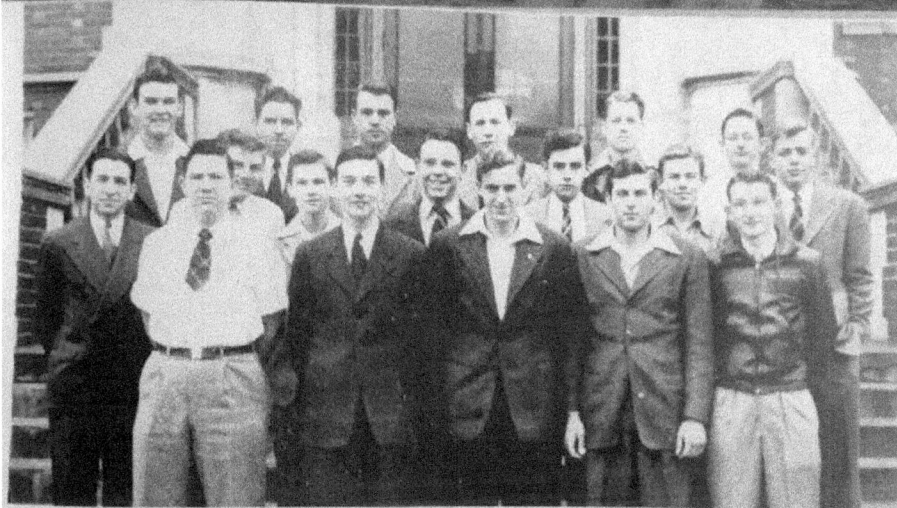

WARBLERS

Mr. Light, sponsor; James Brown, President; John Nickolson, Vice President; Cleveland Hunt, Secretary; Richard Ward, Lamar Smith, Reporters; Henry Randall, Bill Farrar, Joe Black, Bill Davis, Jack Forsiman, Whitten Weadow, Rayburn Ferguson, Charles Hagler, Robert Herring, Auman Burnett, Billy Watson, Shaffer Gregory.

———————

PEN AND INK

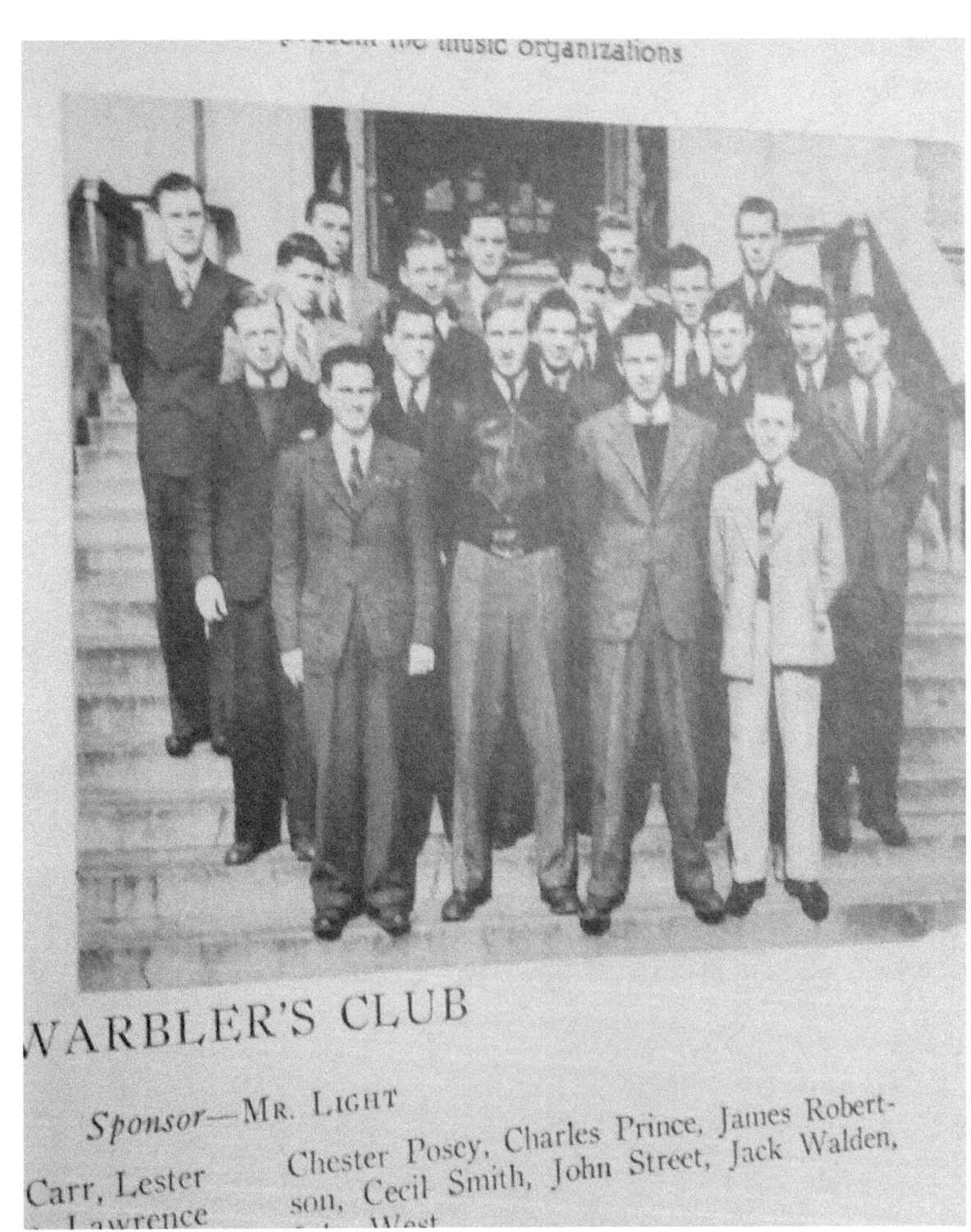

WARBLER'S CLUB

Sponsor—Mr. Light

Carr, Lester Chester Posey, Charles Prince, James Robert-
Lawrence son, Cecil Smith, John Street, Jack Walden,
West

1941

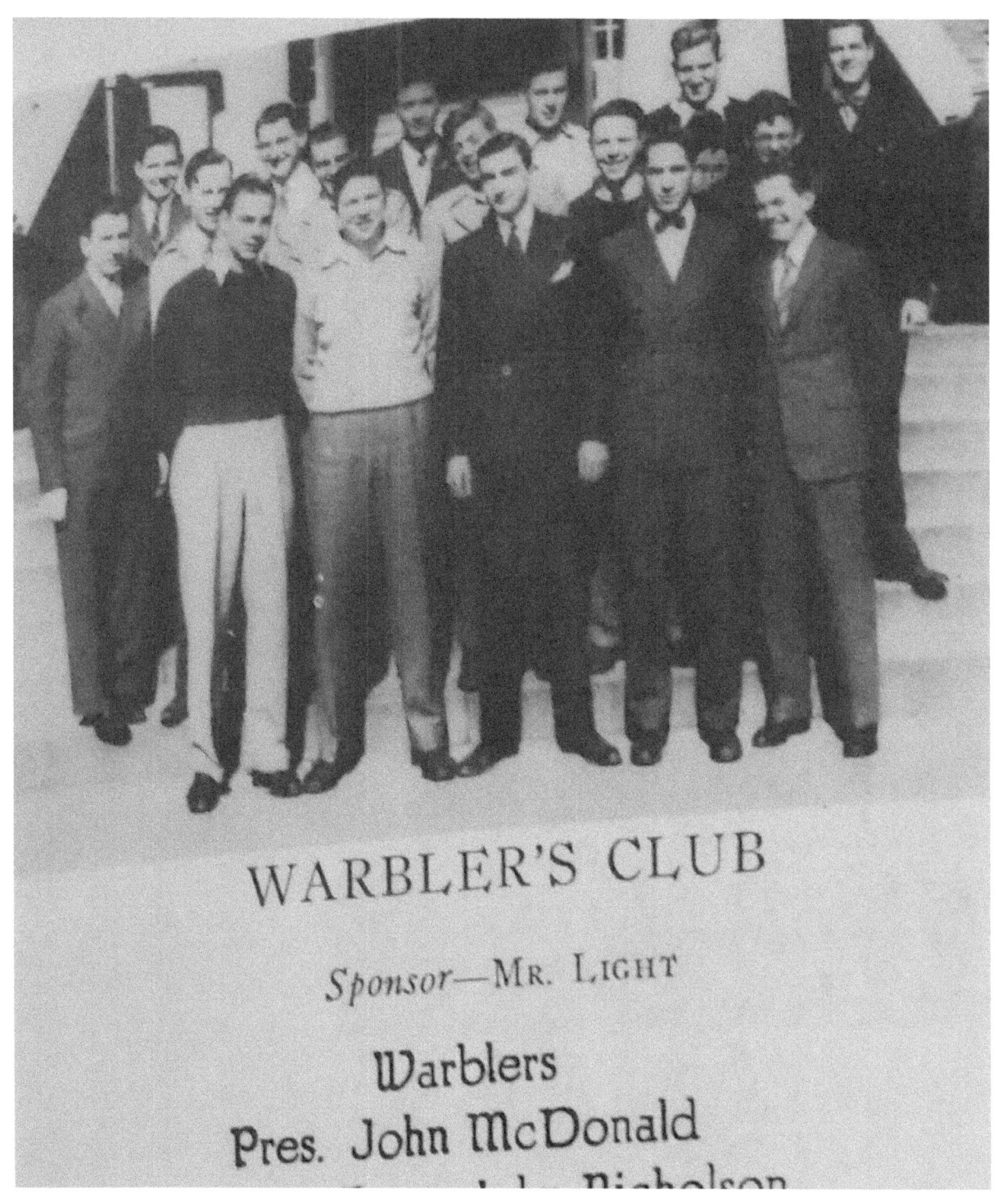

WARBLER'S CLUB

Sponsor—MR. LIGHT

Warblers
Pres. John McDonald

1943

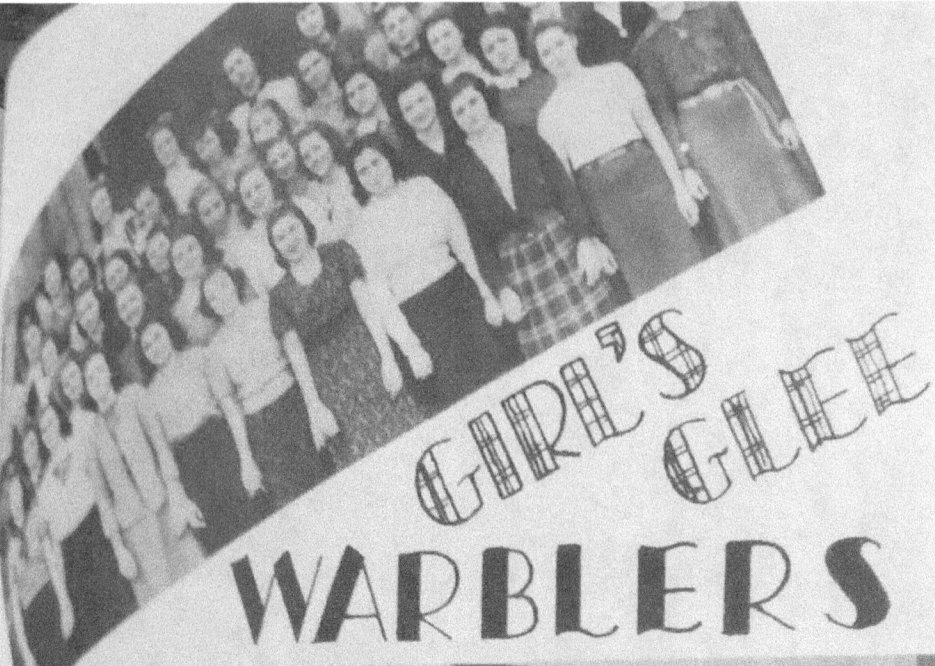

GIRL'S GLEE

WARBLERS

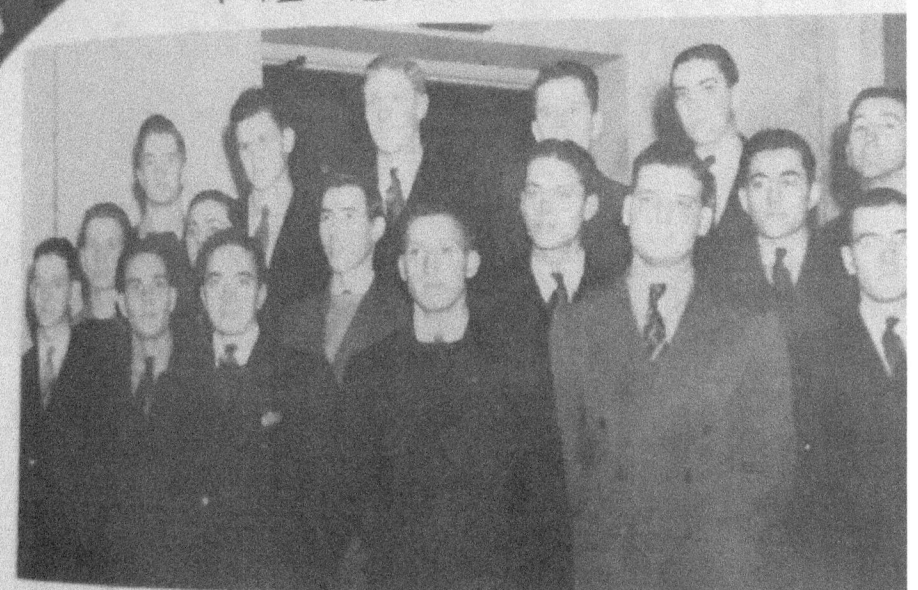

THE CAVALIERS

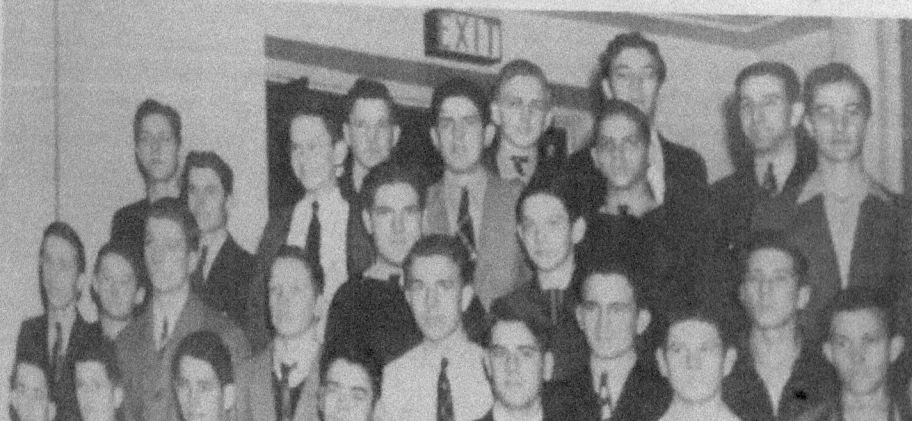

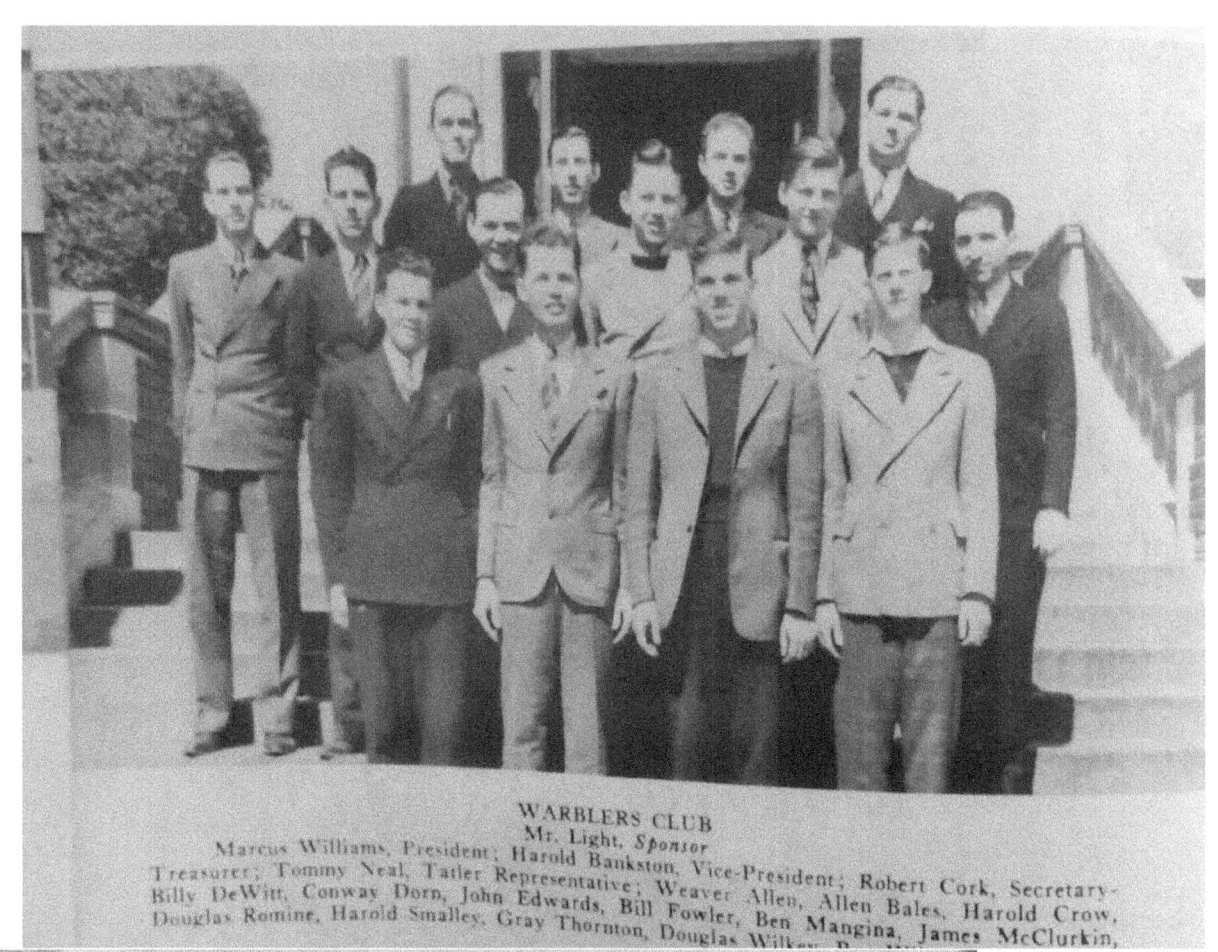

WARBLERS CLUB
Mr. Light, *Sponsor*
Marcus Williams, President; Harold Bankston, Vice-President; Robert Cork, Secretary-Treasurer; Tommy Neal, Tatler Representative; Weaver Allen, Allen Bales, Harold Crow, Billy DeWitt, Conway Dorn, John Edwards, Bill Fowler, Ben Mangina, James McClurkin, Douglas Romine, Harold Smalley, Gray Thornton, Douglas Wilke...

1939 Top, 1938 Bottom

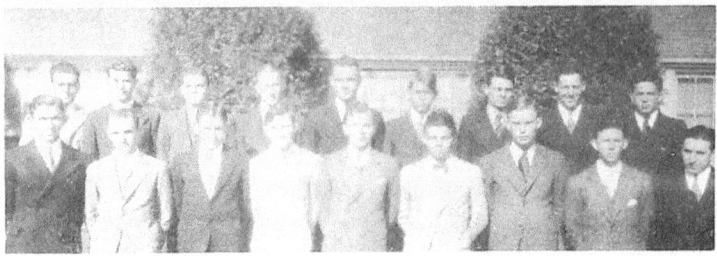

Warblers

Charles Brewer, *President;* Fred Vann, *Vice-President;* John Prescott, *Secretary and Treasurer;* James Black, *Reporter;* Ernest Davidson, Pelham Fowler, Robert Knapp, Travis Gattana, Maurice Richards, Dick Smith, Herbert Counts, Tolbert Barry, Paul Patten, Cecil Kiser, J. B. Barrow, Elmer Holland, George Weaver, Joe King. Mr. Light, *Sponsor.*

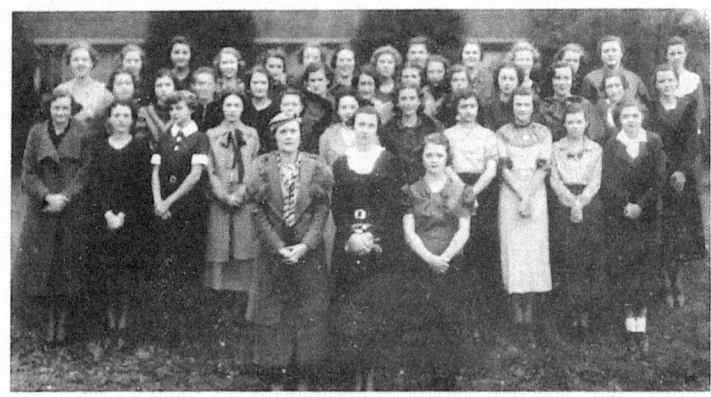

Girls' Glee Club

Vera Aderholt, *President;* Mildred Hanlin, *Vice-President;* Julia Mae Stacey, *Secretary;* Edith Bailey, Eleanor Bernhard, Bernice Boyd, Elizabeth Cagle, Hilda Mae Carter, Martha Childers, Mildred Claffelter, Margaret Dentin, Marie Finney, Evelyn Fowler, Millie Frances Faulkner, Mildred Gilby, Sarah Hoover, Eva Janes Lovelace, Cathryn McKibbin, Burnadette Montgomery, Hazel Morrow, Evelyn Morrow, Edna Morris, Eleanor O'Hara, Frieda Riesl, Ruth Roberts, Elizabeth Powell, Frances Ray, Marilyn Saxon, Jeanette Sims, Myra Summers, Billie Suttles, Frances Smith, Jamie Taylor, Mary Francis Taylor, Dorothy Thomas, Mary Elizabeth Van, Lucy Vann Williams, Dorothy Wood. Miss Dowling, *Sponsor.*

Forty-seven

1935

1
9
3
2

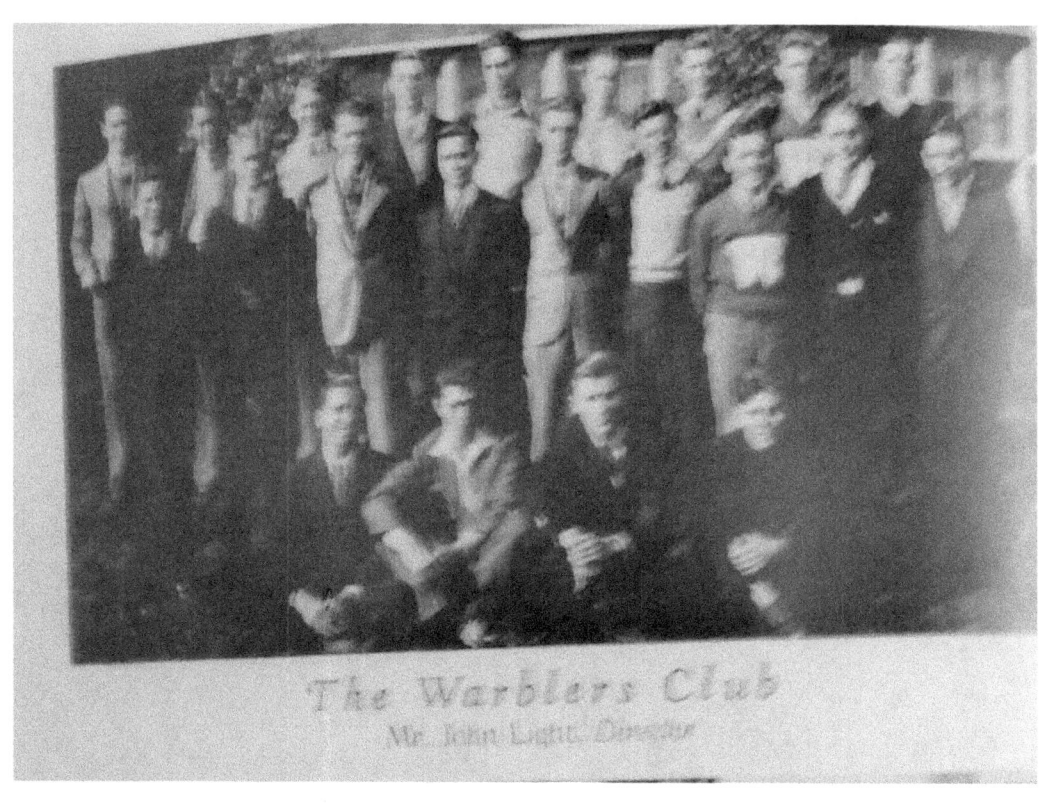

The Warblers Club
Mr. John Light, Director

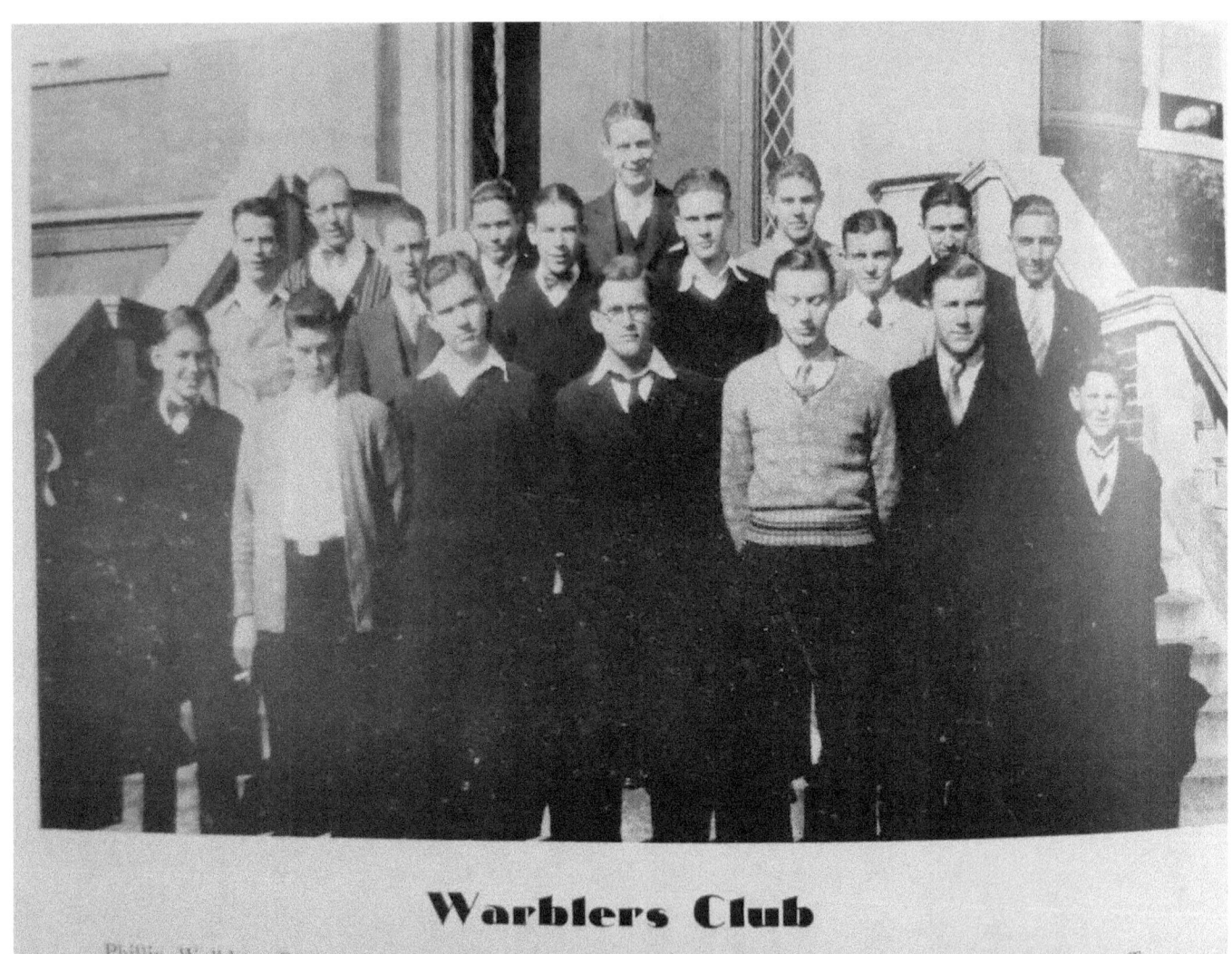

Warblers Club

Phillip Walkley, *Pres.*; A. A. Vines, *Vice-Pres.*; John West, *Sec'y*; John C. Calhoun, *Treas.*

1931

WARBLERS CLUB

President	MORGAN GILLESPIE
Vice-President	HOOD KILLEBREW
Secretary	J. B. KING
Treasurer	OTTICE SCHIELE
Reporter	MALCOLM JACKSON

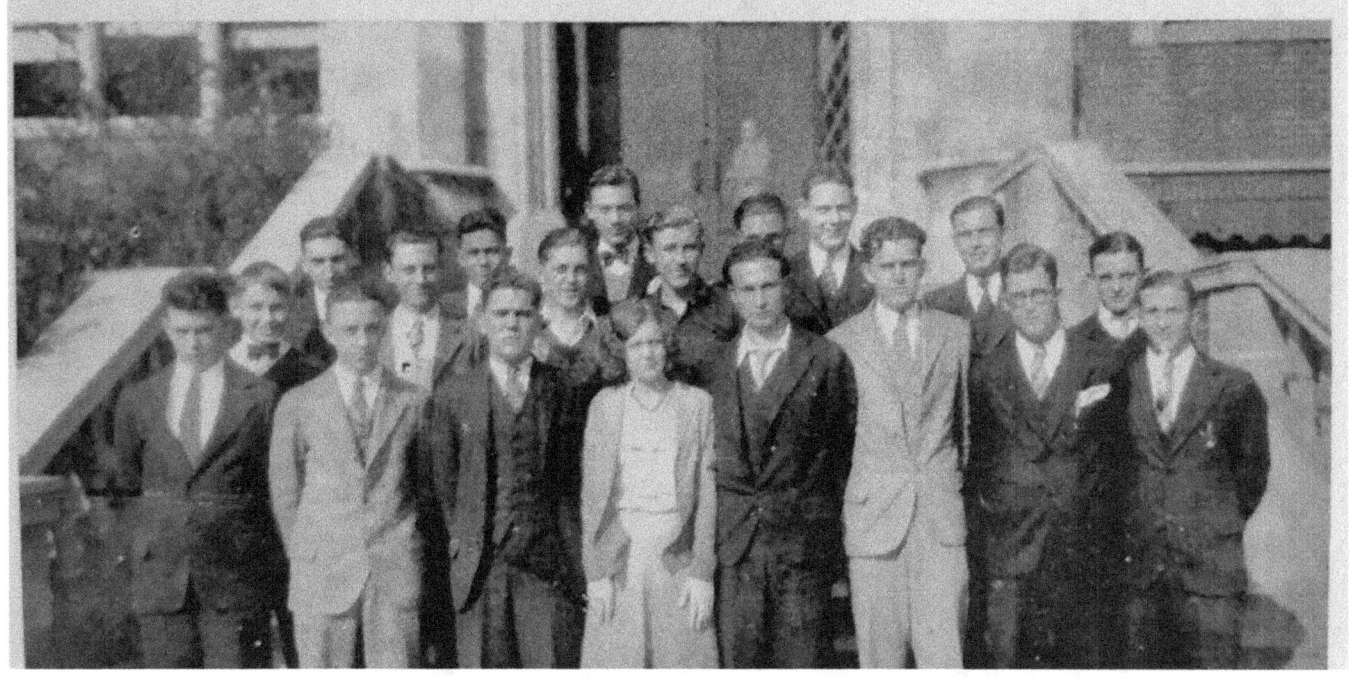

1930

THE BOYS' GLEE CLUB

VERNON NOAH, *Director*

JEFF POWELL
ELLIE McCLAIN
ALFRED BELLSNYDER
BOB BODINE
JOHN NORMENT
JAMES BONE
CUDELLIOS SIMMONS
JACK KING
SAM WILCOX
HUBERT ALLBROOKS
HUGH JONES
WILLIAM STROUD
GUY McKINLEY
ALGENE McKINLEY

FORNY HUGHES
DONALD LUNDBOM
CLAYTON ALLEN
DOUGLAS WALL
WALTER HOLT
JIMMIE LASSETER
MAX OESER
CHARLES NESBITT
A. A. VINES
EDWARD POWELL
NORMAN CRANFORD
AL RAY CRUMPLER
E. T. WALDROND
MORGAN GILLESPIE
HAROLD CRANFORD

VENT SPEAKER
RALPH ROSS
EDWARD GAYLORD
DEWITT SHELTON
PAUL MATTOX
HAROLD HASSELL
PERRIN CRANFORD
MOWARY HILLIARD
EDWARD OLDHAM
JOHN ROPER
PAUL MASON
J. B. KING
JOHN WHATLEY
BILLY SHARPE

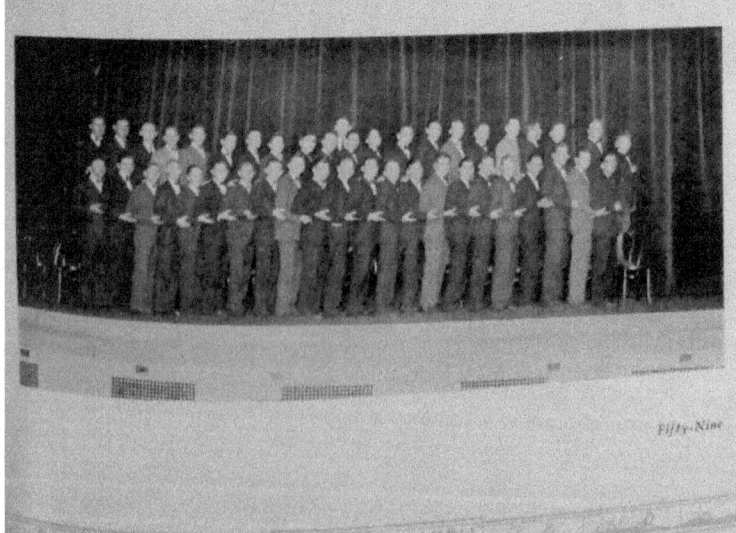

Fifty-Nine

1929

112

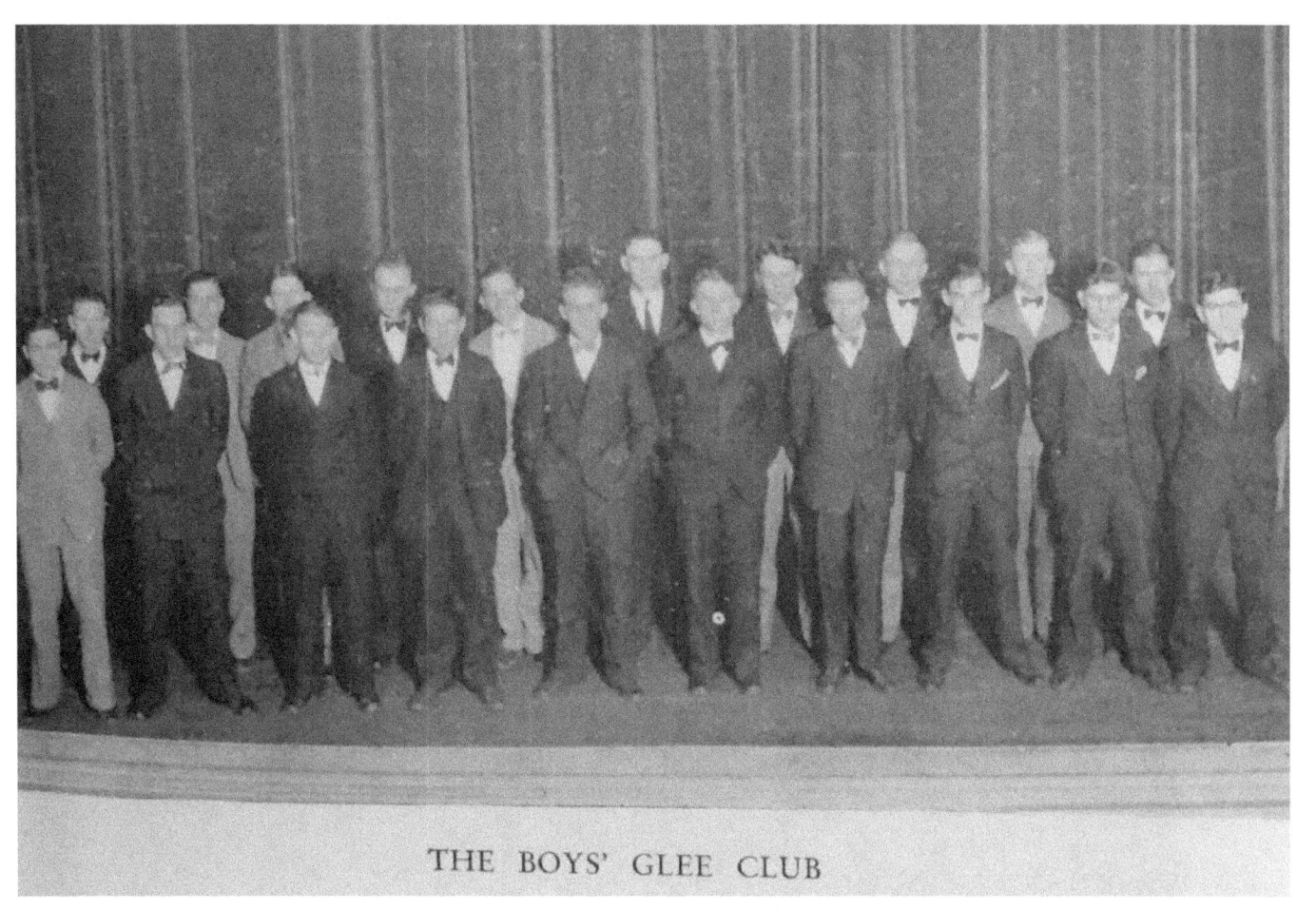

THE BOYS' GLEE CLUB

1929

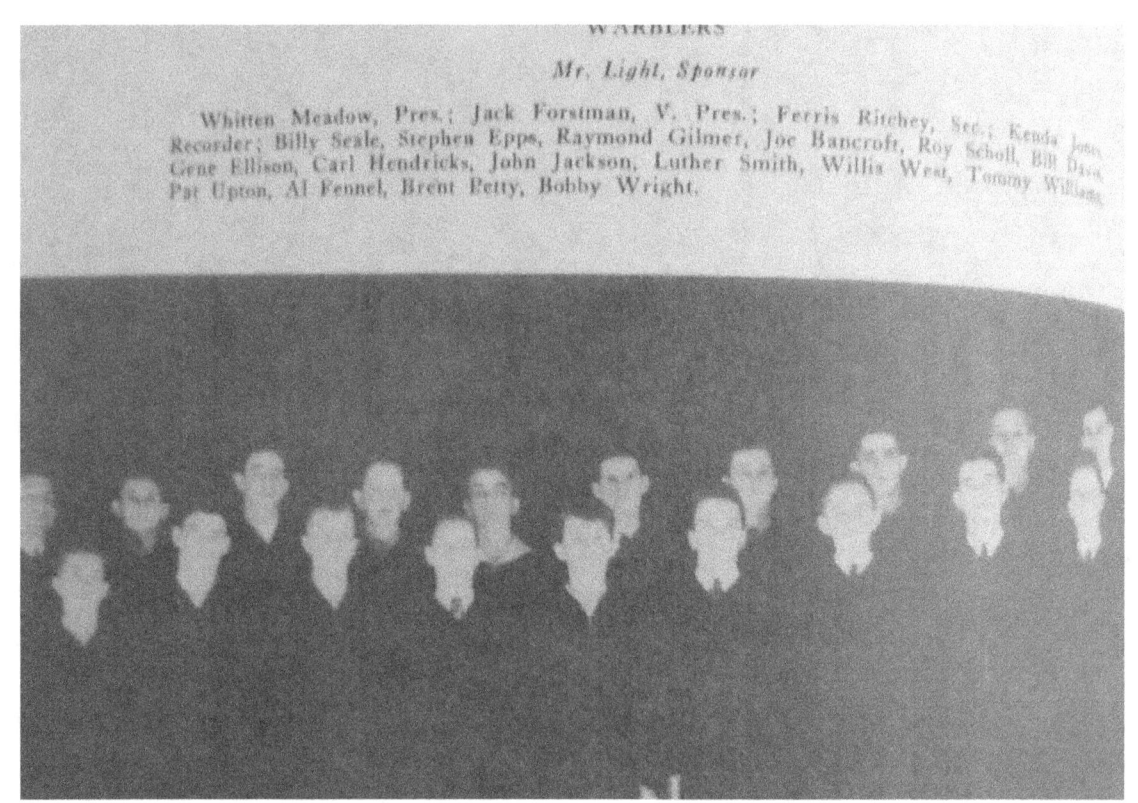

WARBLERS

Mr. Light, Sponsor

Whitten Meadow, Pres.; Jack Forstman, V. Pres.; Ferris Ritchey, Sec.; Kenda John Recorder; Billy Seale, Stephen Epps, Raymond Gilmer, Joe Bancroft, Roy Scholl, Bill Dixe, Gene Ellison, Carl Hendricks, John Jackson, Luther Smith, Willis West, Tommy Williams, Pat Upton, Al Fennel, Brent Petty, Bobby Wright.

1946

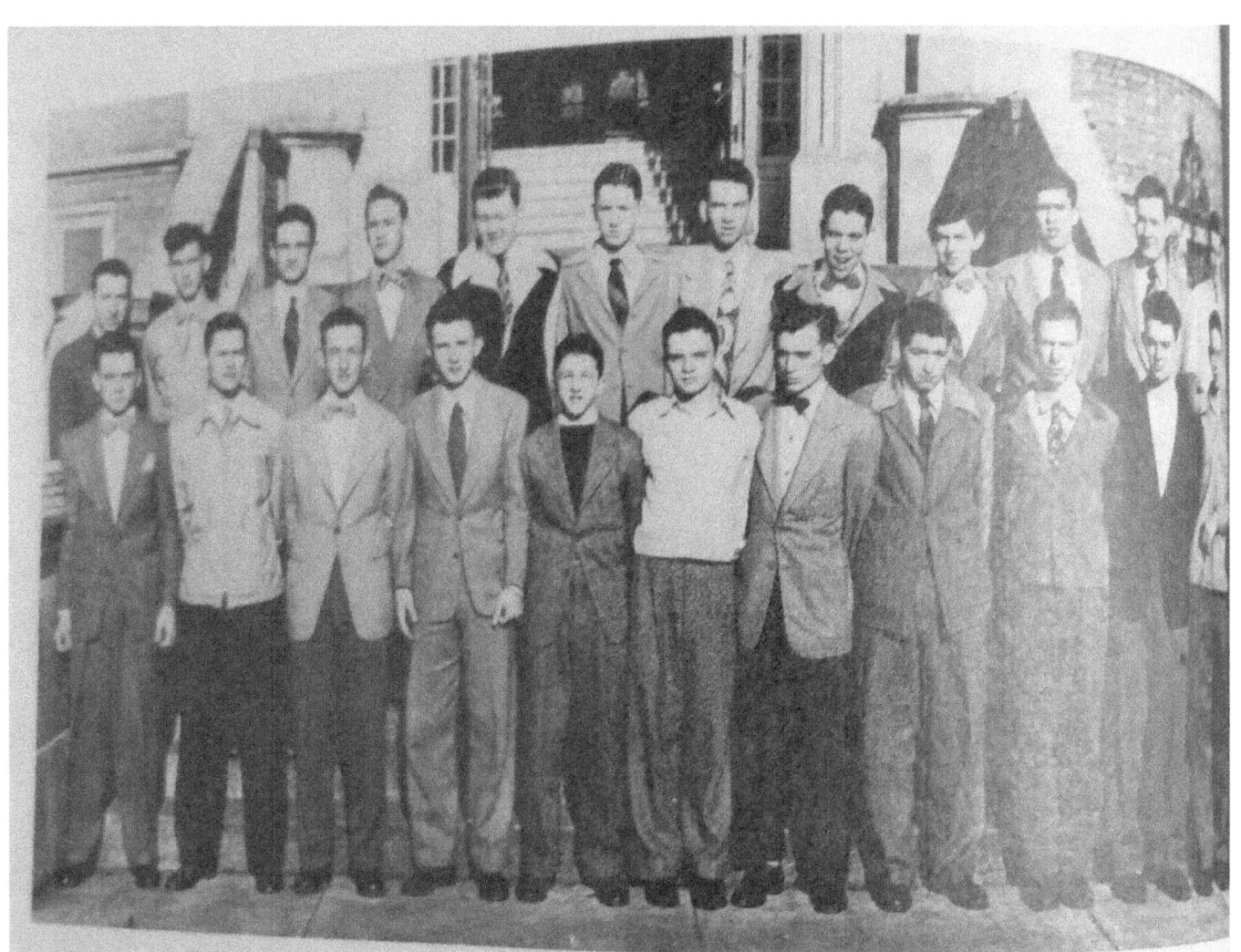

THE WARBLERS CLUB · Mr. Light, Sponsor

Bill Bancroft, Joe Bancroft, Don Burbank, Billy Cather, Don Crow, Jim Cumb, Stephen Epps, Al Fennell, Joe Flarity, Raymond Gilmer, Ed Hall, Frank Hull, Brown Matthews, Vincent McAllister, Johnnie McDonald, Lanier Smith, Ronald Nash, Chandler Smith, Luther Smith, George Sparks, Frank Sutherland, Beasley Williams, Bobby Wright.

1947

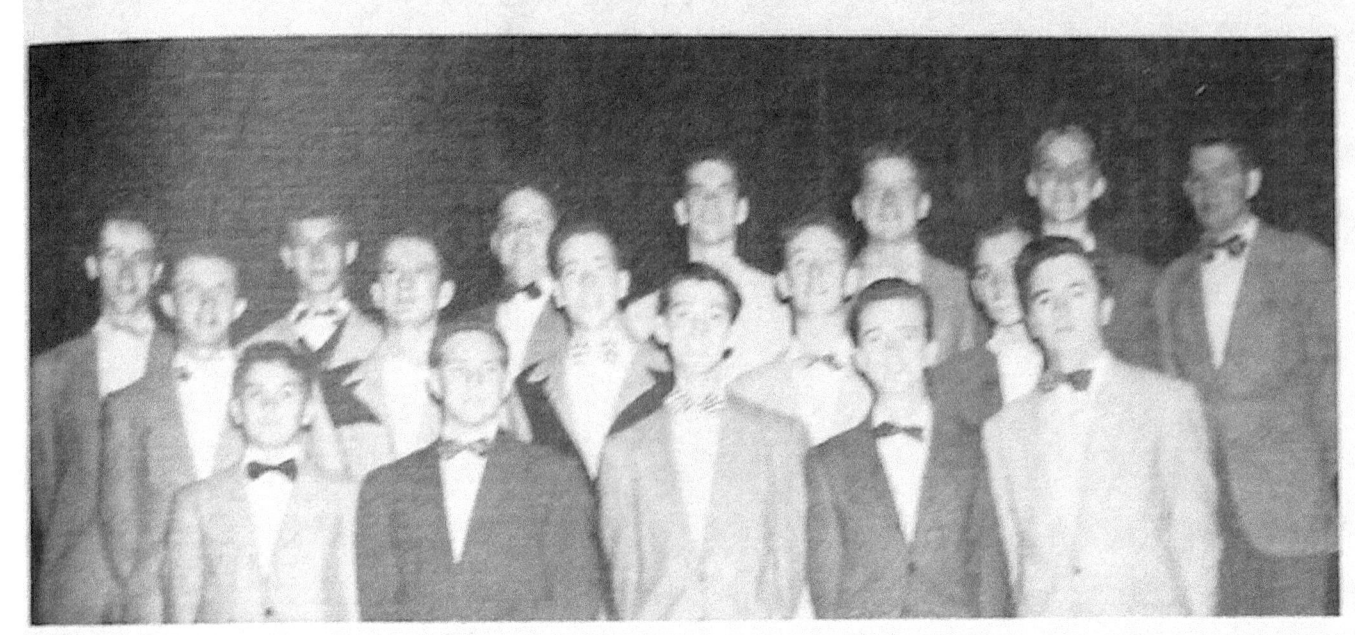

THE WARBLERS

MR. HUDSON, *Sponsor*

Jake Anconin, Russell Bishop, Milton Bullard, Bill Cacher, Nelson Cole, Joe Flaherty, Davis Gibson, Gregory Holcomb, Clif Holman, Jimmy Keel, Dan Jordan, Ed Montgomery, Melvin Mooney, Danny Newman, John Ed Ramsey, Tommy Randall, Richard Rogers, Chandler Smith, George Sparks, John Paul Tate, Bill Walker, Beasley Williams, Ronnie Nash.

1948 Warblers

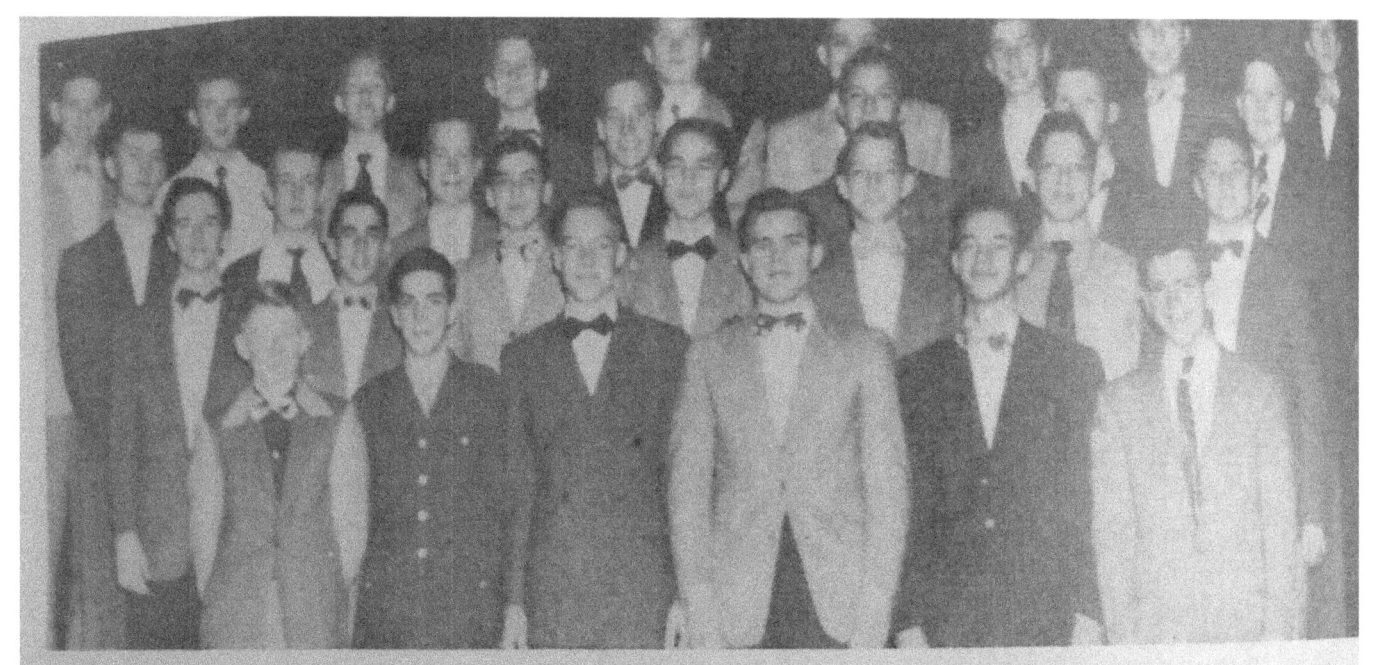

WARBLERS
MR. HUDSON, Sponsor

Jimmy Alford, Willard Benefield, Walter Brand, Milton Bullard, Bill Cather, Jimmy Coker, Charles Crenshaw, Herman Dumas, Bill Emerson, Bobby Griffis, Gayle Hobbs, Robert Jones, Roland Jones, Dan Jordan, David Jordan, Fritz Kirchner, Ladell Milan, Melvin Mooney, Ed Montgomery, Felix Montgomery, Elbert Morris, Mace Myers, Ronnie Nash, Goff Owens, Millard Petty, Richard Poe, John Ed Ramsey, George Reed, Richard Rogers, John Paul Tate, Kenneth Thomas, Bobby Wynne.

1948 Cavaliers (Picture says "Warblers" but it is actually the Cavaliers)

JAKE ANTONIO

Warblers' Minstrel

1949

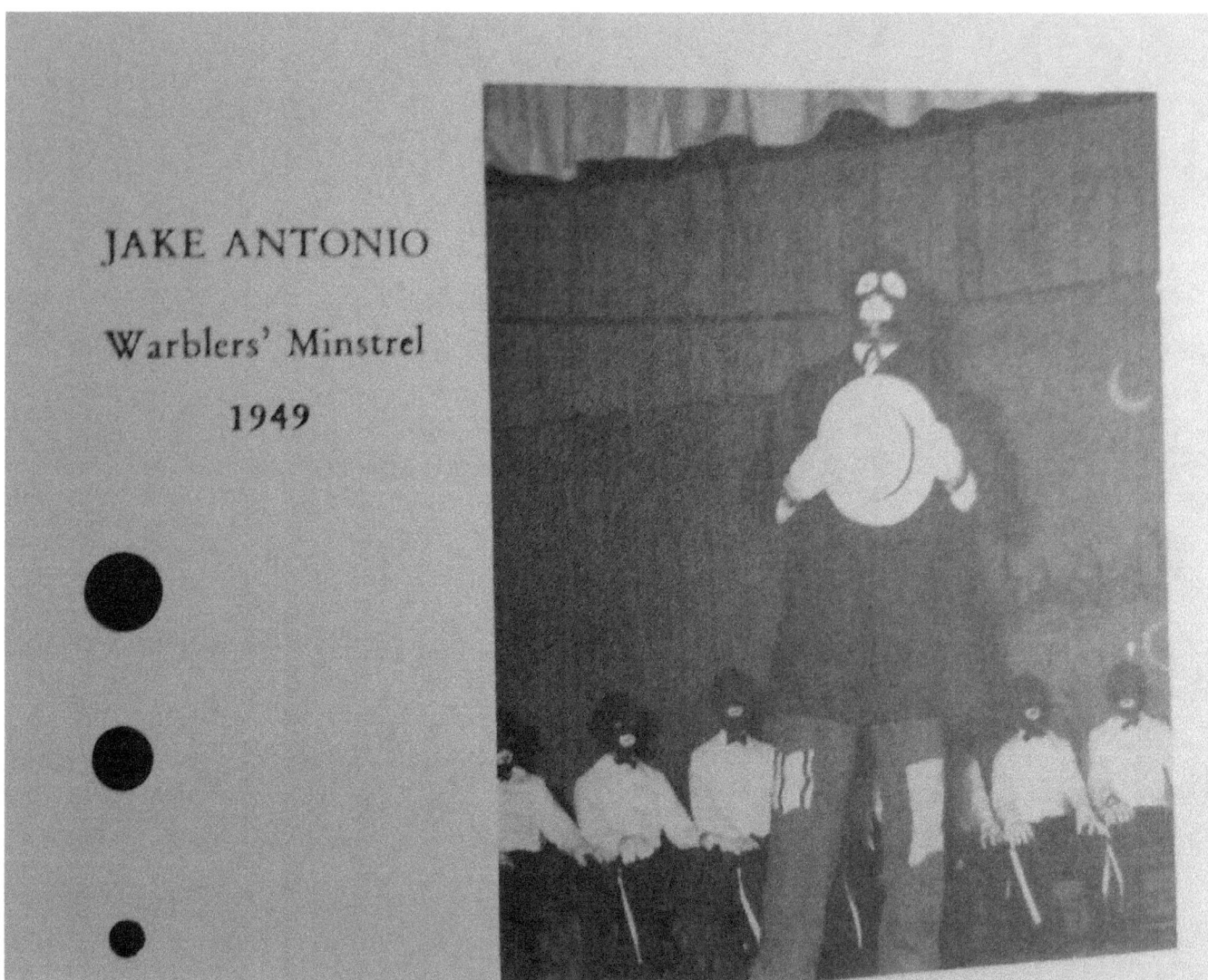

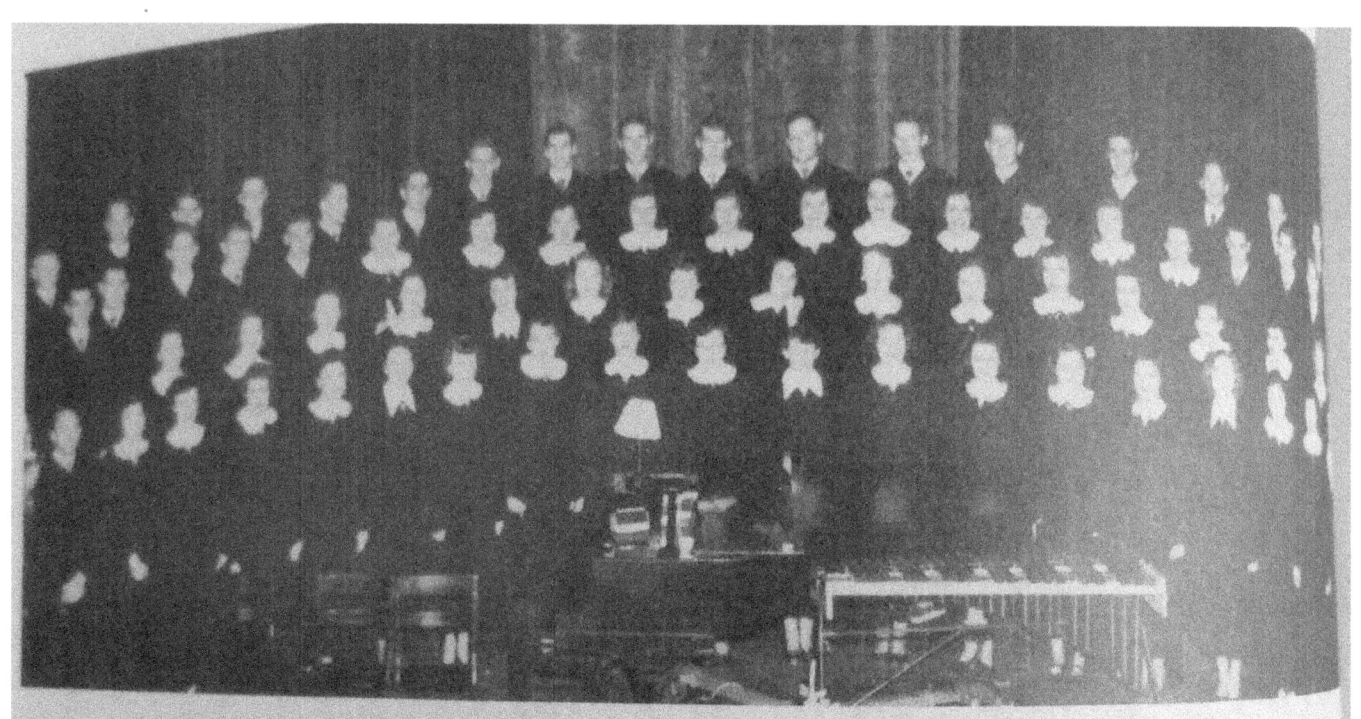

THE WOODLAWN HIGH SCHOOL CHOIR

Directors
Claude Dowling and Joseph Turner

President—John Paul Tate

Vice-President—Peggy Taylor

Accompanists
Barbara Fenn and Betty Lee Krueger

Treasurers—Frances White and Jean Smith

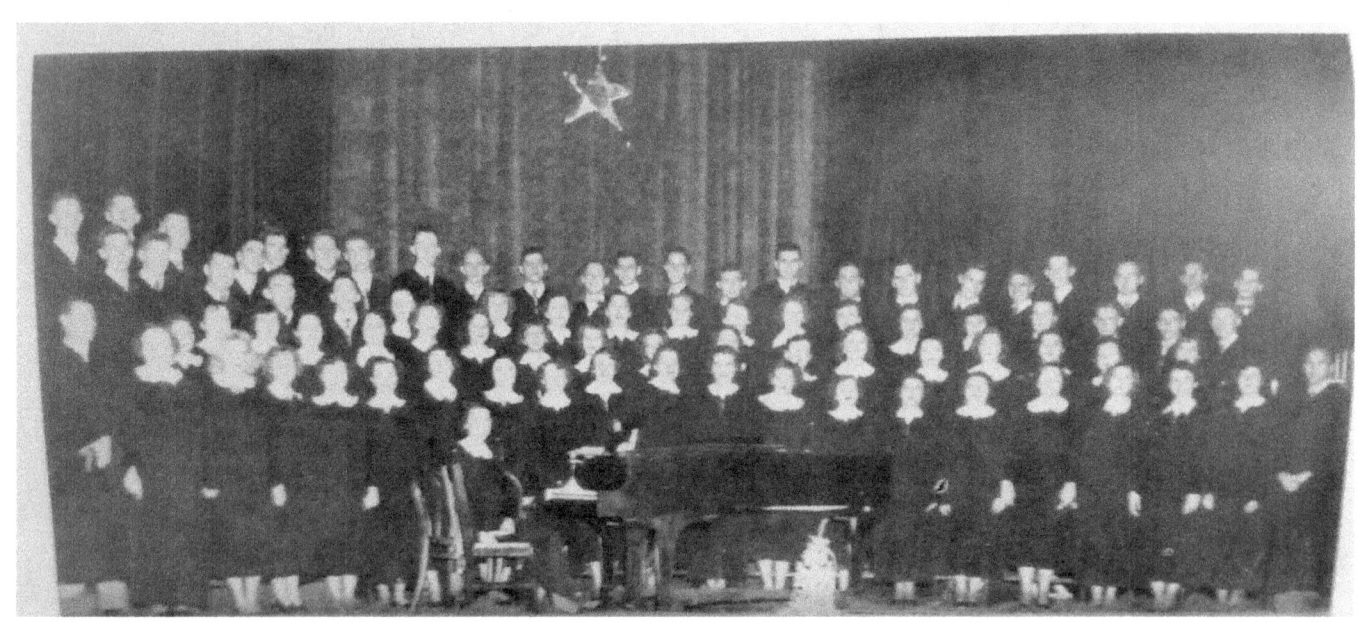

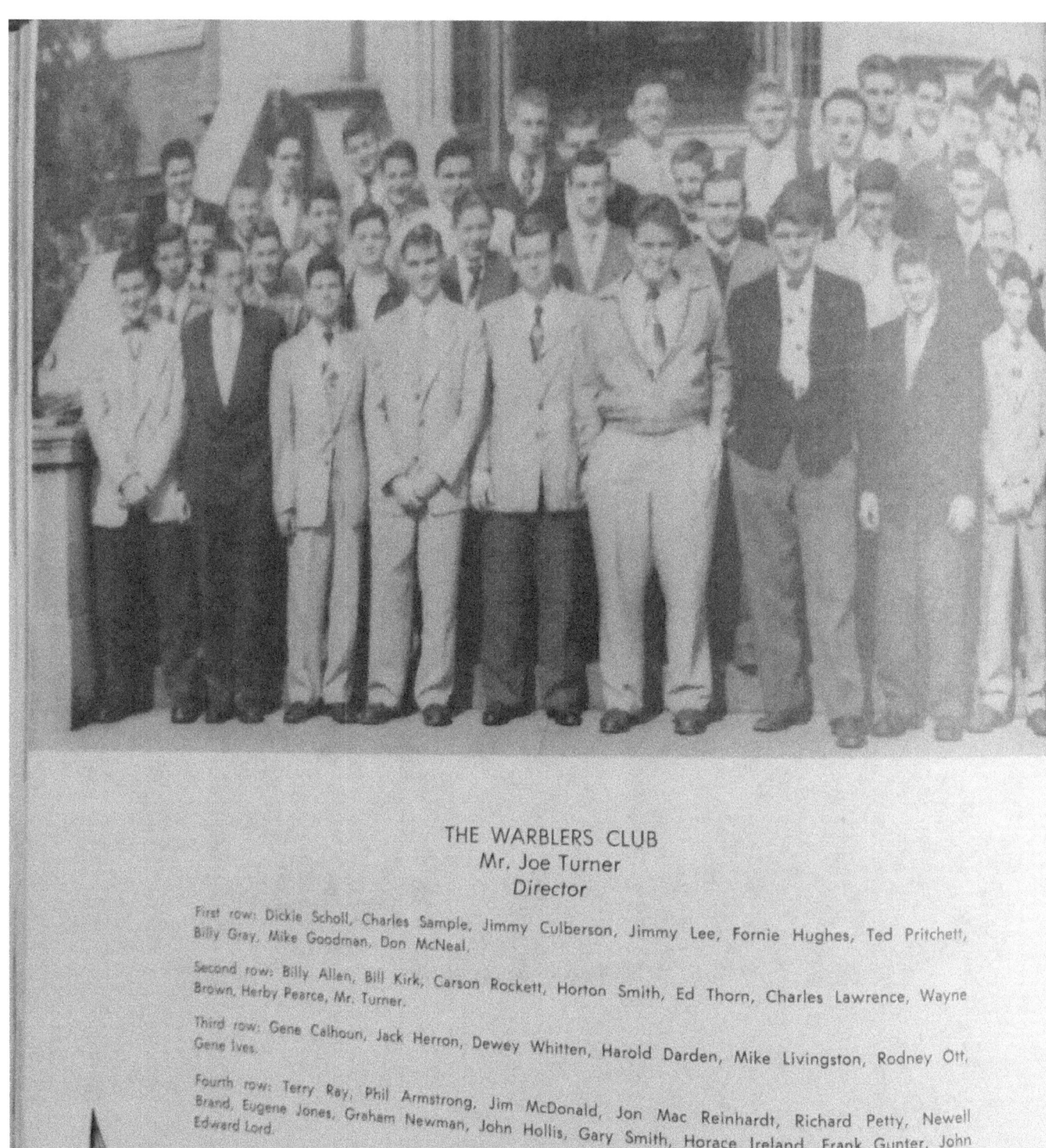

THE WARBLERS CLUB
Mr. Joe Turner
Director

First row: Dickie Scholl, Charles Sample, Jimmy Culberson, Jimmy Lee, Fornie Hughes, Ted Pritchett, Billy Gray, Mike Goodman, Don McNeal.

Second row: Billy Allen, Bill Kirk, Carson Rockett, Horton Smith, Ed Thorn, Charles Lawrence, Wayne Brown, Herby Pearce, Mr. Turner.

Third row: Gene Calhoun, Jack Herron, Dewey Whitten, Harold Darden, Mike Livingston, Rodney Ott, Gene Ives.

Fourth row: Terry Ray, Phil Armstrong, Jim McDonald, Jon Mac Reinhardt, Richard Petty, Newell Brand, Eugene Jones, Graham Newman, John Hollis, Gary Smith, Horace Ireland, Frank Gunter, John Edward Lord.

1952

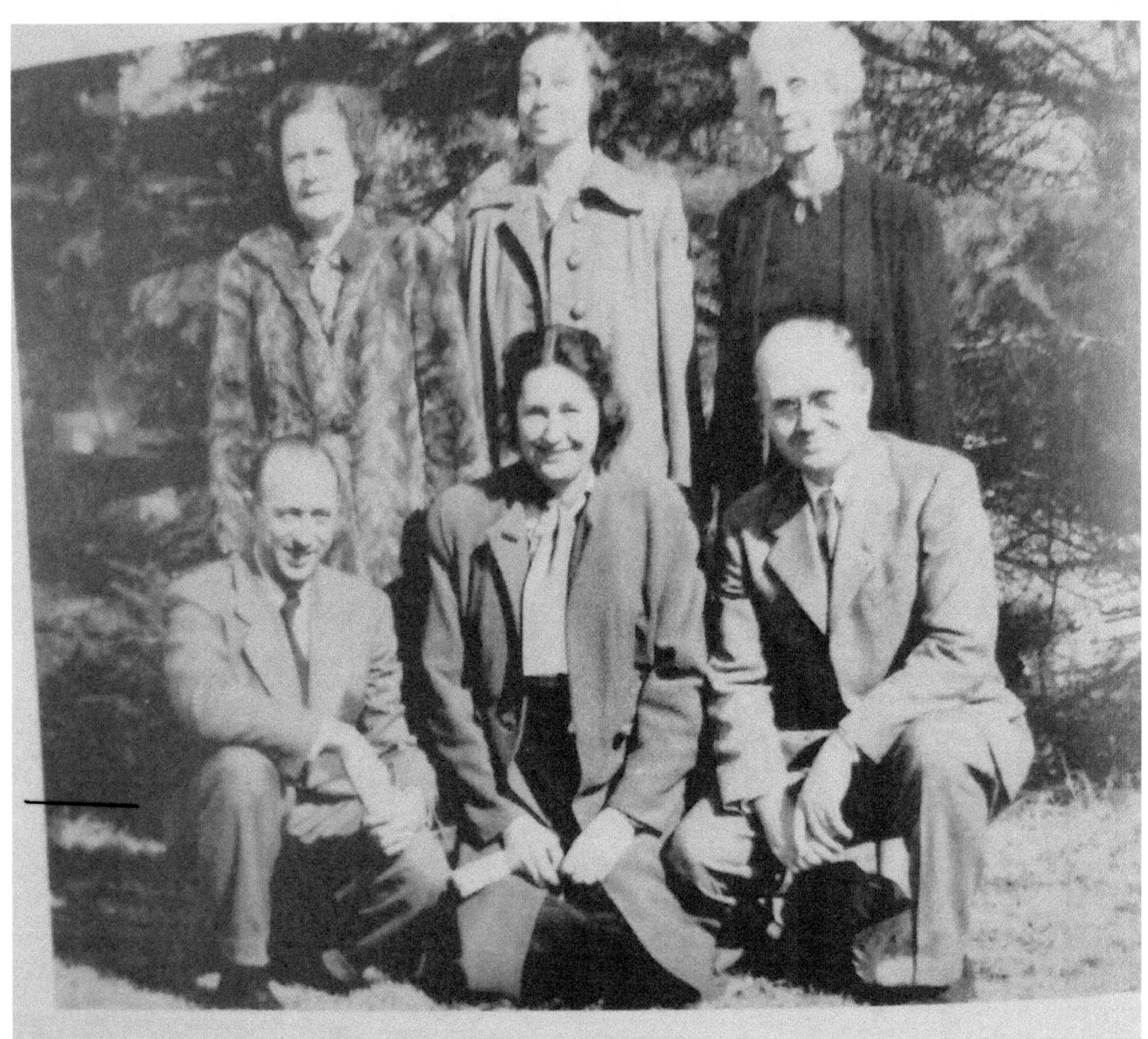

The Music Teachers

First Row: Mr. Turner, Miss Zinser, Mr. Smith.
Second Row: Miss Dowling, Miss Ogden, Mrs. Nabors.
Not Pictured: Mr. McLain.

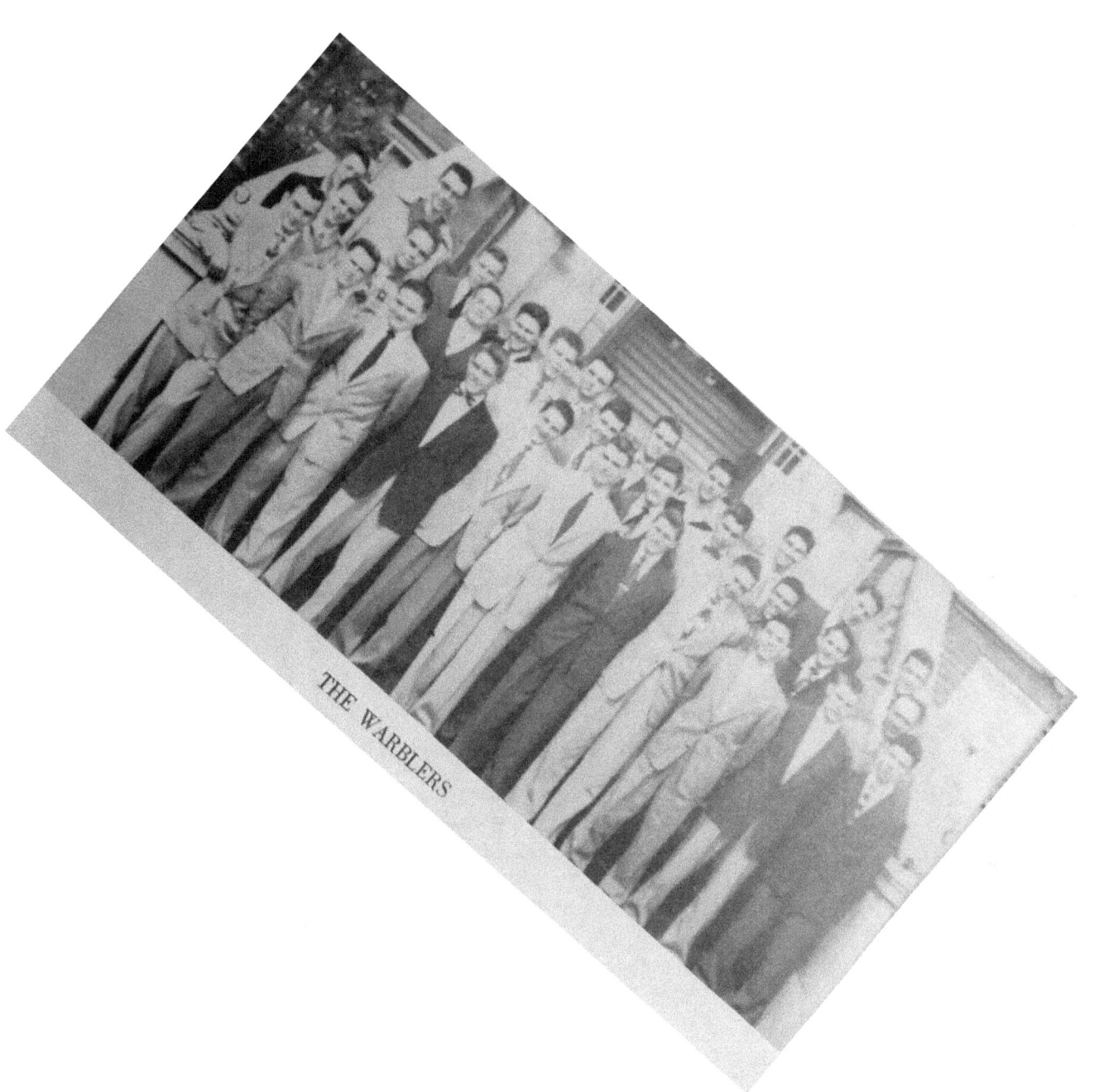

THE WARBLERS

1953

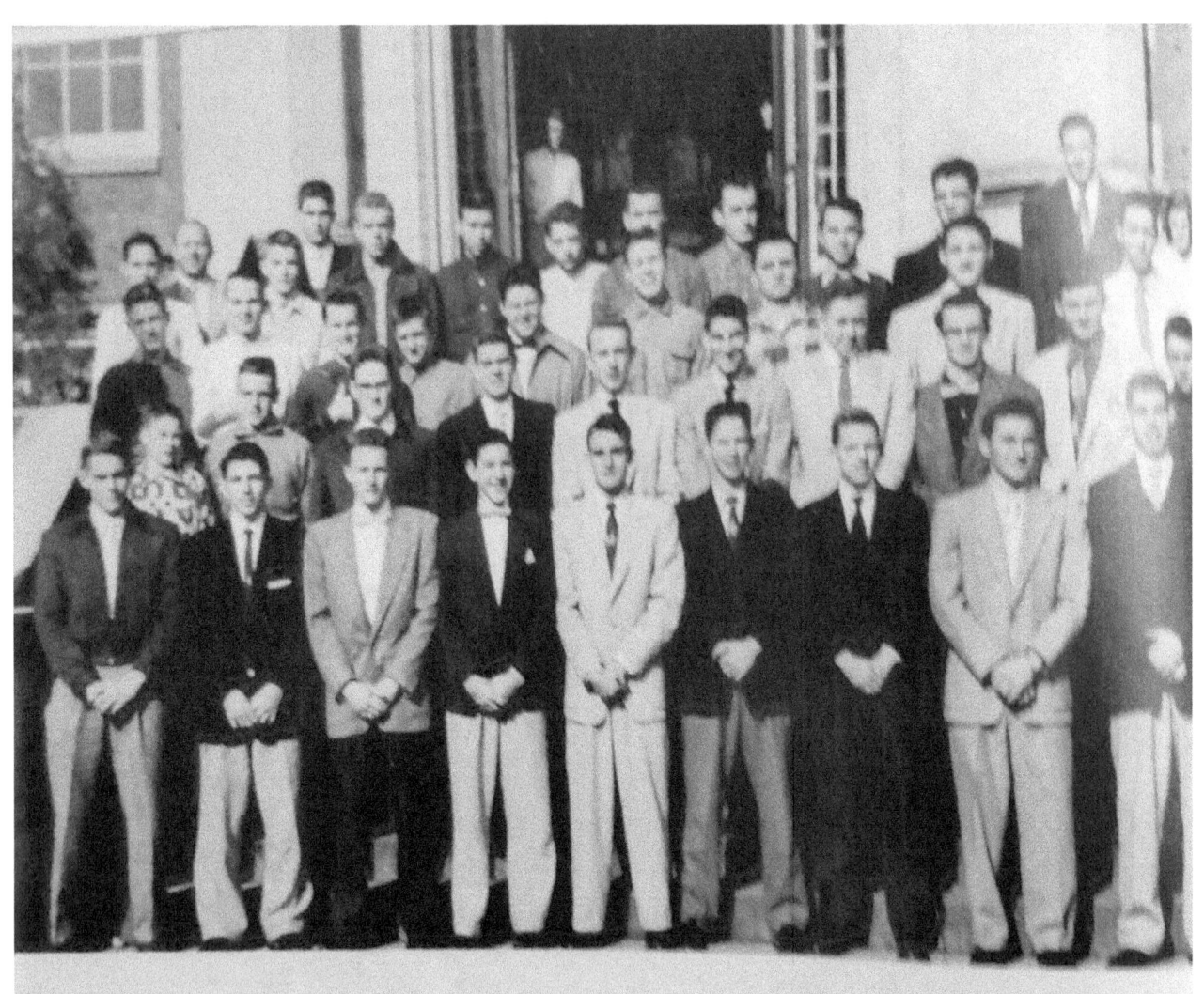

THE WARBLERS

First row: Welbey Smith, Andy Powell, Don Williams, Sammy Dameron, Bobby Hendricks, Ronnie Bryant, Kirby Godsey, Bill Johnson, Frank Bankson.
Second row: Wallace Crittenden, Gene Calhoun, John Earl Reaves, Charles Montgomery, John Childers, Bill Moore, Horton Smith, Burton Walker, Jim Burton, Roland Smith.
Third row: Bernard Clem, Terry Dunn, Don Shockley, Terry Ray, Gene Stover, Paul Dover, Richard Petty, Ed Bryant.
Fourth row: Paul Chandler, Richard Wood, Graham Newman, Bill Smith, Lelias Kirby, George Grubbs, Doug Fegenbush, Jim Powers, David Adams, Ed Myers, Mary Jim Ellis, Accompanist; Mr. Turner, Sponsor; Gary Smith.

1954

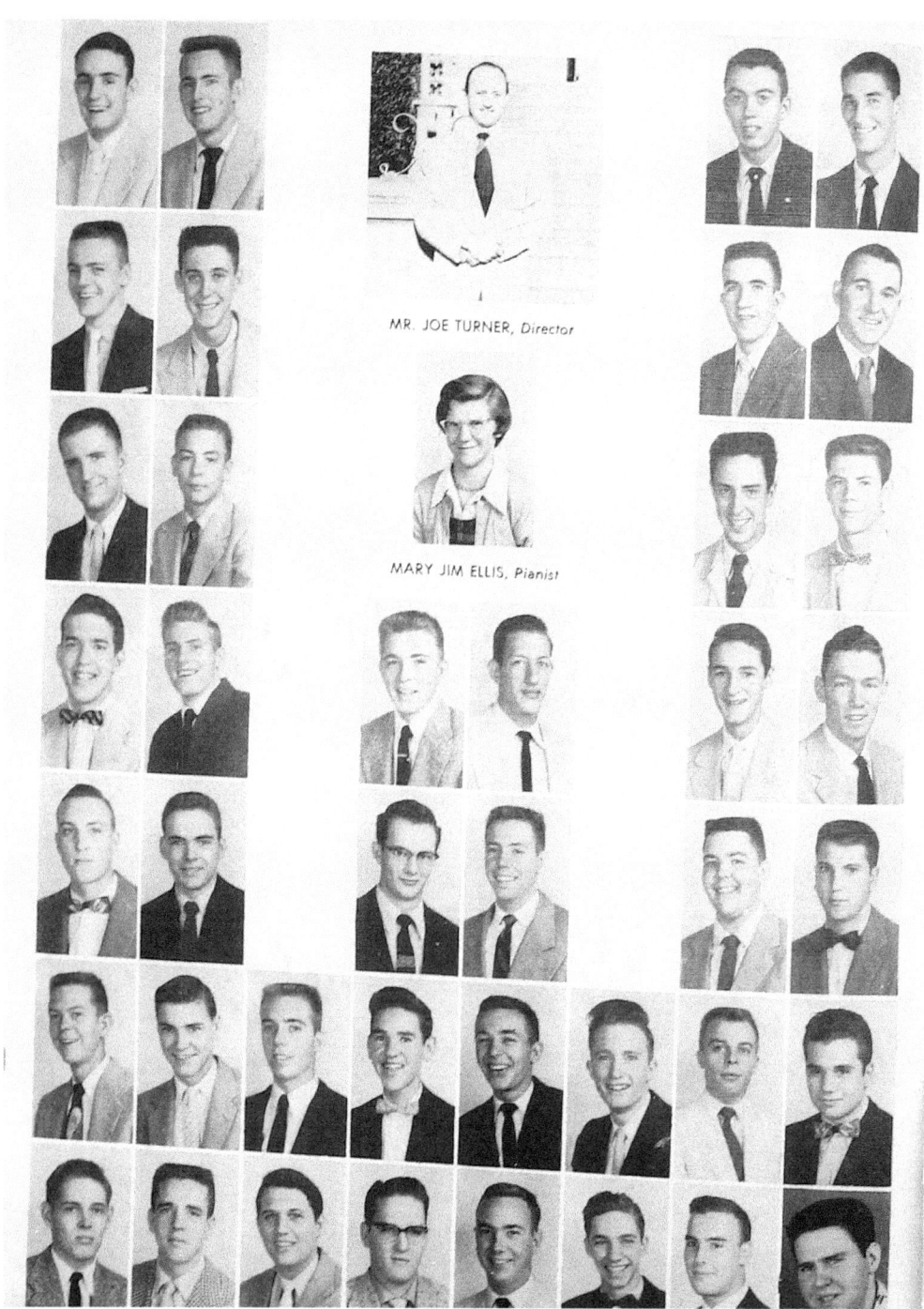

MR. JOE TURNER, *Director*

MARY JIM ELLIS, *Pianist*

1955

WARBLERS 1958

Without music, life would be a mistake.

F. W. NEITZSCHE

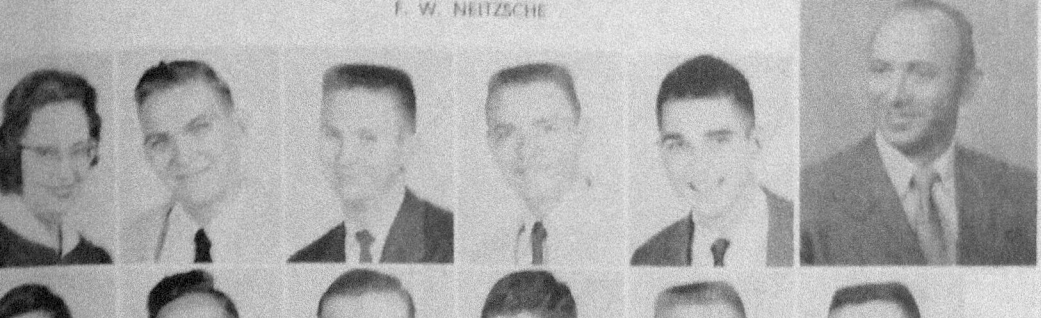

Pianist,
Robbie Terral
John Abbott
Conrad Allen
Hobart Arnold
Ted Beason
Mr. Joe Tuми

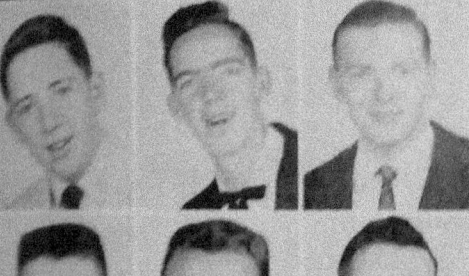 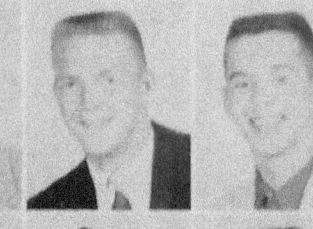 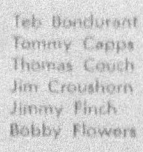

Teb Bondurant
Tommy Capps
Thomas Couch
Jim Croushorn
Jimmy Finch
Bobby Flowers

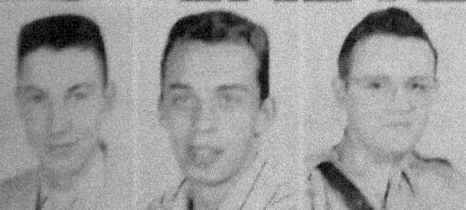 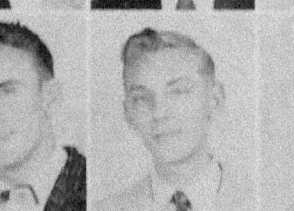 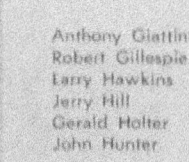

Anthony Giattina
Robert Gillespie
Larry Hawkins
Jerry Hill
Gerald Holter
John Hunter

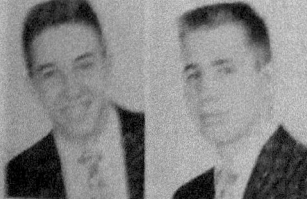 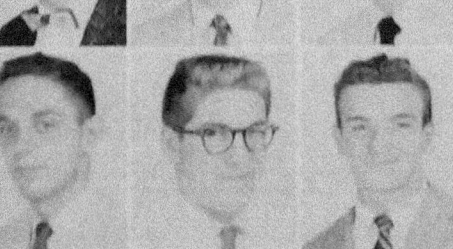 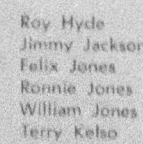

Roy Hyde
Jimmy Jackson
Felix Jones
Ronnie Jones
William Jones
Terry Kelso

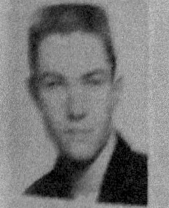 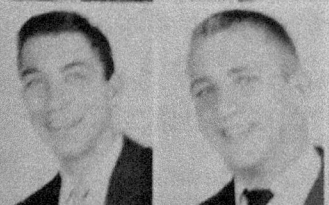 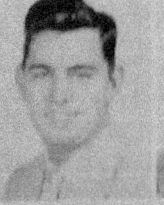 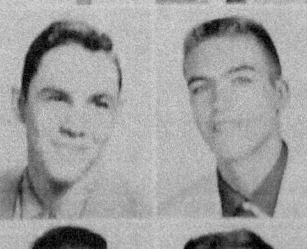 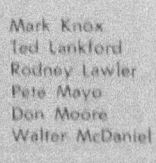

Mark Knox
Ted Lankford
Rodney Lawler
Pete Mayo
Don Moore
Walter McDaniel

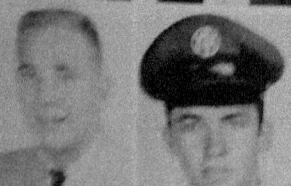 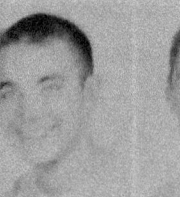 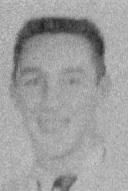 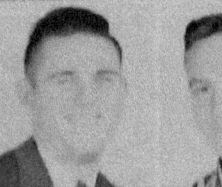 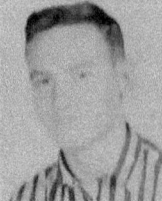

Wayne Neugent
Paula Newman
Walter Nichols
Jack Pyle
Leroy Sharp
Bill Sprouse

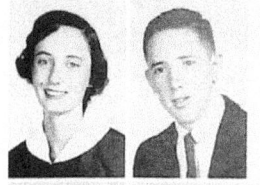
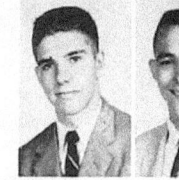
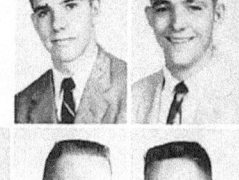

WARBLERS CLUB
1959

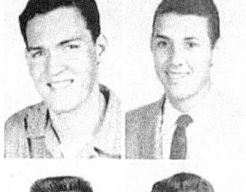
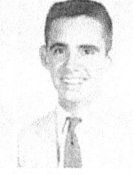
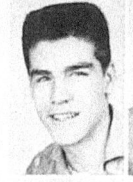
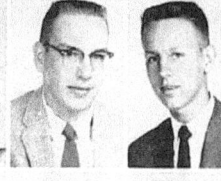

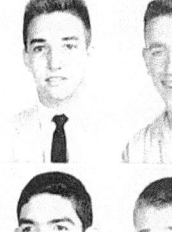
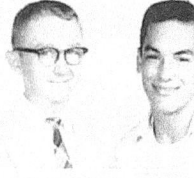
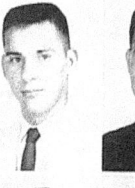
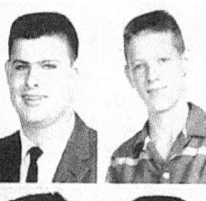
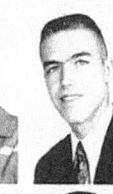
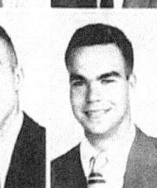

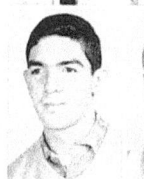
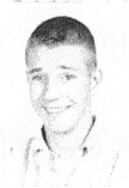
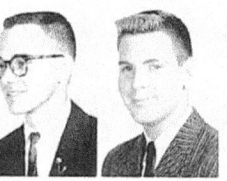
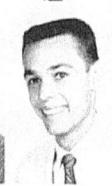
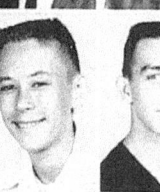
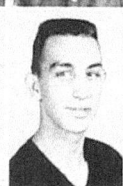
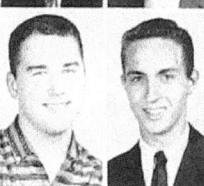
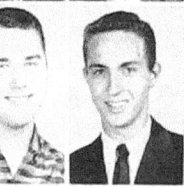

Anne Gray, pianist	Sam Dennis	David Kennedy	Charles Ferrell	Allen Colburn
Wallace Courington	Andy Keith	Dicky Smith	Alan Loyd	La Mar Henry
Roy Hyde	Wayne Self		Wayne Thrasher	Rodney McKinley
George Quiggle				Cecil Ward

Teb Bondurant	Olin Kelso	Bill Lardent	Bill Cardwell
Billy Davis	Neal Shepherd	Bill Stout	Donald Harper
Jimmy Ives			Walter McDaniel
Wayne Russell			Jerry Vines

The members of the Warblers Club are the best male vocalists of Woodlawn. Boys in the Cavaliers try out for positions in the Warblers Club and are selected by members of that club. The Warblers Club meets every day. With the Glee Club, it provides good music and entertainment for auditorium, Stunt Night, P.T.A., and graduation. This year, the Warblers will give a minstrel. Glee Club and Warblers participate in an annual Spring competition with other schools..

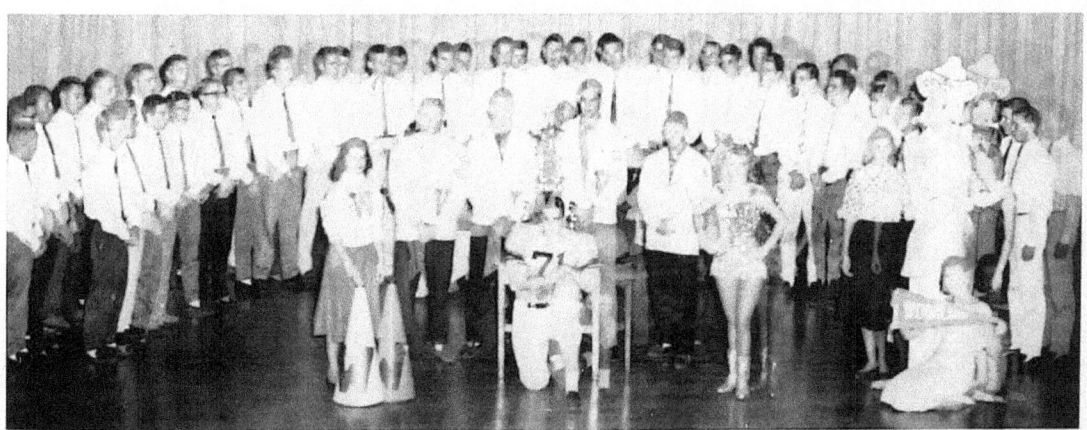

The Warblers sing in Auditorium for the Sportsmanship Program.

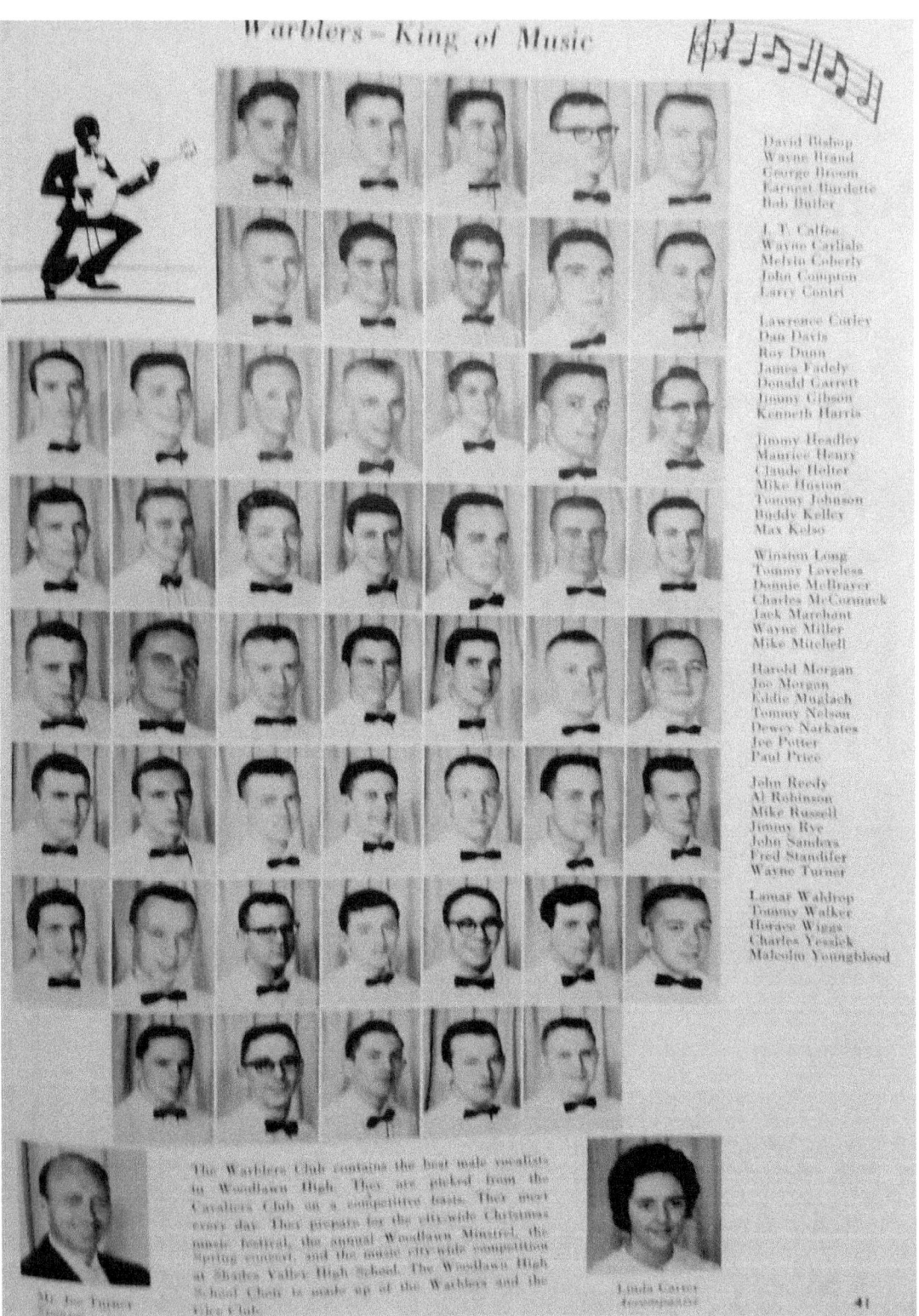

Warblers – King of Music

David Bishop
Wayne Brand
George Broom
Earnest Burdette
Bob Butler

J. T. Calfee
Wayne Carlisle
Melvin Coberly
John Compton
Larry Contri

Lawrence Corley
Dan Davis
Roy Dunn
James Fadely
Donald Garrett
Jimmy Gibson
Kenneth Harris

Jimmy Headley
Maurice Henry
Claude Helter
Mike Huston
Tommy Johnson
Buddy Kelley
Max Kelso

Winston Long
Tommy Loveless
Donnie McBrayer
Charles McCormack
Jack Marchant
Wayne Miller
Mike Mitchell

Harold Morgan
Joe Morgan
Eddie Muglach
Tommy Nelson
Dewey Narkates
Joe Potter
Paul Price

John Reedy
Al Robinson
Mike Russell
Jimmy Rye
John Sanders
Fred Standifer
Wayne Turner

Lamar Waldrop
Tommy Walker
Horace Wiggs
Charles Yessick
Malcolm Youngblood

The Warblers Club contains the best male vocalists in Woodlawn High. They are picked from the Cavaliers Club on a competitive basis. Their meet every day. They prepare for the city-wide Christmas music festival, the annual Woodlawn Minstrel, the Spring concert, and the music city-wide competition at Shades Valley High School. The Woodlawn High School Choir is made up of the Warblers and the Glee Club.

Mr. Joe Turner

Linda Carter
Accompanist

41

1962

128

Warblers

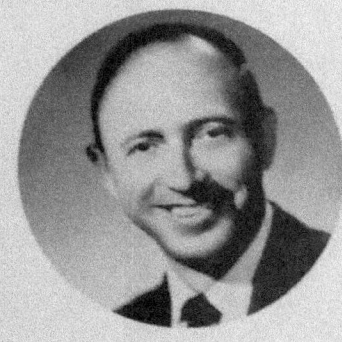

MR. TURNER

It was in the year 1928 that eight boys met and formed what is now known as the WARBLERS CLUB. Under the able leadership of the past sponsors—Mr. John Light, Mr. Amos Hudson, and the present sponsor, Mr. Joe Turner, the WARBLERS CLUB has grown to its present membership of forty-five.

The WARBLERS are often called upon to sing at various civic functions. Also they have sung in the Choir Competition at Shades Valley, the annual Music Festival at Woodlawn, the Spring Concert at Woodlawn, and the city-wide Christmas Music Festival. But the main attraction of the WARBLERS is their annual minstrel, which is looked forward to by everyone.

Membership is on a competitive basis. Auditions, held once each semester, are limited to those who have served at least one semester in the CAVALIERS CLUB.

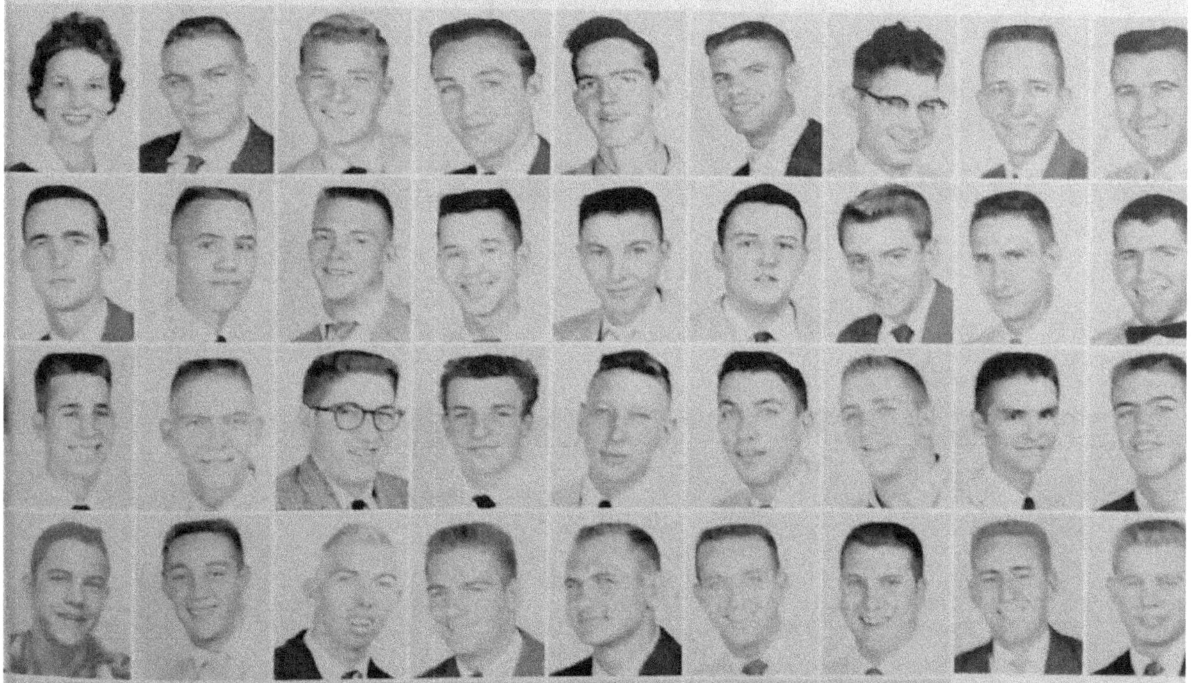

Bobby Davis Earl Edwards
David Hearn Buddy Ives
Jack Light Walter McDaniel
Mike Sheddix Bob VanHooser

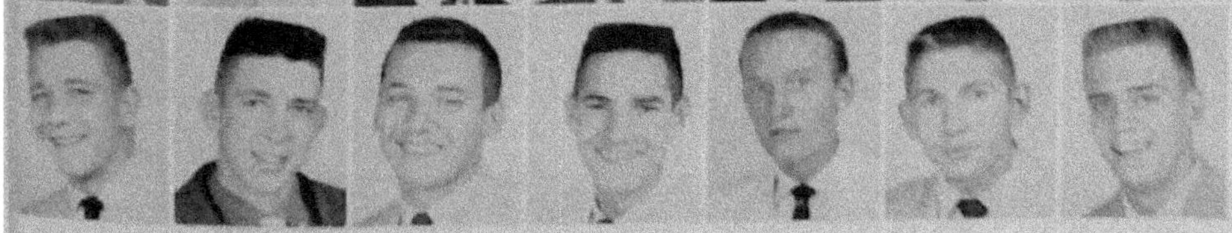

Pat Barnes John Abbot Ronald Boyer Horace Brady Tommy Capps Orville Chandler Don Crow
Noel Edwards Gene Estill Jimmy Finch Bobby Flowers Tony Giottina Larry Hawkins Connie Haydock
Jim Jackson Ken Johnson William Jones Terry Kelso George King Ted Lankford Rodney Lawler
Don Moore Jack Pyle Frank Richard Hubert Riggins Jack Rutledge Harlay Scogin Travis Simmons
Hubert Wade Dick Wamba____ Mike Whatley Bruce White Ted Williams Bill Wilson Joe Woods

183

1957

The best male vocalists in Woodlawn make up the membership of the Warblers' Club. Membership is on a competitive basis. Boys from the Cavaliers try out for positions in the Warblers and are selected by members of that club. The Warblers participate in the Choir Competition at Shades Valley High, the annual Music Festival at Woodlawn, the Spring Concert at Woodlawn, and the City-Wide Christmas Music Festival. This year, the Warblers will be presenting their minstrel.

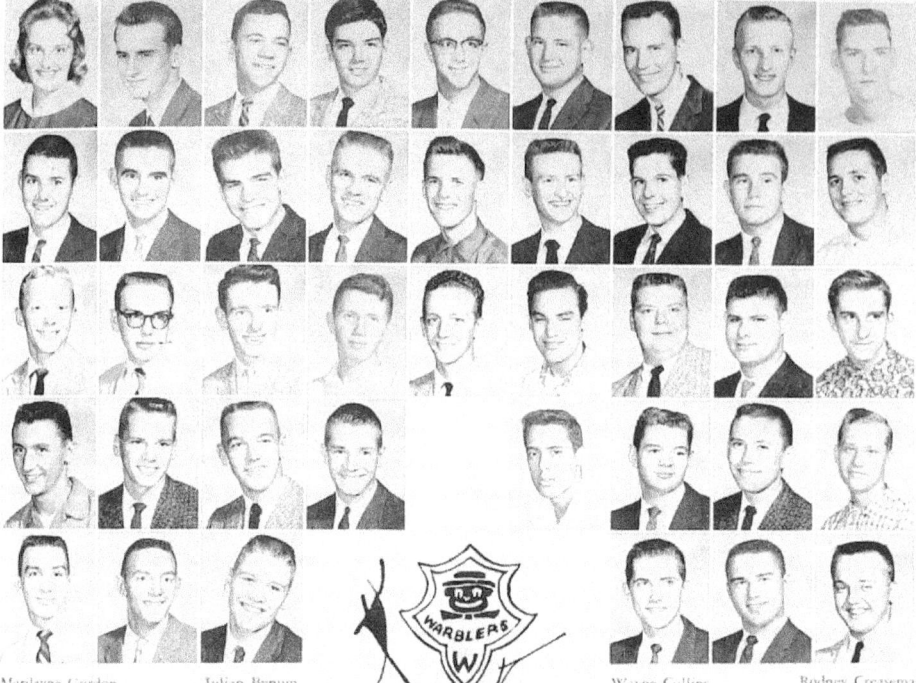

WARBLERS

Marilayne Gordon
Bill Davis
Butch Hargrove
Winky Moore
Wayne Thrasher

Julian Bynum
Charles Ferrell
Jimmy Ives
Wayne Pugh
Wheeler Vice

Anthony Bedsole
Sammy Dennis
Don Harper
George Nichols
Eddie Vanderburg

Wally Carlisle
Ernest Fife
Johnny Ives
Wayne Russell

Tommy Clements
Roy Gable
Johnny Johnston

Wayne Coggin
Bill Garrison
Olin Kelso
Brian Savage

Wayne Collins
Bobby Gentle
Joe Lackey
Hal Shelton
Wayne Villadsen

Ed Cook
Tommy Godwin
Bill Lardent
Bill Stout
Jerry Vines

Rodney Creaseman
Ronnie Hamm
Harry Looney
Joe Thrasher
Joe Wallis

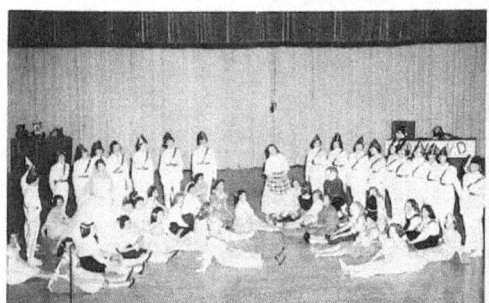

A scene from the Glee Club's Toyland for Stunt Night in November.

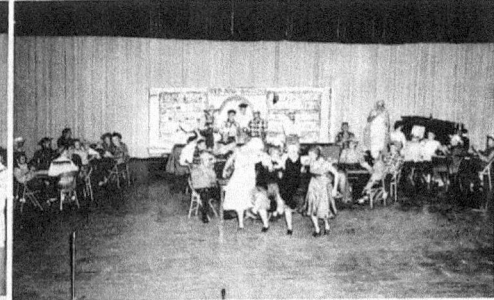

This western scene was the Warblers' winning stunt at Stunt Night.

47

1960 Warblers

Warblers Club Members Kings of Music

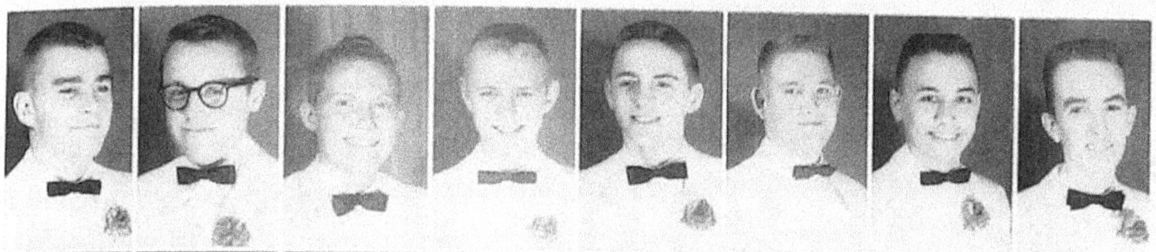

Wallace Allison
Robert Brown
David Bullock
J. T. Calfee
Jim Cobb
Wayne Coggin
Larry Contri
Lawrence Corley

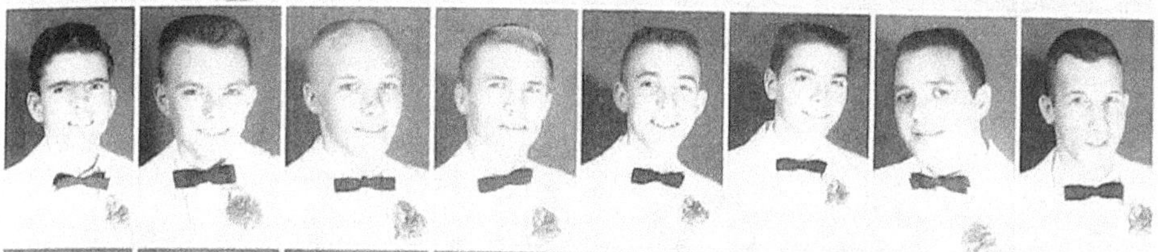

Charles Drake
Bill Dunsmore
John Freeze
Roy Gable
Jimmy Gibson
Terry Gilpin
Ronnie Hamm
Larry Harris

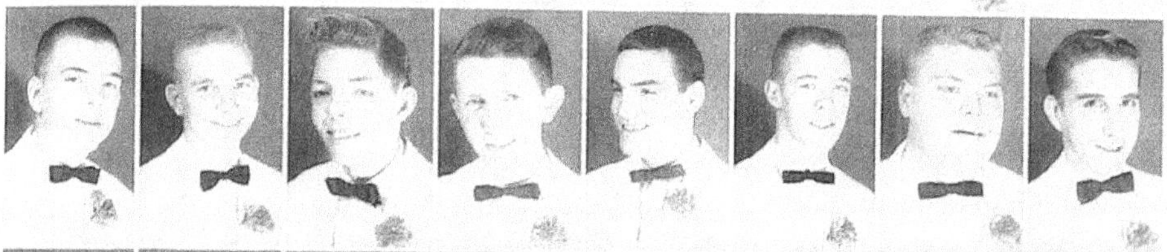

Jimmy Headley
Maurice Henry
Claude Holter
Johnny Ives
Olin Kelso
John Kimbrough
Joe Lackey
Harry Looney

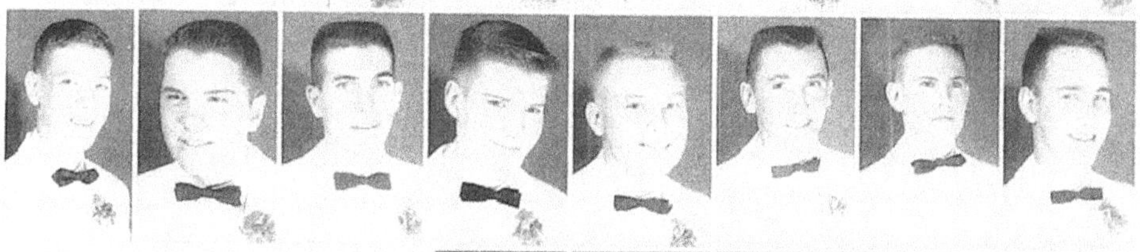

Alan Loyd
Guy Lytle
Jack Marchant
Eddie McCarley
Wayne Miller
Winky Moore
Jim Newman
Joe Potter

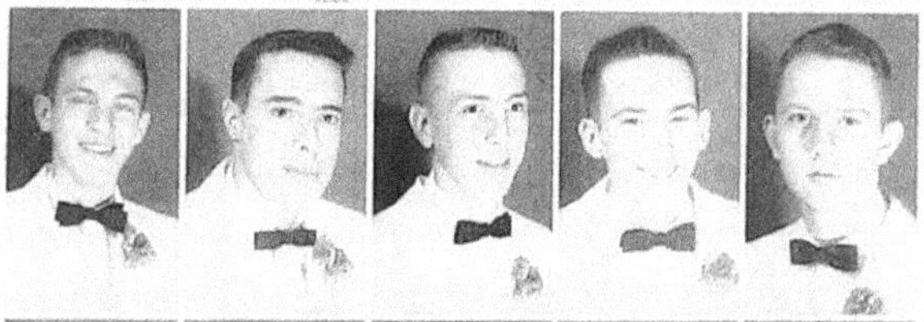

Jim Reese
Brian Savage
Ronnie Smith
Jerry Sparks
Doug Stegall

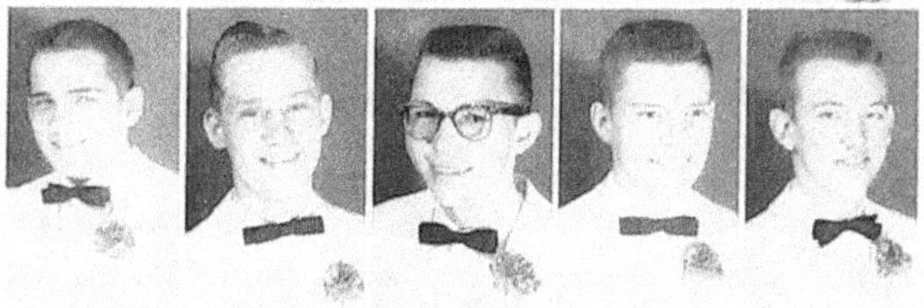

1961

John Thomas
Joe Thrasher
Richard Turner
Ronnie Viars
Charles Yessick

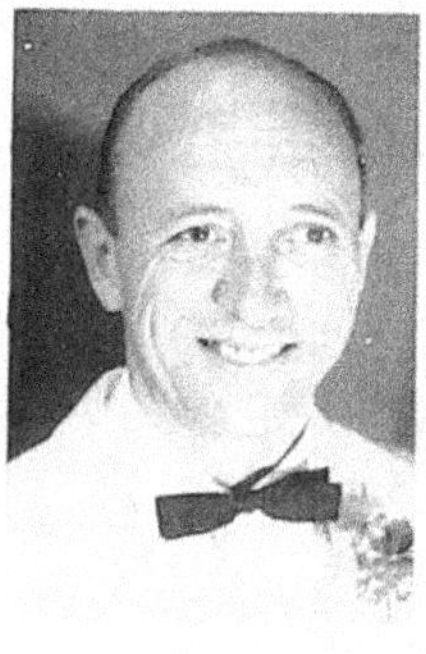

Sponsor
MR. JOSEPH TURNER

The Warblers Club contains the best male vocalists in Woodlawn High. They are chosen from the Cavaliers Club on a competitive basis. At their daily meetings they prepare for the city-wide Christmas music festival; the Spring concert and the music festival at Woodlawn; the annual Woodlawn Minstrel show; and city-wide competition at Shades Valley High. The Warblers and the Glee Club make up the Woodlawn High School Choir.

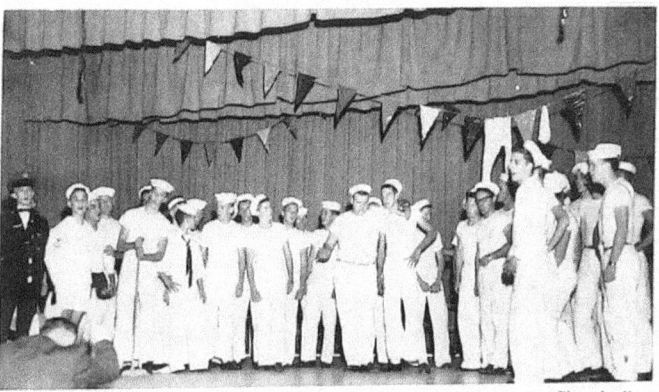

Photo by Kent

The Warblers are singing "Eight Bells" from their Stunt Night skit.

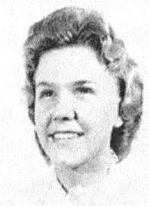

Accompanist,
CAROLYN MAGNUSON

"WARBLERS"

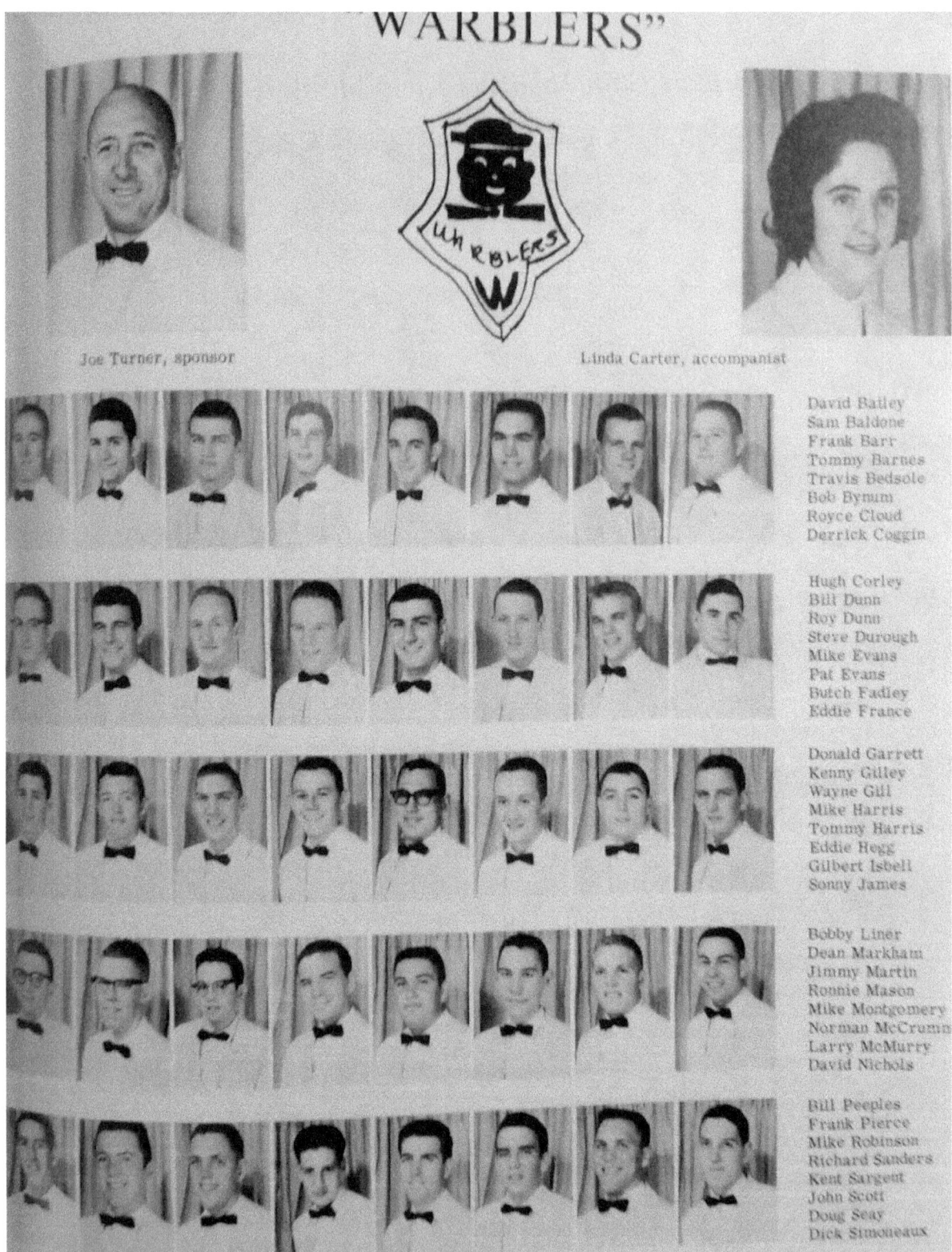

Joe Turner, sponsor

Linda Carter, accompanist

David Bailey
Sam Baldone
Frank Barr
Tommy Barnes
Travis Bedsole
Bob Bynum
Royce Cloud
Derrick Coggin

Hugh Corley
Bill Dunn
Roy Dunn
Steve Durough
Mike Evans
Pat Evans
Butch Fadley
Eddie France

Donald Garrett
Kenny Gilley
Wayne Gill
Mike Harris
Tommy Harris
Eddie Hegg
Gilbert Isbell
Sonny James

Bobby Liner
Dean Markham
Jimmy Martin
Ronnie Mason
Mike Montgomery
Norman McCrumm
Larry McMurry
David Nichols

Bill Peeples
Frank Pierce
Mike Robinson
Richard Sanders
Kent Sargent
John Scott
Doug Seay
Dick Simoneaux

1964 Warblers

CHOIR
WARBLERS

The Warblers Club contains the best male vocalists in the city. They are picked from the Cavaliers Club on competitive basis. The Woodlawn High School Choir is made up of the Warblers and the Girls Glee Club. They prepare for the Christmas Music Festival, the Spring Concert, and the City-wide Music Competition.

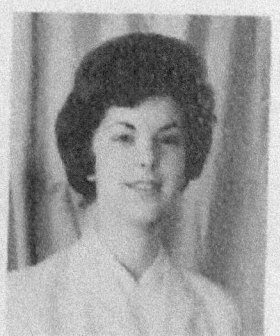

Joseph D. Turner
Sponsor

Elaine Cordes
Accompanist

Rick Allison
Jerry Bailey
Richard Barnes
Travis Bedsole
Wayne Gill
Dick Bradley
Ronnie Burnett
Bob Bynum
Royce Cloud

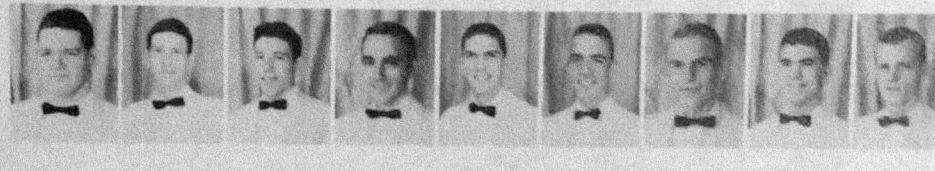

Derrick Coggin
Joe Allen Cook
Bob Corley
Dale Cottrell
John Dawson
Steve Dorough
Larry Ethridge
Pat Evans

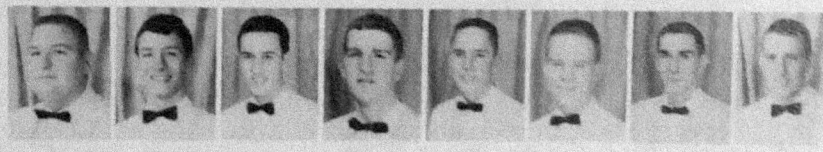

James Faulkner
Freddie First
Kenny Gilley
Joe Hamilton
Gary Johnson
Tommy Lackey
George Lefoy
Randy Marsh
Bill Martin

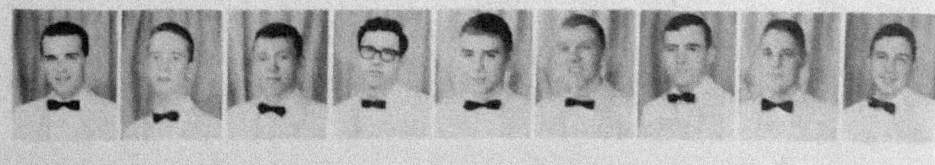

Curt Massey
Norman McCrummen
Johnny McFarlin
Jerry McGukin
Gary Mitchell
Bill Murray
Rusty Murray
Jimmy Nix

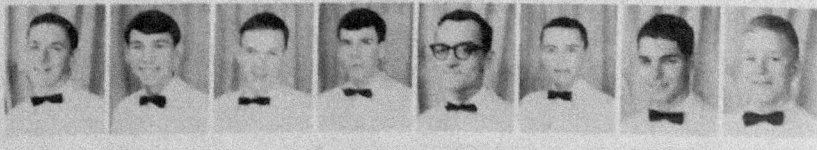

John Norton
Danny Painter
Joe Palmer
Bill Peeples
Doug Phillips
Duane Ready
George Sanders
Danny Scott
John Scott

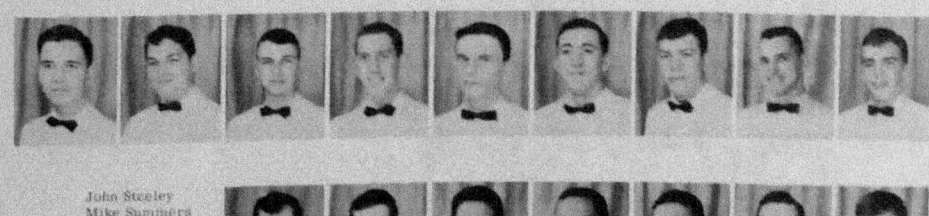

John Steeley
Mike Summers
Bobby Thomas
Bobby Wheat
John White
Tom Woods
Steve Yessick

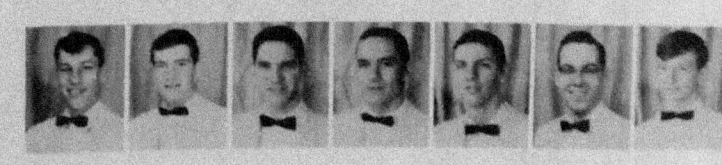

1965 Warblers

Sponsor

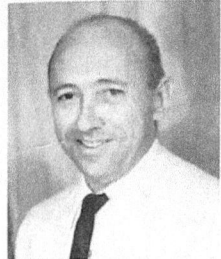

Joseph D. Turner

Warblers

The Warblers are another part of Woodlawn High School's choir. They are picked from the Cavaliers Club on a competitive basis. They prepare for the Christmas Music Festival, the Spring Concert, and the City-wide Music Competition.

Accompanist

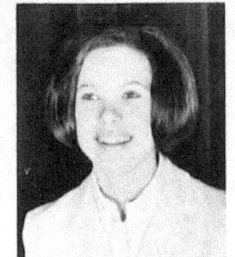

Beverly Adamson

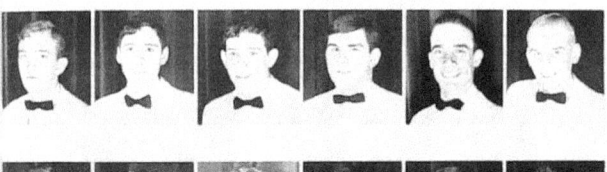

Richard Amberson
Barry Andrews
Richard Barnes
Terry Blackwell
Dick Bradley
Ronnie Burnett

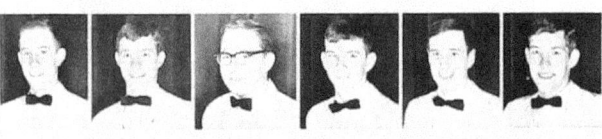

Edwin Camp
Joe Allen Cook
John Cook
Mike Cordes
Bob Corley
Gary Courington

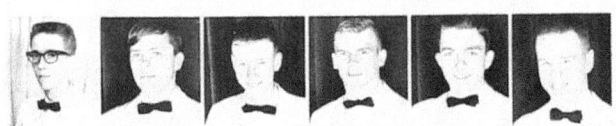

Dennis Craft
Allen Crew
Phillip Crump
Ronny DeLoach
Jim DeVore
Steve Dorough

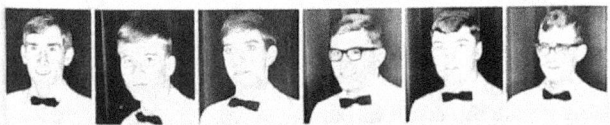

Larry Etheridge
Fred First
Steve Fletcher
Don Garrison
Robert Gregory
Joey Grogan

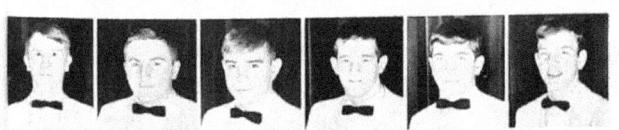

Steve Gruman
Gary Johnson
Lee Herring
Doug McBrayer
Sam McDaniel
Johnny McFarlin

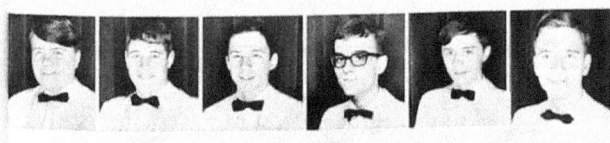

Brad Marsh
Randy Marsh
Bill Martin
Gary Mitchell
Bill Murray
John Norton

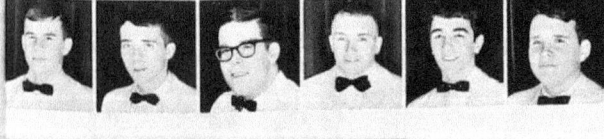

Ronny Pilgreen
Ronald Smith
Bruce Sproull
Ronny Stone
Mike Tribble
Jim Troutman

Larry Walker
Steve Williams
Franklin Wingard
Steve Yessick

35

1966

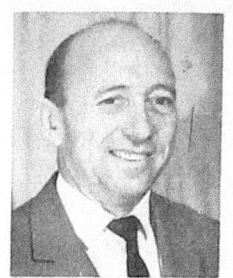

W a r b l e r s

Mr. Joe Turner
Sponsor

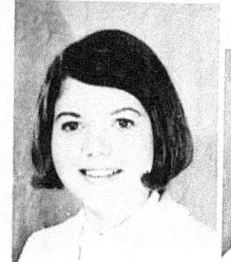

Nancy Adamson
Pianist

Fran Kimberly
Assistant

Gary Allen
Larry Boone
Barry Brokaw
Mike Browning
Johnny Bryant

Rusty Chastain
Mike Cordes
Philip Crump
Jim DeVore
Bill Dimon

Carl Estes
David Garrison
Eddie Gaylord
Robert Greene
Allen Griffin

Steve Gruman
Andy Haynes
Terry Henderson
Bill Henry
Eugene Hobson

Greg Kelley
Ronnie Ledbetter
Danny Lofton
Brad Marsh
Sammy McDaniel

Mike Parker
David Pifer
Jerry Pittman
Eddie Roberson
Jack Shores

Danny Smith
Bill Sorrell
Cary Speaker
Bruce Sproull
Steve Timms

Mike Wanniger
Carlton White
Tracy Wiggs
Johnny Willis
Mike Vinson

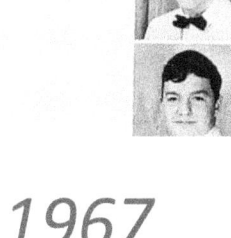

Terry Vinson
Steve Urquhart

1967

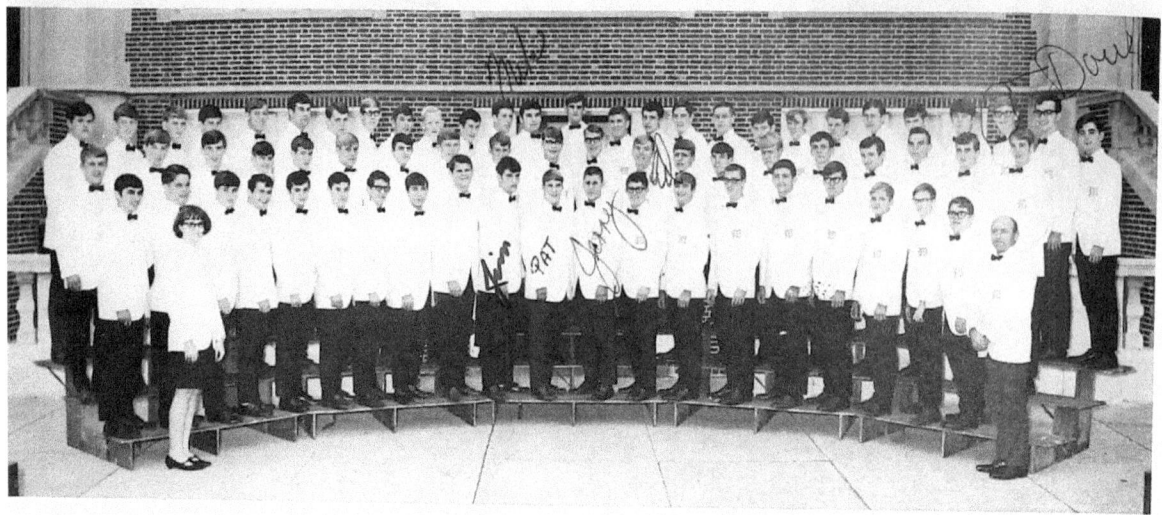

ROW 1: F. Kimberly, Acc., G. Alexander, D. Colee, G. Garrett, M. Musso, M. Murray, D. Lucas, E. Bell, G. Morrison, J. Lester, J. Self, S. Langner, J. Marbut, L. Viars, C. Smith, A. Reid, B. Sorrell, R. Edwards, N. Allen, W. Strickland, R. Vinson, Mr. Turner ROW 2: T. Harris, B. Noblitt, S. Woods, R. Bowman, C. Whitaker, J. Morton, K. Cain, G. Robbins, R. Taylor, R. Lawrence, B. Parker, E. Wharton, M. Wilson, V. Thompson, D. Brown, J. Jernigan, P. McBrayer, T. Bearden, D. Olive, H. Sudderth ROW 3: J. Tapscott, R. Brandon, C. Cramer, S. Garrard, D. Abbott, L. Cokeroft, C. Lowery, L. Price, L. Maples, A. Young, J. Roberson, M. Hale, D. Taylor, D. Nichols, L. Bean, A. Wood, E. Sorrell, C. Frew, R. Rodgers, D. Markham, L. Kinsaul, P. Choate, . Watkins, R. Ledbetter, D. Vinson, R. Stewart, R. Coberly

Warblers

OFFICERS
President - Darell Lucas
Vice-President - Phillip McBrayer
Secretary - Lynn Viars
Treasurer - Ed Wharton
Chaplain - Bob Simmons
Sergeants-at-Arms - Mike Hale
                         Scott Langner
Accompianist - Fran Kimberly

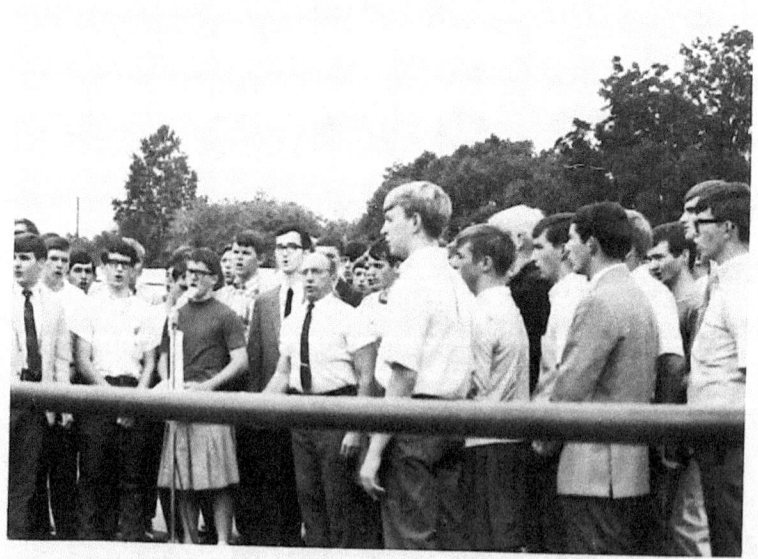

The Warblers inspire others to sing the Woodlawn Alma Mater.

136

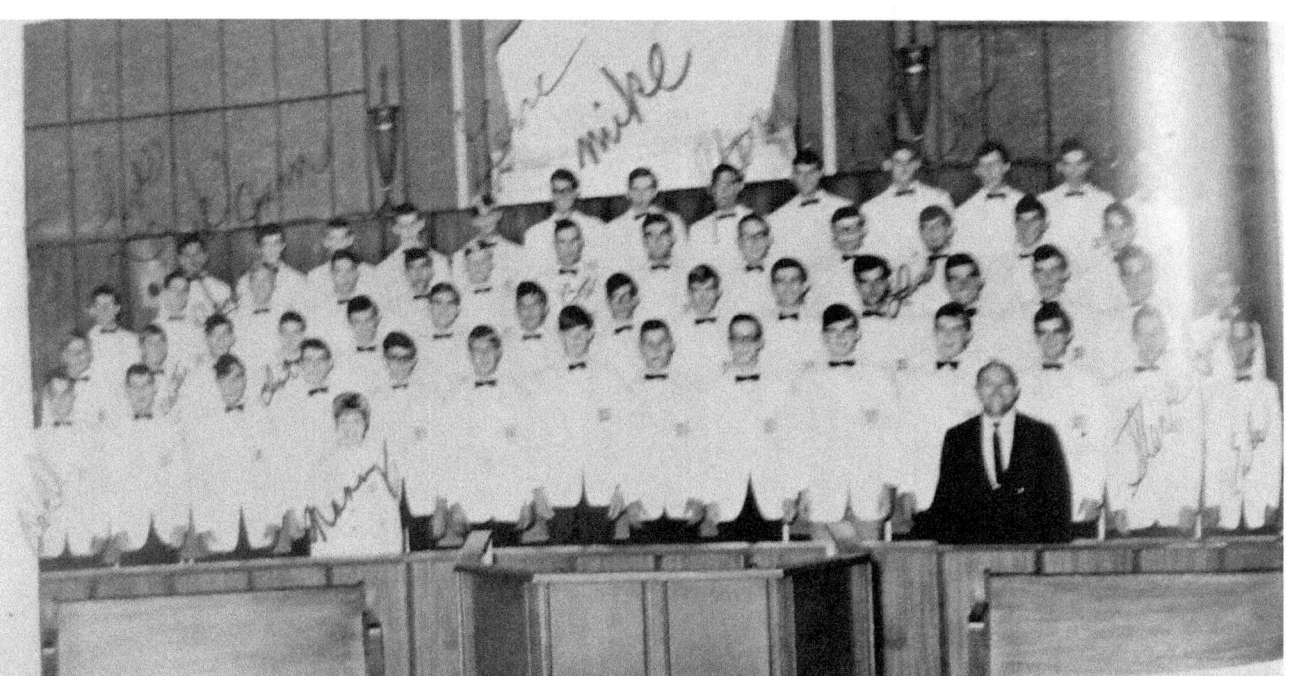

Nancy Adamson, Mr. Turner. ROW 1: D. Lucas, M. Musso, G. Morrison, K. Cain, J. Willis, D. Brown, M. Browning, J. Marbut, A. Reid, D. Olive, S. Langner, M. Murray, S. Uquhart, E. Plummer. ROW 2: M. Wilson, C. Smith, V. Thompson, C. Newman, P. McBrayer, J. Scott, T. Vinson, R. Edwards, D. Markham, B. Simmons, R. Crenshaw, T. Pierce, S. Woods, D. Colee, J. Stewart. ROW 3: L. Viars, R. Chastain, E. Wharton, J. Self, S. Thomas, M. Connors, B. Holley, D. Taylor, J. Shores, M. Vinson, L. Cummings, L. Maples, T. Dunion. ROW 4: G. Tapscott, J. Robinson, C. Lowery, G. Hobson, M. Parker, J. Bryant, G. Allen, A. Griffin, D. Nichols, M. Hale, J. Williams, B. Henry.

1968

1969-1970

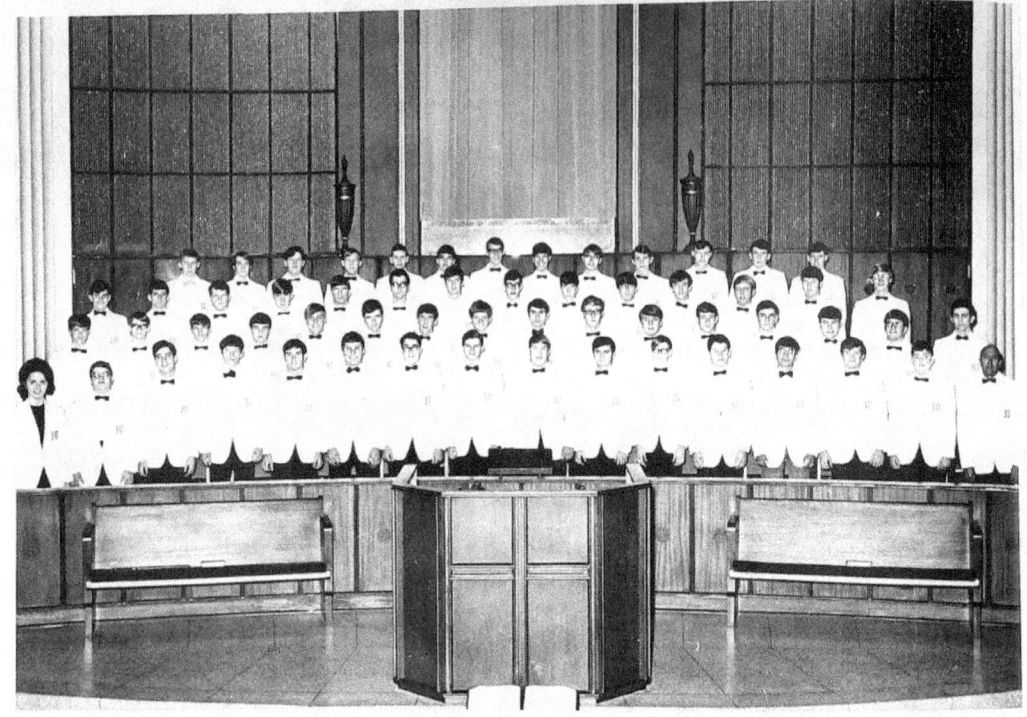

ROW 1: Alice Fuller, pianist, R. Vinson, R. Coberly, G. Clements, V. Thompson, J. Marbut, N. Funderburg, J. Posey, S. Langner, M. Murray, W. Strickland, A. Speaker, J. Caterinichia, N. Allen, F. Vest, Mr. Joe Turner, Director.

ROW 2: B. Lauderdale, F. Hinds, R. Bowman, G. Garrett, J. Morton, L. Bishop, S. Woods, R. Taylor, K. Cain, R. Ray, M. Wilson, C. Whitaker, G. Hallman, G. Robbins, J. Wheat, B. Simmons.

ROW 3: S. Garrard, M. Bishop, L. Kinsaul, D. Dunnaway, L. Bean, R. Stewart, R. Meadows, R. Shores, R. Lambert, R. Dunsmore. J. Jernigan, D. Brown, R. Ledbetter, D. Vinson.

ROW 4: G. Robbins, H. Sudderth, S. Robinson, D. Abbott, J. Perry, A. Wood, B. Parker, D. Hawkins, R. Lawrence, C. Lowery, P. Choate, J. Neel, R. Ousley.

Warblers

OFFICERS

President - VAN THOMPSON
Vice President - MIKE MURRAY
Secretary - RICHARD LAWRENCE
Treasurer - HAROLD SUDDERTH
Sergeants-at-Arms - MIKE WILSON, SCOTT LANGNER, LEE BEAN
Chaplain - JERRY MARBUT

1970-1971

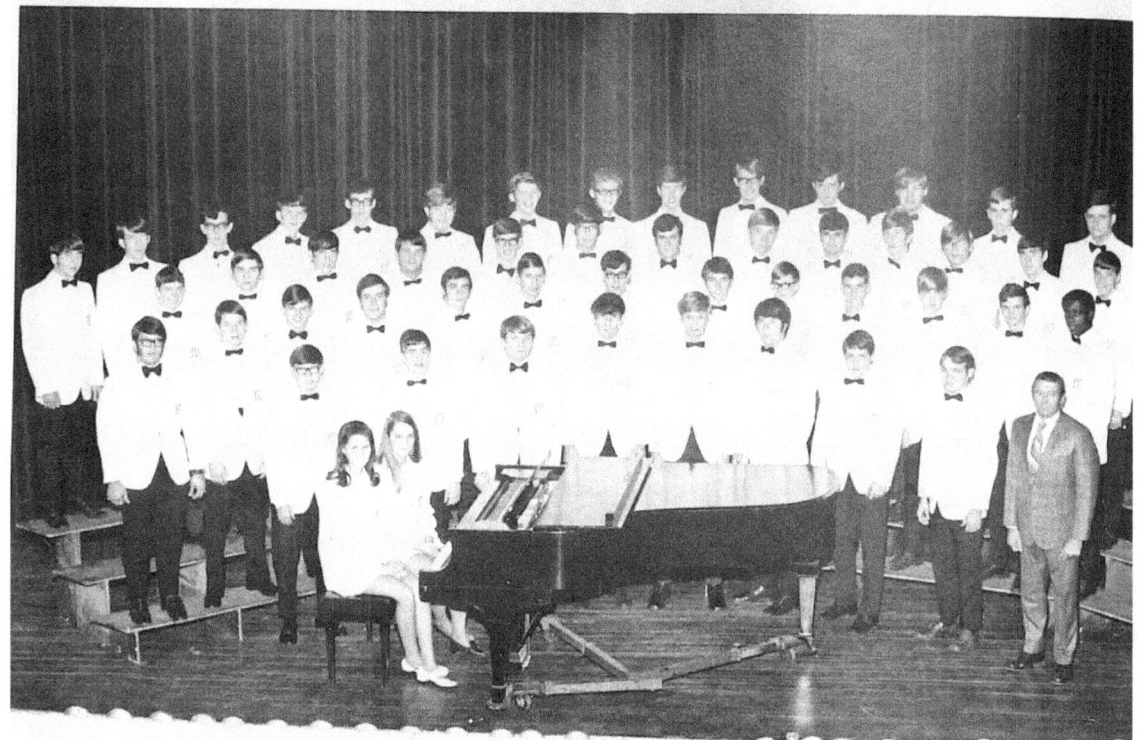

ACCOMPANISTS: Vickie Marsh, Marta Jordan

ROW 1: B. Smith, F. Vest, B. Hill, J. Neel, D. Vinson, R. Ledbetter, D. Kinsaul, R. Hyche, Mr. Joe Turner, Director

ROW 2: J. Wheat, A. Speaker, J. Posey, R. Morrison, G. Hallman, J. Perry, J. Waites, J. Stubbs, W. Strickland, C. Newman, J. Lauderdale, R. McBrayer, L. Thompson

ROW 3: E. Varn, R. Perry, R. Lambert, J. Burkett, T. Corley, D. Mills, R. Harbuck, W. Atkinson, T. Collier, B. King, R. Dunsmore, D. Douglas, L. Culpepper

ROW 4: P. Lee, M. Goldman, P. Cail, W. Whited, R. Shores, C. Martin, G. Robbins, R. Ray, D. Hawkins, B. Parker, H. Cobbs, K. Brechin, S. Dill, K. Tow

Warblers

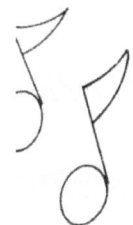

Officers

President - - - - - - - - - - - - - Alan Speaker
V. President - - - - - - - - - - - - Bob Parker
Treasurer - - - - - - - - - - Wesley Strickland
Sgt. At Arms - - - - - R. Ledbetter, D. Vinson
Secretary - - - - - - - - - - - - - Jim Posey

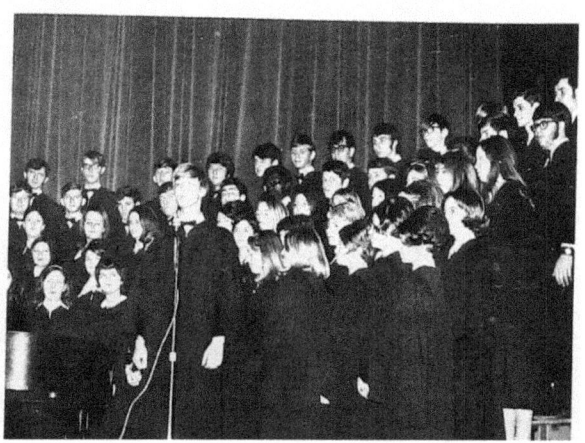

139

Warbler's Club

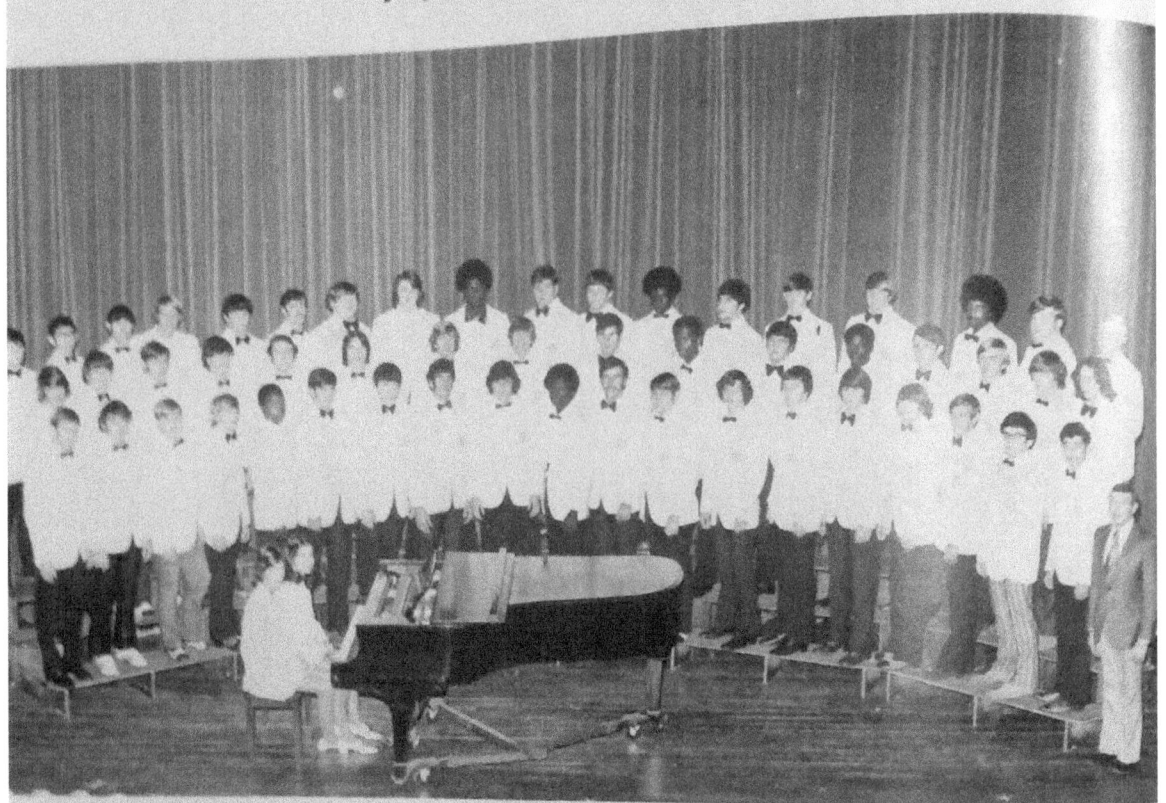

ROW 1: Bill White, Tommy Tuggle, Barry Corbett, Johnny Penfield, Dwight Dillard, Anthony Montalto, Mike Grauel, Bobby Bradley, Seth Poole, Conrad Herlon, Randy Morrison, Jimmy Nunnaly, Roger Lucas, Randy DeRieux, Mark McElroy, Mike Lauderdale, David Edwards, Bill Brewer, John Butler. ROW 2: Chris Lewis, Bobby Richeson, Tommy Robbins, Carson Tingle, Chris Wilson, Robert Coats, Steve Monk, Terry Overstreet, Tommy Reynolds, Tony Henderson, Byron Hill, Steve Washington, Louie KcKnight, Bob Collins, Kent Moe, Robbie Roberson. ROW 3: David McAfee, Frank Buttler, Larry Bowman, Robert Frew, Mike Avery, John Finney, Mike Crawford, Wade Overstreet, Gary Speers, Kenneth Graham, Steve Spenser, Ricky Jones, Peyton Zarzour, Johnny Jordan, Steve Loggins, Ronald Coleman, Steve Henegar, Walter Hunter. Pianists: Julie Knox and Gail Jeff.

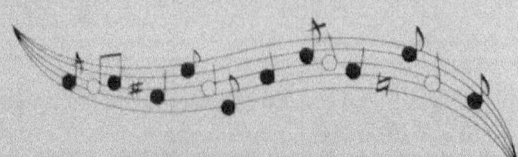

OFFICERS	
Accompanists	Gail Jeff,
	Julie Knox
Chaplain	Bob Collins
Sgt. at Arms	Bobby Bradley
Secretary	Randy Morrison
President	Mark McElroy
Treasurer	Mike Crawford
Sgt. at Arms	Tommy Reynolds
Vice Pres.	Roger Lucas
Sponsor	Mr. Joe Turner

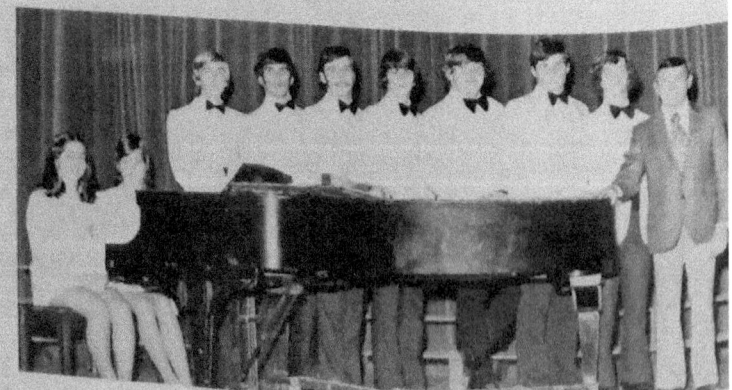

Warblers

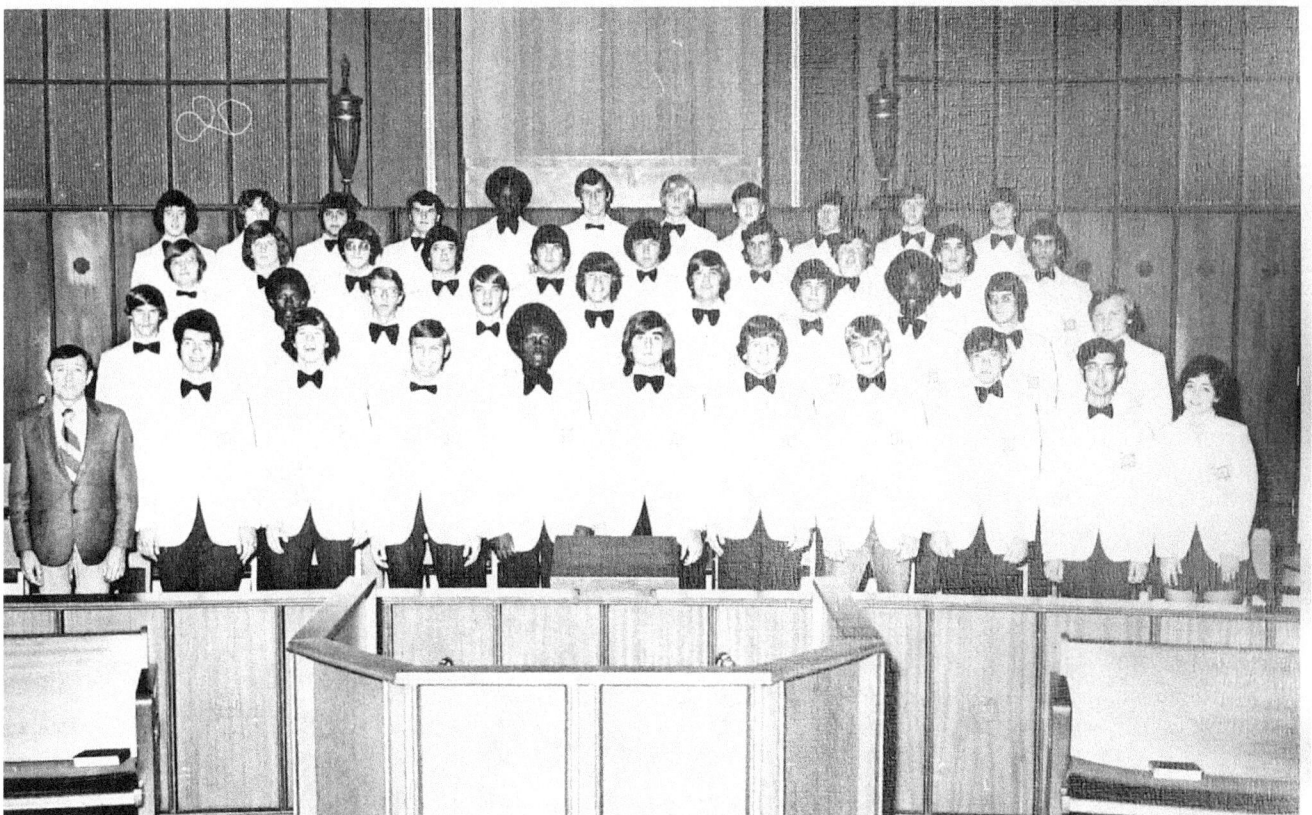

ROW 1: Mr. Joe Turner, H. Bolus, R. Lucas, B. White, C. Herlong, J. Jay, W. White, J. Blackwood, S. Crawford, J. Buttler, Gail Jeff, Accompanist.
ROW 2: D. Edwards, J. Story, D. White, M. Copeland, T. Overstreet, R. Parker, H. Manley, J. P. Rogers, B. Bliss, S. Grantham.
ROW 3: J. Nunnally, J. Baker, K. Hill, C. Tingle, R. Howell, M. Grauel, A. Montalto, S. Henegar, S. Self, B. Bradley.
ROW 4: G. Simmons, B. Richeson, P. Zarzour, D. Ragland, G. Speers, B. Hendrix, D. Davis, B. Walsh, E. Smith, D. Deloach, R. Hunter.

1974

Hail, dear old Woodlawn High,
  noble and strong,
To thee with loyal hearts
  we raise our song;
Swelling to heav'n aloud,
  our praises ring;
Hail, dear old Woodlawn High,
  to thee we sing.

Majesty as a crown rests
  on thy brow.
Pride, Honor, Glory, Love
  before thee bow;
Ne'er can thy spirit die,
  thy walls decay;
Hail, dear old Woodlawn High,
  for thee we pray.

Hail, dear old Woodlawn High,
  guide of our youth,
Lead thou thy children
  on to light and truth;
Thee, when Death summons us,
  others shall praise;
Hail, Alma Mater dear,
  through endless days.